INTO THE
PROMISED LAND

INTO THE PROMISED LAND

Issues Facing the Welfare State

Edited by
Asher Ben-Arieh and
John Gal

Westport, Connecticut
London

Library of Congress Cataloging-in-Publication Data

Into the promised land : issues facing the welfare state / edited by Asher Ben-Arieh and John Gal.
    p.   cm.
    Includes bibliographical references and index.
    ISBN 0–275–96905–3 (alk. paper)
    1. Welfare state. 2. Israel—Social policy. I. Ben-Arieh, Asher, 1963– II. Gal, John.
  JC479.I57   2001
  361.6′5′095694—dc21   00–022342

British Library Cataloguing in Publication Data is available.

Library of Congress Catalog Card Number: 00–022342
ISBN: 0–275–96905–3

First published in 2001

Praeger Publishers, 88 Post Road West, Westport, CT 06881
An imprint of Greenwood Publishing Group, Inc.
www.praeger.com

Printed in the United States of America

The paper used in this book complies with the Permanent Paper Standard issued by the National Information Standards Organization (Z39.48–1984).

10 9 8 7 6 5 4 3 2 1

*To Abraham Doron
A mentor, a colleague, and a friend*

Contents

Preface

Into the Promised Land: Issues in the Welfare State is dedicated to Professor Abraham Doron to mark his retirement from the Paul Baerwald School of Social Work at the Hebrew University in Jerusalem. This book contains fifteen chapters dealing with issues of major importance to all welfare states, along with a special focus on developments in the Israeli welfare state. The chapters in this collection were written by leading scholars in the field of welfare state research and by Israeli students of the welfare state from a number of different universities and research institutes.

These works are the pick of a much larger number of papers first presented at a conference on the future of the welfare state held at the Hebrew University in Jerusalem in June 1998 in honor of Professor Abraham Doron. As such, we would like to express our appreciation to all those who participated in the conference, and in particular, to the scholars who presented papers on that occasion. The conference itself was held under the auspices of the Paul Baerwald School of Social Work at the Hebrew University in Jerusalem, the Israeli National Insurance Institute, and the Israeli National Council for the Child. Special thanks are due also to the JDC–Brookdale Institute in Jerusalem, the Israeli Association of Social Workers, and the Hallbert Center for Canadian Studies at the Hebrew University and the British Council for supporting the conference.

The goal of this volume is twofold. First, it is intended to enrich the knowledge and data on social policy and the welfare state, in general, and on the Israeli welfare state, in particular. Second, it seeks to enhance public discussion and the study of various aspects and issues facing the welfare state and relating to social policy, its formulation process, and its implications and outcomes.

This book is divided into an introduction and three parts. In the introduction, Uri Yanay discusses Abraham Doron's work and views in the context of the changing face of social rights in the welfare state in an era of globalization. The first part of the book presents different approaches to the welfare state. This is followed by a section devoted specifically to the Israeli welfare state and the formulation of social policy in Israel. The third and final part of the book focuses on developments within welfare states.

We are convinced that the unique nature of this volume—a collection that includes both the leading lights in welfare state analysis and a number of related chapters that deal with the relatively unknown welfare state in Israel—will provide an interesting and enriching experience for readers. We hope that it will encourage additional debates and studies. If so, it will serve as a fitting recognition of Abraham Doron's academic endeavors and his contributions to the study of the welfare state.

Introduction

Uri Yanay

Developments in a wide range of "welfare states" indicate clearly that the very nature of this form of state orientation has undergone marked changes in recent years. Certainly, the contemporary debate over the preferred form of welfare services and the level and type of social security that society should provide its citizens has taken a very different form from that which characterized the years of the "welfare state crisis." However, the implications of current changes in the welfare state are no less, and indeed perhaps even more, dramatic than those in the heyday of the New Right offensive against the welfare state. This is certainly the case with regard to the Clinton administration welfare reforms in the United States and with New Labour's efforts to introduce structural innovations in the British welfare state. It is also true of a wide range of welfare states in continental Europe, Australasia, and, as the chapters of this book will show, of Israel as well.

Into the Promised Land seeks to examine the nature of contemporary changes in the welfare state by focusing upon different levels of investigation. Many of the works included here focus on general trends that have resonance for all welfare states. Others focus on the implications of change in the context of a single welfare state, and one that has been the subject of very limited academic scrutiny—the Israeli welfare state.

The rather unusual content of this book is a result of the fact that it is based upon contributions presented in an international

seminar, "The Future of the Welfare State: International and Israeli Perspectives." This seminar, held at the Hebrew University
of Jerusalem, was dedicated to Professor Abraham Doron upon his
formal retirement from the Paul Baerwald School of Social Work.
The seminar brought together an international group of distinguished scholars and researchers to discuss three major themes:
new perspectives on the welfare state; issues related specifically to
the study of the Israeli welfare state; and issues pertaining to the
development of the welfare state.

These different themes reflect the areas that Professor Doron
has studied, taught, and written about. Since the early 1950s, Professor Doron has been involved in the making of the Israeli welfare
state, first as a rehabilitation worker and later as a planner and a
social insurance analyst. Over the years, in addition to his academic contributions, Professor Doron has been and still is deeply
involved in the making of social policy in Israel, influencing and
shaping the Israeli welfare state.

Professor Doron has undertaken numerous studies that have focused upon the needs of a wide range of social groups, ranging literally "from the cradle to the grave," and upon the policies aimed
at dealing with these needs. His studies have focused upon low-
wage earners, the unemployed and the aged, and children and
mothers, to name but a few. In his writings, Professor Doron has
always displayed a deep commitment to the less powerful groups
in the population.

Professor Doron has clear-cut views on the welfare state and the
role it plays in our ever-changing era. He makes his views explicit
and shares them with others in his writings and teaching. His contribution to this book, entitled "Fifty Years of Social Security in the
Making: A Participant's Journey," highlights his professional views
and values. Clearly, he favors a more caring, egalitarian society.
He argues that the state should be involved in "promoting social
solidarity, strengthening social cohesion and bringing about the
integration of the underprivileged classes into the mainstream of
societal life [through] a mixture of social insurance principles and
progressive evolution of the social rights of citizenship."

Professor Doron admits that he has always had a "somewhat naive
yearning for a better world" and a belief that this could be achieved
by means of progressive social policies. He argues that the welfare
state in many Western, industrial societies as well as in Israel has
never reached this social goal. He states, "One must bear in mind
some of the significant failures. The main failure of welfare state
politics and policies was that it left almost without change the distribution of wealth and power in capitalist societies."

Professor Doron's observations are somber but valid. They reflect his endless commitment to the welfare of people. The stronger this commitment, the more he challenges society and the political system and the more direct and severe is his criticism. Professor Doron identifies a crisis in political values, leadership, and social commitment. He claims that "the origins of the current counter-revolution against the welfare state can be located in the original sin of its failure to change the distribution of wealth and power in capitalist societies when it could do so." This argument reflects, first, an expectation of change in the distribution of wealth and power in society, and second, an observation that the postwar welfare state failed to do so.

In his writings, Professor Doron lays bare the tension that exists between two central social values: equality and freedom. While politicians often tend rhetorically to combine the two and indeed to commit themselves to achieving both equality and economic freedom, these concepts do not coincide. In fact, they form two poles of an abstract continuum. There is an unsettled, almost unbearable, tension between achieving social equality and reaching economic freedom with free enterprise as its underlying principle.

In its ideal type, capitalism is based on free market principles and encourages little if any state intervention through taxation or other means of redistribution of wealth. The search for equality, on the other hand, is based on a pursuit of distributive justice. Inevitably, this implies employing administrative tools for the redistribution of income to achieve a more just society and to even out the ownership of wealth and, perhaps, power. The more equality one seeks to pursue, the more state intervention it requires.

Indeed, research evidence shows that countries that have adopted a more radical liberalization strategy do better in terms of employment but suffer a high cost in terms of inequality and poverty. In contrast, those resilient to change pay the price of high unemployment, as is the case in much of continental Europe (Esping-Andersen 1996, 25).

In Britain, New Labour is rapidly finding itself in an impossible situation. On the one hand, it is committed to its traditional welfare ideology, while on the other it is trying to desperately to change this image and maintain a sparkling "Cool Britannia" economy. Instead of its traditional "commitment to welfare," the British government published in 1998 a Green Paper which described eight principles for welfare reform under the title "New Ambitions for Our Country: A New Contract for Welfare." This so-called contract is portrayed as an effort "to rebuild the welfare state around the work ethic: Work for those who can, security for those who cannot."

The traditional Labour commitment to welfare seems to have been eroded.

The establishment of the postwar welfare state was followed by an attempt to secure basic social and welfare "rights." One ought to question not only if social rights exist, but to ask what is their nature and how robust are they in an ever-changing environment.

Dworkin (1977, 98) distinguishes between "abstract" and "concrete" rights. Abstract rights, such as the right to speak on political matters, "take no account of competing rights, and there is no price tag attached. Concrete rights, on the other hand, reflect the impact of such competition . . . in the language of economics." Applying them costs money that governments are unready to commit themselves to, especially if the volume of social needs cannot be defined and budgeted.

Following a similar line, Raymond Plant (1992, 18) distinguishes between civil, political, and social rights. Civil rights are those securing an individual from coercion and assault. Political rights secure free voting and political participation. Social rights secure standards of health, education, and welfare. Such rights, according to Plant, involve resource allocation and therefore depend on being financed. Financial cuts will ultimately undermine or negate these rights. Plant argues that if governments do not want or cannot allocate the resources needed to secure them, social rights have little, if any, practical or legal value.

One could argue that the concept that comes nearest to a social right in contemporary welfare states is that of entitlements. Administrative in nature, entitlements can be claimed and even legally argued; they cannot, however, substitute for a right. They can be withdrawn whenever a political or administrative decision is made or when resources are exhausted.[1]

In many cases, what were considered solid social rights have been eroded and traditional welfare entitlement have been negated. Some traditional rights have been redefined as abstract rights insofar as no government is ready to fund or secure them. While governments tend to limit social rights and entitlements, however, the public may find a new source for such rights and a leverage for acquiring them. It would appear that an alternative framework has emerged which will enable the establishment of a new type of welfare state that will eventually secure social and welfare rights. Unlike the traditional model, in which most changes in welfare legislation were attributed to "bottom-up" pressure or to public demand, the new type of rights stems from outside the nation-state.

It was Archimedes who said that given leverage outside the globe, he would lift the earth. Perhaps we are now witnessing the emergence of a new type of welfare state—states in which standards are secured from the outside. These standards will no longer be a creation of the state and its people; rather, norms and rights will be set by international bodies.

International declarations, conventions, and covenants have been signed to establish a universal caring society that will secure basic human and social rights. The problem is that in legal (or legalistic) terms, such rights have only partial merit. In order to take effect in most countries, such rights must be enacted as state laws or must be challenged and established by courts, sometimes as precedents.

One example of an emerging set of welfare rights can be attributed to the United Nations Covenant on Economic Social and Cultural Rights (1966). To illustrate, the first rights in this covenant relate to self-determination (article 1), state responsibility and non-discriminatory cooperation (article 2). Article 3 of the covenant deals with the prohibition of discrimination between men and women. Article 6 relates more directly to social policy in that it stipulates the "right to work." Article 7 specifies the right to "just and favorable conditions of work," including collective labor rights (article 8). The right to social security is specified in article 9 of the covenant, followed by familial rights in article 10 of the covenant. Article 11 sets the right to adequate standard of living, followed by the right to the highest attainable standards of health (article 12) and the right to education (article 13).

The United Nations Covenant on Economic Social and Cultural Rights is only an illustration of one document which underlines the right to work, to adequate standard of living, and to high health and education standards. Experts in the field also point to other international documents, such as the United Nations Declaration of the Rights of the Children, which are not only quoted frequently but also seem to be applied nationally. Such is the case with some International Labor Organization (ILO) standards that deal with indigenous and foreign workers.

International declarations, conventions, and covenants do not compel a government. No individual can argue his or her right to welfare based on any such international document. However, international declarations, conventions, and covenants do set standards. By ratifying an international document, a government is implying that it has accepted its principles, at the very least, as guidelines to policy and legislation. Such principles have special value especially if a person wishes to use them when challenging her or his case legally. Moreover, a principle anchored in an international document can trigger a "bottom-up" political process and attempts at legislation on a national level. Furthermore, governments that ratify international declarations, conventions, or covenants are required to report regularly on efforts to abide by the document and apply it nationally.

Individuals or groups may wish to make use of international declarations that have been ratified by their government and apply them locally. They can mobilize outside, international bodies to urge their government to abide by the principles enshrined in the document, be it a declaration, convention, or covenant. It has become common practice in the European Court to deal with matters agreed upon in the European Union countries and not applied locally.

The European Court appears to be overwhelmed by cases presented by individuals and groups that are petitioning the court to secure and apply some of their personal political and social rights. The court's decisions have become guidelines that serve as precedents to European governments.

As a consequence of these developments, we may witness in the future a dual process. Even as there is decline and erosion of the postwar welfare state, with a reduction of entitlements to public and private goods and the erection of barriers to public funding of welfare programs, a new type of a welfare state may be emerging, in which "social rights" and entitlements are set by international standards and guidelines. These guidelines do not originate from a notion of citizenship, social justice, or equality, but from basic human rights, the standards of which are set by international bodies. If this observation is valid, then the welfare state has not failed, even though its foundation may have changed. From a national welfare state based on civil society and citizenship, we seem to be witnessing the emergence of a new type of a welfare state based on universal human and social rights secured from the outside.

Many of the chapters in the first part of this book relate directly to the issues raised in this discussion. In his opening piece, Ian Gough discusses the two types of justifications often invoked in debates over the future of the welfare state. By employing a universal definition of need, he argues that there is strong evidence for both normative and consequentialist claims for the welfare state, despite the changes that have taken place on the national and global levels. In a direct response to issues raised in this chapter, in their contribution John Carrier and Ian Kendall focus upon the notion of need, which plays a major role in Gough's arguments on behalf of the welfare state. Reviewing the social policy literature and citing current case-law examples, they conclude that both relative and absolute definitions of need should always be used at the same time in order to ensure that the administration of welfare programs is perceived as legitimate by clients and professionals alike. Graham Room's chapter focuses upon the notion of social exclusion in contemporary welfare states, in particular in the context of change in these states and the rapid process of the globalization of the economy. His conclusion is similar to the one proposed in this introduction—that only international institutions can provide an adequate framework for arresting the process of erosion of the structures established by welfare states to prevent distress and exclusion. While the focus of Julia O'Connor's chapter is also international, the subject is different from the others in this section of the book. She seeks to understand the way in which gender equality issues have been understood in two liberal welfare states—the United States and Australia. In particular, her analysis deals with the political factors that have influenced change in this field in recent decades. The final chapter in this section is Abraham Doron's. His participant's journey along the path of social policy making enables him to underline the major changes that have occurred in welfare states, and in the Israeli welfare state in particular, over the last half-century, and to pinpoint the reasons for these changes.

The second part of *Into the Promised Land* deals specifically with the Israeli welfare state. In his opening paper, Jack Habib describes the major factors that have influenced developments in the Israeli welfare state over the years since its establishment. He examines the nature of these developments, employing notions such as privatization, decentralization, universalism as opposed to selectivity, and the role of work-related benefits. The following chapter, that of John Gal, focuses upon the social security component of the Israeli welfare state. Gal looks at the distribution of expenditure between the different types of social security programs and examines the major role that noncontributory and nonmeans tested benefits play in the Israeli welfare state. Both Asher Ben-Arieh and Yael Yishai look at aspects of policy making in the Israeli welfare state. Ben-Arieh concentrates on the Israeli parliament, the Knesset, and analyzes the role of Knesset members in the social policy formulation and implementation process. Yishai differentiates between "top-down" and "bottom-up" models of policy making. She finds that despite the fact that Israel has undergone change favorable to the emergence of the second, more pluralist model, the policy process is still characterized by a "top-down" model that emphasizes the role of elites, bureaucrats, and professionals.

The final section of this book focuses upon issues in the development of the welfare state. Francis Castles's chapter looks at the dynamics of postwar welfare state development. His findings indicate that monocausal interpretations of social policy outcomes are inappropriate. Instead, he suggests that various demographic, cul-

tural, and political factors have crucial impacts upon the development of welfare states over time. The issues of privatization and
commercialization, two key ideas in the current welfare state debate, are at the heart of Ernie Lightman's contribution. After distinguishing between these two terms, the arguments in favor of
privatization are reviewed, and questions pertaining to the desir-
ability of privatization are raised. In a chapter devoted to understanding the dynamics of social policy change, Martin Rein presents
a framework for policy analysis over time that takes into account
the changing nature of debate over public policy. Employing a number of historical examples, and in particular the issue of single
mothers, Rein shows how existing policy paradigms can be challenged and indeed changed given the right conditions. In his chapter, Wim van Oorschot looks at the implications of one of the more
popular themes of contemporary social policy—targeting benefits.
Using data from The Netherlands, van Oorschot indicates that various factors can lead to the nontake-up of targeted benefits and as a
result can significantly undermine the effectiveness of targeted
policies. In the final chapter of the book, Hugh Heclo looks at the
future of social policy making. After identifying the major developments that have characterized the development of social policy over
the last century, Heclo argues that the next century will see another movement in the nature of social policy. This will take the
form of a growing realization that making social policy choices does
in fact entail the making of cultural choices.

While this book begins and concludes with contributions that focus upon the conceptual and theoretical analysis of the welfare state
as an institution, the center part concentrates upon developments
in the Israeli welfare state. In its fifty years of statehood, Israel
has dealt with numerous challenges, both from within and without. The establishment of a modern welfare state, modeled upon
those established in other industrialized societies, was perceived
as a means with which to deal with some of these challenges. The
chapters included here should provide the reader with the means
to better understand the Israeli welfare state, and to view its development, its contemporary characteristics, and its future path in
comparison to other welfare state regimes.

NOTE

1. In Israel we have recently witnessed how so-called "rights," or, in
practice, entitlements secured for single mothers, new immigrants, and
discharged soldiers were cut or withdrawn with little, if any, reaction from
the public. Furthermore, our well-publicized National Health Insurance

Act was only partially implemented, though the public pays for its so-called "rights."

REFERENCES

Dworkin, R. 1977. *Taking Rights Seriously*. London: Duckworth.

Esping-Andersen, G. 1996. "After the Global Age?: Welfare State Dilemmas in a Global Economy." In *Welfare States in Transition: National Adaptations in Global Economics*, ed. G. Esping-Andersen. London: Sage.

Plant, R. 1992. "Citizenship, Right and Welfare." In *The Welfare of Citizens: Developing New Social Rights*, ed. A. Coote. London: Institute for Public Policy Research and Rivers Oram Press.

PART I

PERSPECTIVES ON
THE WELFARE STATE

1

Normative and Consequentialist Arguments for the Welfare State

Ian Gough

Arguments for the welfare state can be divided into moral and consequentialist. The former appeal to overiding ethical goals such as equality or justice; the latter to its beneficial consequences for the economy or other subsystems of society.

In recent years both forms of justification for the welfare state have been turned against it. The moral critique of the welfare state can be divided into two camps: one that disputes the contribution of state welfare to ethical values, and the other which denies that there are any coherent ethical values by which to evaluate it or other social arrangements. The two dominant examples of the first are the libertarian and the communitarian. One contends that the welfare state denies individual rights, undermines freedom, and creates dependency; the other that it undermines communal bonds and family mutuality and creates dependency. More persistent is a strong form of philosophical relativism which denies that universal goals can be coherently formulated, let alone justified, and which propounds a strong form of pluralism in public life and social policies.

Consequentialist critiques of the welfare state are encountered in any issue of the *Economist* magazine. The welfare state, it contends, undermines work, savings, innovation, and motivation. The reasoning is at times intrinsic and on other occasions specific to the current stage of world economy. Either way, welfare states today are incompatible with good economic performance; they harm productivity and the competitiveness of enterprises and nations.

Failures in state provision, regulation, and redistribution lend support to minimalist forms of intervention and will condemn the traditional extensive state welfare systems of Europe to slow decay.

I want in this chapter to draw on both moral and consequentialist arguments to defend the welfare state, which I shall define, briefly and assertively, as the public guarantee of rights to the means to human welfare in general and to minimum standards of well being in particular.

THE MORAL CASE:
UNIVERSAL NEEDS AND THE WELFARE STATE

A Theory of Human Need

Let me begin by summarizing some of the arguments put forward by Len Doyal and me in *A Theory of Human Need*. The word "need" is used explicitly or implicitly to refer to a particular category of goals which are believed to be universalizable. Needs in this sense are commonly contrasted with "wants," which can also be described as goals but which derive from an individual's particular preferences and cultural environment.

This imputation of universality rests upon the belief that if needs are not satisfied by an appropriate "satisfier," serious harm of some specified and objective kind will result. We define serious harm as fundamental disablement in the pursuit of one's vision of the good—not contingent subjective feelings like anxiety or unhappiness. Another way of describing such harm is as an impediment to successful social participation. We build a self-conception of our own capabilities through learning from others. Participation in some form of life without serious arbitrary limitations is a fundamental goal of all peoples.

Thus, basic needs consist, at the least, in those universal preconditions that enable nondisabled participation in one's form of life. At the most, they consist of those universal preconditions for critical participation in one's form of life—the capacity to situate it, to criticize it, and, if necessary, to act to change it. We identify these universal prerequisites as *physical health* and *autonomy*. Autonomy of agency—the capacity to make informed choices about what should be done and how to go about doing it—is impaired when there is a deficit of three attributes: mental health, cognitive skills, and opportunities to engage in social participation.

Recognizing that these common human needs can be met in a multitude of different ways by an almost infinite variety of specific satisfiers, we next go on to identify those characteristics of need satisfiers that everywhere contribute to improved physical health and autonomy (Doyal and Gough 1991, ch. 8). These we label "universal satisfier characteristics" or "intermediate needs." We group these characteristics into eleven categories: adequate nutritional food and water, adequate protective housing, a nonhazardous work environment, a nonhazardous physical environment, appropriate health care, security in childhood, significant primary relationships, physical security, economic security, safe birth control and childbearing, and appropriate basic and cross-cultural education. Nine of these apply to all people, one refers to the specific needs of children, and another to the specific needs of women for safe child bearing. All eleven are essential to protect the health and autonomy of people and thus to enable them to participate to the maximum extent in their social form of life, whatever that is.[1]

As developed thus far, our theory of needs is substantive, or "intrinsic" (Hewitt 1992, ch. 10). It also, however, has a procedural dimension. We indentify universal *procedural* and *material* preconditions for enhancing need satisfaction (Doyal and Gough 1991, chs. 7, 11). These are attributes of social systems, not individuals. Procedural preconditions relate to the ability of a group to identify needs and appropriate need satisfiers in a rational way and to prioritize need satisfiers and the need satisfactions of different groups. In the face of radical disagreements over the perceived interests and needs of different groups, how can this best be achieved? To answer this we draw on the works of Habermas and Rawls to sketch out certain communicational and constitutional preconditions for optimizing need satisfaction in practice. Habermas outlines a theory of communicational competence that emphasizes the importance for the rational resolution of debates—including debates about need satisfaction—of the best available understanding and of truly democratic debate. This, we go on to argue, entails drawing on "bottom-up" experiential knowledge along with "codified" knowledge when identifying specific satisfiers and policies to improve welfare.

On these foundations, we can build a normative dimension and relate this to the case for the welfare state. Unfortunate as it may be, it is possible to accept the idea of universal human need without accepting that anything ought to be done about it. The case for moving from the "is" of human need to the "ought" of meeting it must still be made. Briefly, this connection can be developed in the following stages (Doyal and Gough 1991, ch. 6):

1. The membership of any social group implies obligations or duties.
2. To ascribe duties to someone presupposes that they are in fact able to perform these duties.

3. The ascription of a duty thus logically entails that the bearer of the duty is entitled to the level of need satisfaction necessary to enable her or him to undertake that duty.

4. Where the social group is large, this entails similar obligations to strangers, whose needs we do not directly witness and can do nothing individually to satisfy. This will require support for agencies that can act to guarantee the wherewithal to meet the needs of strangers. This is roughly my definition of the welfare state.

5. However, this commitment to support welfare structures cannot stop at the borders of any particular state. The idea of universal human needs leads remorselessly to the global guarantee of their satisfaction. It lends powerful support to contemporary ideas of cosmopolitanism, which sees the entire world as a potential political community (Held 1995; Jones 1998).

CRITIQUES AND REBUTTALS

Let me now turn to four critical responses to our book. First, Drover and Kerans (1993) challenge the "thin" idea of human need and put forward a "thick" alternative. A thick understanding of need attempts to understand the way people name their needs in a specific cultural context. It relies on interpretative methods to grasp the full particularity of need in its everyday context. This approach is more historic, subjective, and authentic. It recognizes the role of social movements, who in the "claims-making process" contest expert and top-down definitions of need and struggle to name their needs through social action. This approach, they claim, avoids the abuses of the concept of need which have been perpetuated by experts and will act as a corrective to various forms of cultural imperialism, which neglect the plurality of discourses that give meaning and moral significance to the lives of individuals within different cultures.

Yet, such a thick account suffers from several problems, well summarized by Soper (1993). If we are to give full due to the variety of claims about needs, what saves their approach from being simply an account of struggle over wants and interests? If, as is almost certain, the communally named needs of different groups conflict, how are we to reconcile them in the name of need? Drover and Kerans draw on Habermas to claim that a group can articulate needs which are universalizable, hence "true" in the sense that in an ideal speech situation there can be a common consensus. But Hewitt (1993) argues that this requires some shared common background to provide the "translation bridgehead" between different social movements espousing different cultural preferences and interests.[2]

But if this much is agreed, it subverts the priority given to subjectivity and authenticity. At a global level, too, there seems no way of addressing the sustainability of the sum of group-defined needs. In other words, thick needs return us via a different route to the well-established problems of wants, preferences, and utility.

A second critique contends that theories of universal need are founded on an individualist notion of agency. Tao and Drover (1997) make this point when contrasting a Chinese notion of need to our "Western" one. They appreciate that we stress the social bases of individual autonomy—the fact that a person's individuality is rooted in their role relationships. They claim, however, that this idea is not followed through and that it sits uneasily alongside the idea of critical autonomy, which may entail individuals up-rooting themselves and turning against their culture of origin. But we do this deliberately. Their alternative is the rigid set of five cardinal relationships of Confucianism: "The father is righteous and protective, the mother is loving and caring, the elder brother is fraternal, the younger brother is respectful and the son is filial." In this relational ethic, "Individuals are *never* recognised as separate entities" (Tao and Drover 1997, 10). This is to go too far. It is individuals who are born, suffer, love, and die! As much as avoiding ungrounded individualism, a credible theory of need must avoid social constructionism.

A third critique states that thin theories of need, like our own, can be criticized for being too thin to act as a guide for policy. Objectivity and universality can only be achieved at the cost of such a high level of abstraction from real societies, cultures, and modes of satisfaction that the theory cannot serve as a practical guide to welfare provision. This question is explicitly addressed in Part 3 of this book. Between universal needs and socially specific satisfiers, I posit "universal satisfier characteristics." As Soper puts it, "These provide a standard of reference by which levels of deprivation within particular groups can be charted and specific welfare strategies defended as objectively grounded rather than ethnocentrically motivated" (1993, 74). In this sense our theory, while not thick, is certainly thicker than thin! Yet, Soper claims that this smuggles in dubiously objective claims, especially in relation to the prerequisites for critical autonomy. This is further compounded when we insist on the role of bottom-up experiential knowledge in identifying specific satisfiers.

I do not believe that this criticism stands up. The procedures for identifying universal satisfier characteristics rest on two foundations: (1) the best available technical knowledge articulating causal relationships between physical health and autonomy and other factors, and (2) comparative anthropological knowledge about practices in the numerous cultures, subcultures, states, and political systems in the contemporary world. Both natural and social sciences, including social policy, play their role in rationally determining policies to meet needs. But in identifying and improving *specific* satisfiers, experiential knowledge grounded in the "lifeworld" is essential. At the former level, the codified knowledge of physical and social sciences is nonnegotiable. At the latter level, the two forms of knowledge should ideally enter into a dialogue within a communicative situation that is as unconstrained and informed as possible. Social policy as an academic discipline embraces both forms of enquiry; but that does not mean that their differing epistemological groundings cannot be distinguished.

Finally, Wetherly (1996) accuses our theory of incoherence when identifying the standards of *basic* need satisfaction. What levels of physical health and autonomy are required to secure minimally disabled social participation? We reject both the "minimum" and the "adequate" standard in favor of the "optimum." Reflecting the distinction between personal autonomy and critical autonomy, this is divided into two: the "participation optimum" and the "critical optimum." The latter comprises those levels of health and cognitive, emotional and social capacities which permit critical participation in one's chosen form of life. In practice, however, we go on to posit a third variant, the "constrained optimum": the best level of need satisfaction presently achieved in the world or a better feasible level (Doyal and Gough 1991, 160–161). I suggest that present Swedish levels of health and autonomy provide a practical exemplar of this constrained optimum.

Soper and Wetherly criticize this proposed standard on related grounds. Soper contends that this standard may actually be too high, in that the extravagance of Swedish energy use and socioeconomic institutions is not generalizable to all other peoples in the world or to future generations. Insofar as this is true, it is accommodated within our definition of constrained optimum. But this raises a difficult issue. We have narrowed our focus from a concern with the universal requirements for minimally disabled social participation to whatever is universalizable across time and place in practice (Soper 1993, 78). This raises more issues than can be dealt with here, but at the end of the day "ought" must imply "can." If due to past industrialism, population growth, and environmental degradation we can achieve less than optimal generalizable satisfaction of basic needs, then so be it. We will be forever living in a world of constraint. Wetherly goes on to claim that this reintroduces relativism. The constrained optimum standard remains "historically—and so socially, culturally—relative" (Wetherly 1996, 58). But the "and so" does not follow. The concept of human need we develop is historically open to the continual improvements in understanding that have characterized human progress. But at any one time, there is a body of best knowledge to which international appeal can be made. Our theory is relative in time but absolute in space.

If these rebuttals of criticisms of our theory are sound, I would claim that the case for a strong, rights-based, and wide-ranging conception of the welfare state still stands. The existence of universal human needs justifies support for an institutional framework guaranteeing sufficient provision of resources to deliver their (constrained) optimal satisfaction. We need to go beyond, however, the best welfare states at the international level. However difficult it is to conceive of this in practice, this commitment should be generalized to all the peoples of the world, subject only to ensuring the need satisfaction of future generations.

THE CONSEQUENTIALIST CASE:
THE WELFARE STATE (SOMETIMES) PAYS

At the end of his review of our theory of need, Wetherly speculates that it endorses an "investment" model of the welfare state of the sort articulated by the 1994 Commission on Social Justice in Britain. This is certainly implicit in our model of material production (Doyal and Gough 1991, 231–241) but it is not spelt out. In the second part of this chapter, I want to address the issue of social policies and economic performance, and in particular the sustainable competitiveness of nations. I thus switch attention to the consequentialist case for—and against—the welfare state, but shall return at the end to speculate on some of the links between the two parts of the chapter. It draws on some other work (in particular Gough 1994, 1996, 1999), in which the arguments and evidence are spelt out in greater detail.

The aspect of economic performance I shall discuss is productivity growth. If the principal economic goal of a nation is to produce a high and rising real income for its citizens, then the ability to do so depends on the productivity with which the nation's resources (labor and capital) are employed. In Pfaller, Gough, and Therborn (1991), we equated this with the *structural* or *underlying* competitiveness of nations—their ability to provide high and growing per capita incomes while being exposed to foreign competition.

Outside exceptional circumstances, it is reasonable to assume that the maintenance of reasonable levels of structural competitiveness is a pervasive constraint on national economic and social policy. "Accumulation" remains a central feature of system integration in the modern, postindustrial, global, capitalist world. The impact of national social policies on the competitive advantage of nations is then a critical part of the consequentialist case for or against the welfare state.

The effects of welfare states on productivity and accumulation can be traced through three routes: via their fiscal effort, via the effects of specific social programs, and via their welfare outcomes. Let me discuss these in reverse order (Gough 1996).

First, if welfare states are roughly defined as institutions to secure the satisfaction of (some) human needs at (some) standard, then their imputed outcomes are significant. Insofar as they influence levels of need satisfaction and welfare outcomes, they affect levels of social integration and cohesion. Social integration refers to the orderly relationship between actors (collective or individual) in a social system; social disintegration on their conflictual or anomic relationships (Gough and Olafsson 1999). Examples of social disintegration include extensive social conflict, inequality, crime, poverty, and social exclusion. The *welfare outcomes* of welfare states, in conjunction with labor markets and family systems, may have an important impact on productivity, competitiveness, and accumulation through this route.

Second, welfare states comprise a large set of specific programs and institutions to guarantee access to those satisfiers deemed necessary to secure acceptable levels of need satisfaction. They are a central part of the apparatus of government, imposing heavy fiscal demands and entailing extensive legislation, bureaucratic implementation, and professional and public employment. The relationship between state social policies and the economy is important and potentially conflictual. At this level we need to consider the consequences of individual social programs for the economy.

Third, this in turn requires substantial fiscal inputs, whether through taxation or borrowing. These fiscal efforts, it is reasonably assumed, have further effects on the supply of capital and labor and the productivity growth of the economy.

The following presents a schematic summary of relationships between aspects of the welfare system and national competitiveness analyzed at greater length elsewhere (Gough 1996, 1999).

Aspect of Welfare System	Impact on National Competitiveness	
	Negative	Positive
1. Fiscal effort	1.1 Borrowing crowds out investment	1.4 Macroeconomic stabilization effects of social expenditure
	1.2 Social security charges encourage export of capital	

1.3 Direct taxes reduce
labor supply

2. Welfare outcomes

2.1 Costs of ill health
2.2 Costs of poor
education
2.3 Costs of crime
2.4 Enforcement costs of
inequality

3. Social Programs

3.1 Pay-as-you-go
pensions reduce savings
3.2 Pensions reduce labor
supply
3.3 Unemployment and/or
sickness benefit reduces
labor supply
3.4 Minimum wages,
employment protection
pose barriers to hiring
3.5 Public sector social
services have lower
internal efficiency

3.6 Market failures (e.g.,
unemployment insur-
ance, chronic health
services), favor collec-
tive state provision
3.7 Deregulation of
housing leads to
equity withdrawal and
rising consumption
3.8 Support for women's
employment
3.9 Human capital
improvements via
education and training

First, much economic theory predicts that the huge fiscal effort of present-day welfare states will have an adverse effect on productivity growth and other indicators of competitiveness. Yet the conclusion of a wide range of macrolevel research is that there is no consistent support for either compatibility or incompatibility perspectives. Atkinson (1995) has reviewed the major cross-national studies which have regressed social security transfer spending as a share of GDP, on economic growth rates. Of the nine studies, four find a negative (incompatibility) relationship, three a positive (compatibility) relationship, and two an insignificant relationship. Another survey of studies has been undertaken by Esping-Andersen (1994), this time of those using a broader definition of welfare state effort—total levels of social spending as a share of GDP. Again the studies reveal a mix of positive, negative, and insignificant effects on national output. Given the widespread assertion that the modern welfare state undermines growth and competitiveness, these agnostic findings deserve wider dissemination.

At the second level of welfare outcomes, new institutional economic theories vie with neoclassical theories. The latter contend there is a trade-off between equality and efficiency. According to the former, more equal societies are capable of supporting levels of cooperation and trust unavailable in more economically divided societies; they thus assist the development of cooperative or negotiated forms of coordination alongside competition and command forms (Gough 1994). Rieger and Leibfried (1998) contend that in the face of globalizing pressures, even the biggest states wield a diminished range of economic policy instruments. A near-universal welfare state is now more relevant to economic performance. Acting as a "filter and buffer," the security that it provides reduces opposition to change and flexibilization among workers and other groups and staves off social disintegration and political upheaval.

Some comparative investigations have been carried out on the relationship between levels of equality and economic performance across nations, all of which show a positive relationship (Persson and Tabolini 1994; Glyn and Miliband 1997; Deininger and Squire 1996; Kenworthy 1995). What comparative evidence there is supports the compatibility theory linking growth with high welfare outcomes.

We are thus faced with conflicting theoretical predictions. The consensus is that high welfare expenditures are likely to be disadvantageous to competitiveness, whereas high welfare outcomes are likely to be advantageous. Alongside this are the findings from cross-national evidence. National competitive advantage is not related one way or the other to welfare effort, whereas there is clear evidence of a positive relationship with welfare outcomes (in the form of greater equality).

It is probable that these findings will be resolved at the third level of welfare systems—the specific social programs enacted and implemented by the nation-state. At this point we must move away from macrolevel theory and aggregate evidence to focus on what Atkinson (1995) calls the "fine structure" of particular social programs. The range of possible influences is very wide, including those of pension programs on savings and employment, of labor market regulation on job creation and productivity enhancement, and of education, training, and other social services on human capital. It is difficult to summarize. I conclude that there is evidence for *both* positive and negative relationships between specific welfare state programs and competitiveness. State failures and inefficiencies confront market failures and inefficiencies. It is no easy task to draw up a balance sheet, though many incompatibility arguments do not stand up to scrutiny.

Most striking is the contingency of these relationships. At the end of his survey of the economic impact of welfare states, Esping-Andersen concludes, "The effects of a welfare state cannot be understood in isolation from the political-institutional framework in which it is embedded. . . . There may exist a trade-off between equality and efficiency in countries where the welfare state is large and very redistributive but in which the collective bargaining system is incapable of assuring wage moderation and stable, nonconflictual industrial relations" (1994, 725). In short, the economic impact of welfare *systems* will differ according to the welfare *regime*. The effect of social policy on competitiveness is *contingent* on the institutions of the nation-state, notably its labor market institutions and family structures. Each regime type generates a different set of problems for or threats to national economic performance; these generate different recommended policy solutions, but these in turn generate further dilemmas or contradictions. Let me conclude this section by speculating on the forms of these contingent relationships of Esping-Andersen's (1990) different welfare regimes.

In *liberal* welfare regimes, such as in the United States and, in the last decade, the United Kingdom and New Zealand, the dominant welfare threats to competitiveness are not those of disincentives, crowding out, state redistribution, regulation, and other leading issues in current debates. The dominant threat is of inequality and its effects: instability in demand, a poor quality educational base, and social disintegration (though this is offset, notably in the United States, by higher employment levels). The policy solution almost universally advocated is investment in education and training to improve the skills base and enhance high productivity sectors of the economy. The dilemma is that high quality education cannot coexist with long-term poverty, a growing "underclass," or major community disintegration. These regimes may well need to increase all forms of social expenditure—on infrastructure, social services, and social transfers—in order to realize these gains in competitiveness. The low levels of state expenditure and the absence of major incompatibility threats in this area provides the economic leeway for this to happen. The interest coalitions fostered within liberal welfare regimes, however, militate against this solution.

The problems facing *conservative* welfare regimes, characteristic of the original six members of the European Community and the southern member states, are very different. They are high and rising social transfers and their effects: high social security charges and nonwage labor costs which cannot always be compensated for by high productivity; discouragement of new service sectors with resulting low employment participation rates, especially among women and young people; some labor market inflexibility; (in southern Europe especially) an extensive hidden economy which undermines tax revenues; and, until Maastricht, public sector deficits and rising debt (Esping-Andersen 1996). It is in these countries that several of the predictions of incompatibility theorists bear fruit. The recommended solutions are selectively to deregulate the labor market, to cap insurance benefits (particularly future pensions as in Italy), and to divert social spending toward more productivist ends. The dilemma is that these solutions threaten the interests of the powerful organized sector of the economy and the breadwinner–familist model of welfare which underpins the regime. It is in the interest of families as decision-making units to support generous welfare attached to secure jobs, though these policies exclude many women and young people from access to the same jobs and benefits in their own right.

In *social democratic* welfare regimes, such as Sweden and Denmark, state spending is high on both transfers and social services, unemployment was low until the 1990s, participation rates particularly for women remain very high, and inequality and poverty are relatively low. The threat to this regime today comes from already high rates of taxation continually fuelled by the rising costs of collectively provided services—the result of extensive low productivity service employment at relatively good rates of pay. The recommended solutions include some cuts in transfer benefits and extension of quasi-markets and private provision in the service sector. Compared with the previous two regime types, many of the policies are in place for a productivist welfare state—indeed the idea was developed in Sweden. The dilemma which remains is that to free resources for further investment in human capital further cuts may be necessary in social transfers that could undermine the corporatist institutions and consensual policy making on which the system partly rests.

Japan and the new market economies of East Asia such as Taiwan, Hong Kong, Singapore, and Korea, may represent a fourth welfare regime (but see Esping-Andersen 1997). They combine low levels of state social spending with developed functional alternatives in the corporation, the family, and the private market. A high degree of employment security, a relatively equal distribution of factor incomes, and low tax levels both permit and encourage high levels of savings which contribute to economic security and growth. The basic threats to this apparently successful system stem from the effects of growth on women's employment, family care functions, and the birth rate. A growing double burden on women, especially as the supply of "grandmother welfare" declines, may create pressure for more state services. At the same time, the falling birth rate is creating a rapidly aging population placing greater demands on social transfers. Again the solution points to a more productivist orientation for state policy, but this will require higher taxes, which may undermine the self-financing nature of present forms of private marketized welfare.

Three conclusions flow from this brief and speculative sketch. First, different welfare regimes exhibit different configurations of effects on performance and structural competitiveness. A problem in one may be a solution in another. Second, and despite this contingency, the general goal to which all need to direct themselves is a welfare state that gives due weight to "productivist" considerations. In this sense the Scandinavian welfare pattern still comes closest to a rational resolution of these dilemmas. Third, in all regimes powerful interest coalitions will resist measures to adapt their welfare systems to the competitive requirements of nations in the new globalized economy. There is considerable path dependency in the evolution of welfare policies reinforced by the way that institutions shape the structure of interests in society and the subsequent formation of political coalitions. This institutionalist perspective warns against the wholesale application of neoliberal nostrums to the European social model or the Nordic model. Evidence for it is weaker than many economists make out (Korpi 1996), and many of the policies could not be transplanted anyway.

CONCLUSION: MORALISM VERSUS CONSEQUENTIALISM?

Let me draw four conclusions from the foregoing information. First, a recognition that universal human needs exist and that a powerful case can be made for their common satisfaction provides a firm moral foundation for the welfare state. The institutional guarantee of need satisfiers to strangers enables them to participate and fulfil the duties of good citizenship. It is not so much that rights imply duties, as present-day communitarians stress, but that the common duties of social membership presuppose rights to the satisfaction of basic needs. Only the state can guarantee these rights through its exercise of legitimate power (though this does not entail that the state directly provides the appropriate need satisfiers). There is no obvious alternative to the state guarantee of welfare to its citizens, though debate will forever continue on the best way of achieving this.

Second, the consequentialist case for the welfare state is stronger than is supposed. The minimization of inequality, poverty, and exclusion and the pursuit of solidarity and social cohesion continue to contribute to conflict resolution and to system legitimacy. They are defining features of the European social model, particularly of its Nordic variant. Theory and evidence suggest that higher levels of welfare contribute to economic competitiveness via enhanced human and social capital. Capitalist nations with an effective and just welfare system are likely to be more sustainably competitive than those without.

Third, the consequentialist case is contingent on the interaction between the welfare state as such—the welfare system, its goals, and its institutions—and the broader welfare regime. Not all combinations of institutional arrangements are possible or economically rational; in fact, only a small set of combinations—or welfare regimes—are likely to be found in practice. The most successful are likely to be those that combine proper levels of guaranteed need satisfaction with investment in human and social capital. There is some support here for the argument that a politics of human need entails a productivist welfare state (Gough and Doyal 1989).

Finally, the set of feasible competitive welfare systems can be ranked according to our earlier normative criteria. Kangas (1998) provides some comparative evidence to update our own (Doyal and Gough 1991, 287–293). He uses data on ten countries to compute a Rawlsian measure of the real living standards of the worst off, which has several affinities with our measure of need satisfaction. He shows that on most measures the Nordic countries are superior and the United States is inferior. He concludes, "Rational desire to minimise the risk of ending up in poor circumstances in any of the three stages of the life cycle would push the unborn soul towards the Nordic countries (particulalrly Sweden), in which children are given the best beginning, people in poor positions are offered relatively open opportunities to better their lot, and the twilight of life is less gray than in most other countries. In the Nordic countries, low levels of inequality are combined with high levels of equal opportunity." In other words, of the different models of competitive welfare states, the liberal regime does less well. So too, most probably, would the southern European countries, while the longer-term sustainability of the East Asian model is as yet untested. This leaves the European social model, and its current exemplars such as The Netherlands and Denmark.

Comparative consequentialist lends support to the moral argument made in the first part of this chapter: that strong, extensive welfare states are good for need satisfaction and objective human welfare. The productivist welfare state, most closely approximated by the Nordic model, remains superior on both moral and consequentialist grounds.

NOTES

1. It will be apparent that our approach has much in common with Sen's ideas of functionings and capabilities. For Sen (1992, 4–7), functionings "constitute a person's being," and since functionings are "intrinsically valuable," they amount to states of well-being. Capabilities refer to the set

of functionings that is feasible to that person—that he or she could choose. But what are these functionings? Sen's list includes being happy, being able to choose, having good health, being adequately fed and sheltered, having self-respect, being able to appear in public without shame, and taking part in the life of the community. Though we may well value all these things, it is a rather strange list. It embraces subjective states (being happy) and objective states (being adequately fed), and culturally generalizable conditions (having good health) along with specifically liberal values (being able to choose). It is not self-evident that all these are "intrinsically" significant in defining the social good. I consider that Sen needs a theory of need to buttress his notion of functionings.

2. Both he and I contend that common human needs in their "thin" form precisely provide such a background (Hewitt 1993).

REFERENCES

Atkinson, A. B. 1995. *The Welfare State and Economic Performance.* Welfare State Programme Discussion Paper 109, STICERD, LSE, May.

Deininger, K., and Squire, L. 1996. "Measuring Income Inequality: A New Database." *World Bank Economic Review* 1 (3): 330–357.

Doyal, L., and Gough, I. 1991. *A Theory of Human Need.* London: Macmillan.

Drover, G., and Kerans, P. 1993. "New Approaches to Welfare Theory: Foundations." In *New Approaches to Welfare Theory.* Aldershot, U.K.: Edward Elgar.

Esping-Andersen, G. 1990. *The Three Worlds of Welfare Capitalism.* Princeton, N.J.: Princeton University Press.

———. 1994. "Welfare States and the Economy." In *The Handbook of Economic Sociology*, ed. N. J. Smelser and R. Swedberg. Princeton, N.J.: Princeton University Press.

———. 1996. "After the Golden Age: Welfare State Dilemmas in a Global Economy." In *Welfare States in Transition: National Adaptations in Global Economics*, ed. G. Esping-Andersen. London: Sage.

———. 1997. "Hybrid or Unique? The Japanese Welfare State between Europe and America." *Journal of European Social Policy* 7 (3): 179–190.

Glyn, A., and Miliband, D., eds. 1997. *Paying for Inequality: The Economic Cost of Social Injustice.* London: Rivers Oram Press.

Gough, I. 1994. "Economic Institutions and the Satisfaction of Human Needs." *Journal of Economic Issues* 28 (1): 25–65.

———. 1996. "Social Welfare and Competitiveness." *New Political Economy* 1 (2): 209–232.

———. 1999. "Social Welfare and Competitiveness: Social versus System Integration?" In *Essays on Exclusion and Integration*, ed. I. Gough and G. Olafsson. London: Macmillan.

Gough, I., and Doyal, L. 1989. "Socialism, Democracy and Human Needs." In *The Social Economy and the Democratic State: A New Policy Agenda*, ed. P. Alcock, A. Gamble, I. Gough, P. Lee, and A. Walker. London: Lawrence and Wishart.

Gough, I., and Olafsson, G., eds. 1999. *Essays on Exclusion and Integration*. London: Macmillan.

Held, D. 1995. *Democracy and the Global Order*. Cambridge: Polity Press.

Hewitt, M. 1992. *Welfare, Ideology and Need: Recent Perspectives on the Welfare State*. Hemel Hempstead, U.K.: Harvester-Wheatsheaf.

———. 1993. "Social Movements and Social Need: Problems with Postmodern Political Theory." *Critical Social Policy* 13 (1): 52–74.

Jones, D. 1998. *Ambassadors of Cosmopolitanism*. Unpublished paper.

Kangas, O. 1998. "Distributive Justice and Social Policy Models: Rawls in International Comparisons." Finland: University of Turku, Department of Social Policies Occasional Paper.

Kenworthy, L. 1995. "Equality and Efficiency: The Illusory Tradeoff." *European Journal of Political Research* 27 (3): 225–254.

Korpi, W. 1996. "Eurosclerosis and the Sclerosis of Objectivity: On the Role of Values among Economic Policy Experts." *Economic Journal* 106: 1727–1746.

Persson, T., and Tabellini, G. 1994. "Is Inequality Harmful for Growth?" *American Economic Review* 84: 600–621.

Pfaller, A., Gough, I., and Therborn, G., eds. 1991. *Can the Welfare State Compete? A Comparative Study of Five Advanced Capitalist Countries*. London: Macmillan.

Rieger, E., and Leibfried, S. 1998. "The Welfare State and Globalisation." *Policies and Society* 26: 363–390.

Sen, A. 1992. *Inequality Reexamined*. Oxford: Clarendon Press.

Soper, K. 1993. "The Thick and the Thin of Human Needing." In *New Approaches to Welfare Theory*, ed. G. Drover and P. Kerans. Aldershot, U.K.: Edward Elgar.

Tao, J., and Drover, G. 1997. "Chinese and Western Notions of Need." *Critical Social Policy* 50 (1): 5–25.

Wetherly, P. 1996. "Basic Needs and Social Policies." *Critical Social Policy* 16 (1): 45–65.

2

Welfare States, Universal Human Needs, and Objective Human Welfare: Some Social Science and Sociolegal Perspectives

John Carrier and Ian Kendall

In the preceding chapter, Ian Gough builds to the profound and powerful conclusion that "strong extensive welfare states are good for need satisfaction and objective human welfare" (Gough 2000, 26). Our immediate inclination is to agree with that conclusion, having arrived at a broadly similar one on the narrower terrain of state involvement in health care (see Carrier and Kendall 1998, 154–158, 228–268, 314–330), especially since many of the key themes and issues are relevant to both arguments. However, not only was our analysis of the case for universalist health care less wide-ranging than Gough's case for "strong, extensive welfare states," our conclusions were less definitive. Indeed the differences in the arguments may in the end be quite fundamental. They can be related directly to an essential element in Gough's chapter—the distinction between what have been termed "thin" and "thick" definitions of need (Fraser 1989, 161–187).

A "thin" definition of human need aspires to identify that which is common, objective, and universal. The outcome, while relatively abstract, is presumed, because of its universal application, to provide a secure moral basis for the nonmarket allocation of resources (see, for example, Drover and Kerans 1993, 11; Soper 1993, 70). Hence a key element in Gough's case for "strong, extensive welfare states" rests on the universalist theory of need he has developed with Len Doyal (Doyal and Gough 1991), described subsequently as "the most complete and sophisticated attempt to defend the universality of needs" (Soper 1993, 70). "Thick" definitions of human need are identified with cultural contexts, available resources, legislative powers and duties, and the "moral climate of the day"—the underlying presumption being that needs must in the end be related to particular social and historical contexts (Fraser 1989; see also Drover and Kerans 1993, 12).

The major concern expressed about a "thin," objective, universal definition of human needs is that it "can be won only at the cost of such a high degree of abstraction from the specific and differential modes of their satisfaction, that the theory of need no longer serves as any practical guide to welfare provision" (Soper 1993, 73). The major concern about "thick," subjective, culturally specific definitions of human needs is that they will be disputed at the intellectual level and contested at the practical level with the result that the concept of human needs will be "notoriously loosely employed" (Soper 1993, 69) and "continually if confusingly used at the level of social welfare practice, by the most varied groups" (Doyal and Gough 1984, 8). For advocates of the "thin" approach, there is an inherent instability and impermanence in the nature of welfare institutions and activities if the major organizing concept of need is subject to such disputes and confusion.

It is our contention that "thick" definitions of need are an integral component of operationalizing state welfare activities—and that the case for "extensive state welfare" must in the end be a "thick" case—a case that is relative to a particular social and historical context. Our paper focuses initially on Gough's three organizing concepts of (1) strong, extensive welfare states; (2) objective human welfare; and (3) universal human needs. We follow this by introducing (4) a sociolegal perspective, in which we review some of the ways in which the courts in the United Kingdom have addressed issues relating to the definition of need—providing a context for social policy arguments in the "real world" resolution of a "claims-making process" (Drover and Kerans 1993, 22), directed at "satisfiers" (Doyal and Gough 1984, 33) and their disputed allocation of "provisionings" (Soper 1993, 69).

STRONG, EXTENSIVE WELFARE STATES

Defining "welfare states" is potentially problematic and was recognized as such many years ago, most obviously with Titmuss's concern about the value of this "indefinable abstraction" (Titmuss 1968, 124). We have pursued the argument previously ourselves by suggesting that the validity of analyses of "welfare states" may be significantly undermined if the focus of such analysis is confusingly or ill defined (see Carrier and Kendall 1986, 316–324). Unfortunately Gough's chapter includes inconsistencies of the definition of "welfare state" deployed as part of his argument. Three examples of his definitions of the "welfare state" will suffice:

1. Institutions to secure the satisfaction of (some) human needs at (some) standards (p. 20).
2. The public guarantee of rights to the means to human welfare in general and to minimum standards of well-being in particular (p. 20).
3. Agencies that can act to guarantee the wherewithal to meet the needs of strangers (p. 22).

While these definitions are not incompatible one with another, they are not identical. In particular, while all the definitions can be taken to refer to state welfare, they can be accommodated within different models of "welfare states." In particular, the minimal state welfare of the Poor Law in nineteenth-century Britain could be said to provide the institutions necessary for the satisfaction of "some human needs at some standards" (definition 1). Definition 2 moves us beyond this residual model of state welfare, but might be said to be achieved (in the United Kingdom at least) via the sort of post-Edwardian and pre-Beveridge state welfare activities that were in place by the 1930s—certainly by some arrangements that are less than universalist in conception. Definition 3 does perhaps carry the implication of the sort of "strong, extensive welfare state" in support of which Gough's arguments are deployed. Nonetheless the British Poor Law authorities were not entirely insensitive or unresponsive to the "needs of strangers" (see, for example, Turnbull 1973).

In our view definitions and models of state welfare are a particularly important element in these normative arguments. As Gough indicates, an acceptance of the moral and consequentialist critiques directed at "welfare states" "will condemn the traditional extensive state welfare systems of Europe to slow decay" (Gough 2000, 25). But the "decay of state welfare" is not the same as "the disappearance of state welfare," although it would seem to signify (in the longer term at least) a return to some form of minimal state welfare (the residual model of state welfare). For the moment at least, the key challenge for the moral and consequentialist arguments is not the case for some state welfare to meet some human needs at some standards, for this has been part of a long-term, near-consensus for all "industrial societies"—that there should be a commitment to the residual model of state welfare. The challenge is whether the force of those arguments restricts the state to "weak and limited" welfare activities, rather than something "stronger and more extensive."

Conclusions

There is an important issue of categories and categorization at the heart of this debate. The variable nature of Gough's definitions of "welfare state" focuses attention on what sort of "welfare state" can be supported by his moral and consequentialist arguments—for there are two critical dimensions to such arguments. First, the inherent strengths and weaknesses of the arguments themselves, and second, the outcomes from the arguments; that is the relative "strength" and "extensiveness" of those state welfare activities which can be justified by these arguments.

OBJECTIVE HUMAN WELFARE

Gough's consequentialist argument is based on an established tradition in welfare theory—evidence-based responses to that part of the liberal anticollectivist position characterized as the public burden model of welfare (see, for example, Harris 1990; Barnett 1986). This public burden model sees "public welfare expenditure—and particularly expenditure which is redistributive in intent—as a burden; an impediment to growth and economic development" (Titmuss 1968, 124–125). Gough continues in this tradition, drawing on his own work (including that with Pfaller, Gough, and Therborn 1991) and that of Atkinson (1995) and Esping-Anderson (1994). The work of the latter reveals "a mix of positive, negative, and insignificant effects on national output." The recording of "positive" and "insignificant" effects is significant.

The liberal anticollectivist critique ("the public burden of welfare") is very much an "all swans are white" argument—a case against "strong, extensive welfare states" that is universalist in its application. A "widespread assertion" is clearly and forcibly made that "the modern welfare state undermines growth and competitiveness" (Gough 2000, 21). Of course it takes but "one black swan" to disprove this assertion—that is we need only one society which has over a lengthy time period combined a relatively good economic performance with a substantial state welfare regime and the associated consequences for quality of life, to disprove the simple relationship posited by the "public burden model." A number of analyses (including those cited by Gough) have located several "black swans." The implication is clear—the "public burden" case against state welfare is not well founded in evidence. As Gough concludes, "Many incompatibility arguments do not stand up to scrutiny" (Gough 2000, 22), and indeed similar conclusions can be drawn about the incompatibility arguments relating to "social well being" and "freedom" (see, for example, Carrier and Kendall 1998, 258–263).

But if the "universalist" public burden case for restricting state welfare activities to something "weak" and "limited" is not well founded, the "agnostic findings" relating to "economic well being" expose an obvious limitation in Gough's consequentialist argument for something "stronger" and "more extensive." For this argument relies on a form of contingency theory—an admission of not knowing which factors in welfare regimes are linked to and support production. While the outcome is fatal to the simpler "universalist" public burden contentions, it cannot sustain an unchallenged nexus between economic performance and high levels of state social welfare spending.

Perhaps it is an impossible task to seek and arrive at a direct relationship between economic production and welfare, the intervening variables being too numerous and too diverse to place values upon their contribution to improved states of welfare. As far back as 1967, Titmuss integrated this limitation of explanatory theory (the problems surrounding "multiple causality") into part of his normative case for universalist state welfare. This limitation led, he argued, to our inability to disentangle and identify with any degree of precision the causal agencies of "socially caused diswelfare . . . (the) . . . social costs and social insecurities which are the product of a rapidly changing industrial–urban society." Titmuss then linked our conceptual difficulties to tangible operational problems with his conclusion that we could not, in many of the circumstances in which we might wish to do so, "legally name and blame" the agents of diswelfare. This leads to a moral dilemma of either allowing "the social costs of the system to lie where they fall" (on particular individuals, households, and communities) or of providing "social services." It was the range, complexity, and diffusion of these "socially caused diswelfares" allied to "unidentifiable causality" that formed the basis of Titmuss's case for the extensive state welfare implicit in "non-discriminating universalist services." It was his contention that the latter offered our best hope of minimizing those circumstances where "the social costs of the system" lay where they fell (see Titmuss 1968, 133–134). But whereas Titmuss's argument does offer us a justification for universalist state welfare, it is not clear that Gough's consequentalist argument takes us that far, especially given his conclusion that "there is evidence for both positive and negative relationships between specific welfare state programs and competitiveness" (Gough 2000, 22).

Conclusions

For explanatory welfare theory, Esping-Anderson has stressed the importance of Polanyi's "embedded approach" (1959) which he describes as "a major inspiration for latter day welfare state theorists, precisely because it promotes an embedded, relational analysis of the welfare state–economy nexus. This kind of analysis permits us to understand why the egalitarian or economic growth effects of welfare states depend so much on welfare state type" (Esping-Anderson 1994, 726).

This case for an embedded, relational mode of analysis can be translated to normative welfare theory as the case for constructing "thick" justifications for "strong, extensive welfare states." This is not to say that the resulting arguments are so context-laden that they cannot be transferable to other times and places; indeed much may be transferable. The potential, however, for transferability will be dependent on "national political and institutional structures" and "the behaviour of collective political actors" (to use the phrasing of Esping-Anderson 1994, 726).

Gough's consequential case, being "thin" and "universalist," is inconsequential—being little more than a case for the residual model of state welfare. It gains strength if it is "thickened," but it is still not clear that it provides the basis for sustaining "strong, extensive welfare states" without the more "embedded, relational" analysis and arguments of the sort developed by Titmuss (e.g., the limitations of the legal system).

UNIVERSAL HUMAN NEEDS

"By talking of needs, welfare theory directs us to the fact that it deals not in desiderata, but in essentials, not in options but in musts, not in what it would be nice to have, but what there is an obligation to provide" (Soper 1993, 69). If welfare is about an obligation to provide, then presumably the resulting claims to scarce resources have to be based on eligibility criteria which are agreed—"some common denominator which all people share" (Doyal and Gough 1984, 9).

Such criteria may relate to the need for a range of resources— cash income or services in kind such as health care or education. The resulting ("thick") concepts of human need can be seen as legitimizing a particular scale and scope of state welfare activities in a particular time and place. In the context of normative welfare theory, this raises the question of whether it is possible to conceptualize human needs in terms of the "levels of health and autonomy which are generalisable to all people in all societies" (Doyal and Gough 1984, 31); that is to arrive at a "thin" definition of need which refers "to a particular category of goals which are believed to be universalisable" (Gough 2000, 16) and which can sustain a "universalist ethical and conceptual framework" (Gough 1997, 86). Gough summarizes the argument from Doyal and Gough (1991) in his contribution to this book (Gough 2000, 14–16). The argument is lausible but problematic. In particular the initial assumption that the membership of any social group implies obligations and duties sounds like a sensible starting point, but could clearly embrace a very wide range of such obligations and duties—libertarians would keep both to a minimum, and thus keep group obligations to the individual at a minimum. So with the very first strand in the argument we have identified the moral basis of some, minimally nonmarketized, compulsory communal (state) welfare, but no more.

Old Welfare Theory

Has the concept of human needs been "either dismissed or elided at the level of theory" (Doyal and Gough 1984, 8), or does this assertion rest on a dismissal or elision of earlier contributions to the debate? One classic historical example is Beveridge. He was certainly concerned with the conceptual consistency of his "plan for social security," the implementation of which "should be dominated by unity of design" (Beveridge 1942, ¶454). In so doing Beveridge anticipated (by half a century) a variation on Doyal and Gough's theory of "intermediate needs" (Doyal and Gough 1991, ch. 8) with his "five giants" and "eight primary causes of need"—the latter being "so general and so uniform as to be clearly fit subjects for compulsory insurance" (see Beveridge 1942, ¶310–319, 456). The following list indicates some of the links between the analysis of Gough and Doyal on the one hand and Beveridge on the other. Some areas match more readily than others, and this might be taken as a further indication of the "thick" nature of the assumptions that underpin such analyses.

Gough and Doyal's intermediate needs (see Doyal and Gough 1991, ch. 8)	Beveridge's eight primary causes of need and five giants (see Beveridge 1942, ¶311, 456)
Economic security	Unemployment; "idleness"
Nonhazardous work and physical environments	Disability
Economic security	Loss of livelihood
Economic security	Retirement

Economic security	Marriage needs of a woman
	Funeral expenses
Security in childhood	Childhood
Appropriate health care	Physical disease or incapacity
Safe child-bearing	Disease
Appropriate basic and cross-cultural education	Ignorance
Adequate nutritional food and water	Want
Adequate protective housing	Squalor
Significant primary relationships	
Physical security	

The absence of "significant primary relationships" and "physical security" from Beveridge's model might also be taken as a recognition that while these may be essentials rather than desiderata, they are beyond the scope of "state welfare activities" to guarantee to any significant degree. Indeed, Beveridge specifically pursued a rationale for the limits of state welfare by identifying needs and risks "suited for voluntary insurance" (e.g., fire, theft, accident) (Beveridge 1942, ¶312). This case for voluntary insurance links to one of Titmuss's contribution to the moral arguments for "strong, extensive welfare states." Titmuss indicated the limitations of voluntary insurance with his strongly evidenced-based case against the efficiency and choice cases for markets in blood. The former was both widely accepted and influenced policy and practice beyond the United Kingdom.

Titmuss also built on the work of Arrow and others to construct a powerful case for the limitations of consumer choice and sovereignty in the medical care markets. The resulting vulnerability of the health care consumer—hoping s/he can trust the ethics and expertise of the health care professional and facing up to the inevitable uncertainties of health care consumption—provided a case for state intervention in health care beyond the residualism of a "poor law medical service." This is because, in the end, a higher income is no guarantee of ethical and expert health care, and can certainly do nothing to diminish the uncertainties of health care—do I need it, how much will I need, how long will I need it, how much will it cost, and what will be the outcomes?

What is clear from some "old welfare theory" is that even a "universalist" concept of need has to be complemented by a consideration of operational issues if it is to serve as a rationale for any state welfare activity. For example, we can note first that it is not clear how some unmet (even if universalist) needs could be met by state welfare activities (e.g., significant primary relationships). Second, that something more than a "universalist" concept of need is required to argue in support of moving beyond residual, safety-net state welfare to something "stronger" and "more extensive." For example, the relative limitations of the nonstate elements in the social division of welfare need to be clearly established (e.g., Titmuss's health care market limitations argument).

In our view, the market limitations argument is powerful and can have an enduring relevance across a substantial time period and in different cultures. For the moment the essentials of Titmuss's arguments on blood remain valid (see for example Martlew 1997, especially 52–53; Le Grand 1997). Similarly the parallel Beveridge case relating to the pension consumer (Beveridge 1942, ¶188) was not only restated effectively by Titmuss a quarter of a century later (Titmuss 1974, chs. 7, 8) but received a continuing validation in the United Kingdom with first the problems of occupational pensioners relying on business acumen and ethical standards of Robert Maxwell; and second, the recognition of the massive "misselling" of personal pensions in the United Kingdom in the 1980s. Nonetheless it is also difficult not to conclude that these are "powerful but thick" arguments. They are culturally specific relating most obviously to a social construction (retirement from work due to age), to say nothing of specific demographic conditions, as well as technological constructions (the capacity to utilize human blood for large-scale transfusion services). For example, presumably one cannot rule out the potential of artificial blood substitutes to diminish the need for human blood and the significance of the arguments against "human blood markets." The concept of the "relative needs-indifference of commodity society" (Soper 1993, 69) needs to be turned into an "everyday discourse" about, for example, the tangible problems of the consumer in contemporary health care and pension markets.

New Welfare Theory—Down the Yellow Thick Road?

Is it possible to develop a universal concept of need without moving from "ought" to "is"—can the intended universal, objective "is" (of human need) avoid the subjectivity of "ought" arguments? In Gough and Doyal's arguments, this problem is most obvious in their recourse to the best available technical knowledge articulating causal relationships between, for example, physical health and autonomy and other factors to underpin their "universal satisfier characteristics." It is not necessary to adopt an extreme subjectivist approach to note that there is much technical knowledge (for

example, on matters of health) which is to varying degrees conten-
tious and disputed (especially in relation to mental health issues).
Even the seemingly more tangible "nonhazardous physical environment" has been intensely controversial, for example, in relation
to safe levels of exposure to radiation since we have had a significant nuclear power industry (and indeed the "official" safety limits
have been subject to significant redefinition). This raises the question of whether this need—a genuinely nonhazardous physical environment—can be the subject of consensual definition, and
therefore universally met, in any realistic sense in an industrial
society.

The significance of expert knowledge is recognized in Gough and
Doyal's "procedural preconditions" for "enhancing need satisfaction"
which include the "rational identification of needs" involving "ap-
pealing to an externally verifiable stock of codified knowledge, for
example, knowledge about nutrition, child-rearing, or environmental control" (see Gough 1994, 29). But operationalizing "rational
identifications of need" does seem to presume a degree of professional (and interprofessional) agreement which is not always apparent; and such disagreement is not simply a matter of intra and
interprofessional rivalries, but often reflects also the uncertainties
that are an integral part of many "stocks of codified knowledge,"
and indeed can form part of the case for nonmarketized, compulsory communal (state) welfare as in the argument about whether
medical care is a conventional consumer good (see Gough 1994, 29;
Titmuss 1968, 146–147). Furthermore, when we consider that from
"birth, our needs for health and welfare, education and employment,
are defined for us by doctors, social workers, lawyers, public health
inspectors, school principals—experts in the administration of needs"
(Ignatieff 1984, 137), then it may not be possible to disentangle the
"rational identification of need" from "procedural preconditions"
which embrace professional, semiprofessional, administrative, and
street-level personnel making "rational decisions" about "need satisfaction." Subjectivist accounts of need cannot be reduced to minor walk-on parts in the front offices of social security, housing,
education, or health care bureaucracies; rather they are the very
stuff of professional discretion, empathy, the nonjudgmental approach of professionals, and their accountability for the allocation
of scarce resources. All this is not to deny the possibility of "best
understandings" (Doyal and Gough 1984, 22) but that they will be
"somewhat thick best understandings"—understandings that are
comprehensible and justifiable within their own social and cultural
contexts.

Conclusions

What are the implications for incorporating "universal human needs" as a component of normative welfare theory? Once again it is not apparent that a "universalist" concept can sustain much beyond the case for the residual model, especially since it is very difficult to elaborate and operationalize the concept without "thickening" the concept (and introducing subjective elements). Moreover, like "human welfare," "human needs" provide a more substantial argument when related to social context and combined with the sort of contextualized operational analysis undertaken in relation to voluntary insurance institutions by Beveridge and Titmuss.

SOCIOLEGAL PERSPECTIVES

"The law is increasingly used to enter spaces that were previously outside legalistic regulation" (Drover and Kerans 1993, 29). Our sociolegal examples are drawn from the fields of health care, social care, housing, and education. In each area the courts have been called upon to pass judgment on individual need in situations where the individual's need has been denied resources by the public authorities of the welfare state and in one example by a private institution; the latter providing a recognition that "welfare claims are made against institutions other than the state" (Drover and Kerans 1993, 3). See Table 2.1 for a summary of the cases.

The outcome of the cases could have a most dramatic effect on the lifestyles, life chances, and indeed the very life of some of the claimants. All the cases provide us with an insight into the outcomes of challenges in the judicial system to the low-level administrative denial of need. They serve as an illustration of judgments of disputes about resources, and which needs are recognized and seen as legitimate by this decision-making process. Does the resolution of the disputes support or challenge Gough's moral and consequentialist arguments?

In R v Cambridge Health Authority, ex parte B, the denial by the health authority of a second bone marrow transplant to an eleven-year-old girl (B) was challenged successfully in the High Court but overturned on appeal the same day. Could such a denial of resources be accommodated within Gough's framework of autonomy and the right to health care? The relevant officer (the Health Authority's director of public health) of the authority had concluded that the proposed treatment, using the Department of Health's guidelines,

Table 2.1
Sociolegal Understandings of Need

Case	Resource / service area	Issue	Decision
R v Cambridge HA, Ex parte B (March 1995)	Medicine Health authority	Resource denied	Health authority denial approved
R v Gloucestershire County Council and Another, ex parte Barry (March 1997)	Social services	Resource denied	Local authority decision upheld; resources relevant in assessing need
R v Sefton (April 1997)	Social services	Resource denied	Local authority decision upheld; resources relevant in assessing need
R v Fisher (Sep.1997)	Medicine Health authority	Resource denied	Retake decision; central government guidance ignored
Polonski v Lloyds Bank Mortgages Ltd (May 1997)	Financial Housing	Pressing social needs and the freedom to love; who loses?	Domestic need; right to move upheld; bank loses £12,000

Table 2.1 (continued)

Case	Resource / service area	Issue	Decision
In re Payatt (May 1998)	Bankruptcy declared Education	Private school fees as a reasonable domestic need	Approved - private school fees considered a reasonable need
R v East Sussex County Council. Ex parte Tandy (May 1998)	Education home tuition	Resource denied	Education authority acting illegally - duty to provide not power to provide - resources not relevant

was experimental: "The doctors to whom I spoke were consistent in their advice that the proposed treatment was neither standard nor had been formally evaluated" (see R v Cambridge Health Authority, ex parte B 1995, 904); would not be an appropriate use of the authority's limited resources; and was not in the best interests of the child. With regard to the latter it should be noted that the physician who had the responsibility for treating B since her illness was first diagnosed had come to the view "that it would not be right to subject (B) to all this suffering and trauma . . . (associated with the proposed treatment) . . . when the prospects for success were so slight" (R v Cambridge Health Authority, ex parte B 1995, 903). Another medical opinion was that a course of palliative therapy "would enable . . . (B) . . . to enjoy several weeks or months of normal life prior to progression," whereas a further course of intensive chemotherapy and a second transplant "would mean several uncomfortable and distressing weeks or months in hospital which in all probability (B) would not survive" (R v Cambridge Health Authority, ex parte B 1995, 903).

In proceedings for judicial review, the judge concluded that the officer had failed to take account of the child's and her father's wishes; was mistaken in describing the treatment as experimental; had not explained the authority's funding priorities adequately; and "had wrongly treated the whole sum (£75,000) as that required whereas the initial requirement was limited to £15,000" (R v Cambridge Health Authority, ex parte B 1995, 898). The authority's appeal against this decision was upheld on the grounds that it was obvious that the director of public health was aware of the family's wishes; that the description of the treatment as experimental was justified ("it was, on any showing, at the frontier of medical science"); that the authority could not reasonably confine its consideration to the first stage of expenditure: and that "it would be totally unrealistic to require the authority to come to the court with its accounts and seek to demonstrate that if this treatment were provided for B, then there would be a patient C who would have to go without treatment. No major authority could run its financial affairs in a way which would permit such a demonstration" (R v Cambridge Health Authority, ex parte B 1995, 906).

In particular it is relevant to note that the need might be recognized and met in the private sector, most obviously in the United States. The judge's observations on this fact are interesting. "Certain doctors there (in the United States) differed from the view which had been expressed by the English doctors and thought there was a substantial chance of further treatment being successful. Unhappily, however, medical treatment in the United States does not come free and does not come cheap. The cost of treatment by these experts in the United States was, at least to English eyes, prohibitive" (R v Cambridge Health Authority, ex parte B 1995, 900–901).

Two implications follow from this. First, that expert knowledge is clearly influenced by the economic and social context, raising yet again the objectivity and universality of definitions of need that are reliant on such knowledge. Second, it is clear that a combination of communal (state) welfare and noninfinite resources pose dilemmas relating to the ethics and effectiveness of health care and that it is not clear that any relatively universal concept of need will assist in resolving these dilemmas.

In R v Gloucestershire County Council and another, ex parte Barry, services to Mr. Barry had been reduced by the Social Services department in September 1994 because of a reduction in a central government grant to the local authority, and not because of any change in his officially recognized need, which had been assessed in September 1992 and was confirmed to be the same by another assessment in August 1993. There was support for the appeal against the reduction in service from Lord Lloyd, who asked "how resources help to measure the need," and continued by observing that it could not have been Parliament's intention "that a local authority should be able to say 'because we do not have enough resources we are going to reduce your needs'. The needs remained exactly the same. They could not be affected by the authority's ability to meet them. . . . Nor could Parliament have intended that there should be a different standard for measuring the needs of the disabled in Bermondsey and in Belgrave Square" (R v Gloucestershire County Council and another, ex parte Barry 1997, 34).

As part of the majority judgment, upholding the decision of the Social Services Department, Lord Clyde said that "necessary" and "needs" were relative expressions and therefore "in the framing of the criteria, the severity of a condition might have to be matched against the availability of resources" and that such an exercise accorded with "everyday domestic experience in relation to things that one did not have." Lord Nicholls in a similar vein concluded that while one important factor in deciding "whether the disability of a particular person dictated a need for assistance, and at what level," what constituted "an acceptable standard of living" and the need for services, "could not sensibly be assessed without having some regard to the cost of providing them" (R v Gloucestershire County Council and another, ex parte Barry 1997, 34).

To some extent these themes were replayed in R v Sefton Metropolitan Borough Council, ex parte Help the Aged and others, which concerned the provision of home help services. Here again the judgment was that a local authority was entitled to take account of its own resources, financial or otherwise, when assessing whether a person was in need—in this case a person seeking accommodation under Section 21 (1) a of the National Assistance Act, 1948. Lord Justice Jowett in support of the decision referred to R v Gloucestershire County Council and another, ex parte Barry, noting that "the reasoning was that need was not an absolute concept and had to be considered in the context of all relevant factors of which the local authority's own resources was one" (R v Sefton Metropolitan Borough Council, ex parte Help the Aged and others 1997, 36).

In R v North Derbyshire Health Authority, ex parte Fisher, the Health Authority was shown to be operating a policy in effect opposed to that contained in a National Health Service circular, and in so doing, was acting unlawfully and would be ordered to put in place a policy conforming with that set out in the circular. In this case the patient (Mr. Fisher) was diagnosed as suffering from multiple sclerosis in December 1989 and on referral to the Royal

Hallamshire Hospital was assessed by a consultant neurologist to be suitable for the drug beta interferon. The drug had been "red-lined" by the Health Authority, which meant that it had to be specially authorized because it was so expensive. The chief executive of the health authority refused to authorize the prescription because the authority had insufficient funds. In the Court of Appeals (2 September 1997) Mr. Justice Dyson concluded that "this was not a case of a health authority considering national policy within a circular and departing from it. The authority was opposed to the policy and decided to disregard it. That was something it was not entitled to do" (R v North Derbyshire Health Authority, ex parte Fisher 1997).

In this case there was possible harm to the patient by the denial of beta interferon, but the court did not order the authority to prescribe the drug—rather it was ordered to follow the correct procedure for decision making. Decision making was to remain in the hands of clinicians and public administrators, but there was an insistence on "due process." This emphasizes again the significance of procedural arrangements and raises the question of whether the "right to due process" might constitute a need. The case seems to demonstrate both a recognition of clinical need by central government and the problem of cash-strapped agencies seeking to evade meeting such needs by rationing and arguments about scarcity.

With the next two cases we move outside, or to the margins, of state welfare. In Polonski v Lloyd's Bank Mortgages Ltd., Mr. Justice Jacob concluded that the "court was not limited to considering purely financial matters when exercising its discretion to order the sale of a mortgaged property. It was entitled to take into account pressing social needs and to look at all the reasons given by an owner for wanting to sell a mortgaged property at a time when the value of the property would be insufficient to pay off the outstanding mortgage and the owner was unlikely to be able to repay the shortfall" (Polonski v Lloyd's Bank Mortgages Ltd. 1997).

The bank had argued, unsurprisingly, that only extreme cases of social need would be enough to outweigh the bank's interests and that the plaintiff's expressed intention of moving to better her social circumstances "was a kind of blackmail." However the judge said that this was an unfair way of describing what she wanted to do, which was "to exercise her undoubted right to live where she wanted"; that she had shown "perfectly good reasons why she should want to move" (the area in which she lived was "fairly rough"); and the plaintiff had, over the years, behaved "thoroughly responsibly financially so far as she could" (Polonski v Lloyd's Bank Mortgages Ltd. 1997).

Almost exactly one year later (In re Payatt), the father responsible for paying private school fees was made bankrupt. Here the court defined the paying of private school fees as a reasonable domestic need for the purposes of Section 310 (2) of the Insolvency Act, 1986. The argument here was without the fees being paid the child's future would be harmed if moved from the school during her public examination year—the official receiver in bankruptcy had said unfortunately, for the father and the child, the fees for children in private education do not form part of allowable expenses. The Court of Appeals disagreed, thereby extending the definition of need to the payment for private school fees (see In re Payatt 1998).

While conventional state welfare was partly involved in Polonski v Lloyd's Bank Mortgages Ltd. through payments to cover the plaintiff's mortgage repayments, the court decisions in this case and In re Payatt, were interesting for the broad-ranging considerations of social need that were recognized as legitimate constraints on a private, for-profit organization and the official receiver. While no direct references were made to the traditional social policy debates, the decisions might be said to represent further evidence of the distinctive status of housing and education as not being "conventional consumer goods."

Our final case returns us to the conventional social policy arena. In R v East Sussex County Council, ex parte Tandy, it was concluded that when a local education authority performed its statutory duty to provide suitable education for children of compulsory school age, it was not entitled to take account of the availability of financial resources when deciding what sort of education was suitable. "A statutory duty was not to be reduced to the level of a discretionary power" (see R v East Sussex County Council, ex parte Tandy 1998). This followed from advice given to parents in October 1996 that for financial reasons the maximum number of hours of home tuition provided under Section 298 of the Education Act, 1993 would be reduced from five hours per week to three hours per week. In the resulting judicial review, the judge held that "the education authority had taken into account an irrelevant factor, i.e. the shortage of resources, when deciding to reduce the number of hours of home tuition, that the decision was made in pursuit of an ulterior purpose, namely the reduction of expenditure and that it was irrational" (R v East Sussex County Council, ex parte Tandy 1998, 769).

The Court of Appeals reversed the decision by a majority on the grounds that it was legitimate for the education authority to take into account the shortage of resources. The appeal to the House of Lords, however, was successful on the grounds that

"suitable education" within the meaning of Section 298 of the Act con-
noted a standard to be determined purely by educational considerations
namely, efficiency and suitability to the child's age, ability, aptitude and
needs; that there was nothing in the Act to suggest that the availability of
financial resources was relevant to the question of what constituted "suitable education"; that a local authority was not permitted to avoid perform-
ing a statutory duty on the ground that it preferred to use its available
resources for other purposes. (R v East Sussex County Council, ex parte
Tandy 1998c, 884)

It is perhaps interesting to note that the judgment was based in
part on the view that "the LEA owes the statutory duty to each sick
child individually and not to sick children as a class" (R v East
Sussex County Council, ex parte Tandy 1998b, 775)—the issue relates not only to the broader, "equality issues" of the allocation of
resources to children, and within that distribution the allocation to
sick children; but the more specific "equity issues" of whether individual needs are being met adequately. In addition the case of R v
Gloucestershire County Council, ex parte Barry featured in the
House of Lords judgment in this case. In particular it was suggested that the statute in R v Tandy "expressly defines what is
meant by 'suitable education' by reference to wholly objective educational criteria" (R v East Sussex County Council, ex parte Tandy
1998c, 776). This was contrasted with the statutory duty to meet
the "needs" of disabled persons where it was held that the lack of
certain benefits enumerated "could not possibly give rise to "need"
in any stringent sense of the word. Thus it is difficult to talk about
the lack of a radio or a holiday or a recreational activity as giving
rise to a need; they may be desirable but they are not in any ordinary sense necessities" (AER, June 3, 1998b, 776).

While social policy references could of course be found to dispute
this "stringent sense" of what is meant by "need," others could be
found to demonstrate that such definitions of "need" and associated definitions of "poverty" remain problematic and controversial.
For the moment, and in these cases, we are at least reminded of
what appears to be a relatively open-ended and "subjective" definition of need in one statute and a relatively precise and "objective"
definition of need in another.

Conclusions

What do our sociolegal perspectives tell us about the social policy
debates relating to human welfare and human need and Gough's
moral and consquentialist case? All the cases were based in the
United Kingdom and naturally demonstrated the importance of that

society's resource allocation decisions, its cultural context, and its dispute resolution procedures. This has led us to a number of conclusions. First and most obviously, the cases are dominated by disputes about resources and the conflicts that arise in the context of scarcity (the public expenditure problem par excellence; see especially Calabresi and Bobbitt 1978). Second, "need" is seen as a legitimate concept within the context of jurisprudence. Even the profit-maximizing bank conceded that "extreme cases of social need" could outweigh its own financial interests. Third, how "needs" should be interpreted and operationalized is problematic and controversial. Fourth, that the reasoning used to adjudicate in the resulting disputes is "thick reasoning," the arguments deployed being clearly contextual. Fifth, the arguments recognize the tension between potentially open-ended or resource-constrained concepts of need; and it is unsurprising that accountable public officials begin from the resource constrained rather than the open-ended perspective of need. But the resulting operationalizing of need is not simply about economic resources, but is rather a complex mix of resource constraints, professional knowledge, flexible administrative imagination, and ethical–moral reasoning. The assumptions were about avoiding foreseeable harm, meeting unexpected disasters, the people's right to enjoy freedom from stress, and rights to support and help based on community resources, and the need to protect the dependent and the vulnerable—children, elderly people, people with disabilities, and the sick.

NEEDS, CONFLICTS, AND CONSENSUS

Despite the inherent forcefulness of the word, needs are elusive. People don't just have needs, they have ideas about their needs; they have priorities, they have degrees of need; and these priorities and degrees are related not only to their human nature but also to their history and culture. Since resources are always scarce, hard choices have to be made. I suspect that these can only be political choices. They are subject to a certain philosophical elucidation, but the idea of need and the commitment to communal provision do not by themselves yield any clear determination of priorities or degrees. Clearly we can't meet, and we don't have to meet, every need to the same degree, or any need to the ultimate degree (Walzer 1983, 66–67). [There are] . . . concrete problems of articulating and defending particular social policies where "need" remains a part of "everyday discourse." (Doyal and Gough 1984, 7)

There would seem to be a contradiction at the heart of the Gough (and Doyal) project. In seeking to establish a "universalist ethical and conceptual framework" and sustain a case for "strong and extensive welfare states," it is far from clear that they have succeeded in reformulating the concept of need in a way that avoids a "collapse into subjectivism" and the "incorrectness [sic] and immorality of relativist arguments" (Doyal and Gough 1984, 9, 32).

Insofar as they have succeeded in diminishing the subjective elements in their concept of human needs, however, so they have succeeded also in diminishing the capacity of the resulting arguments to provide a rationale for much more than the residual model—that is, relatively "weak and limited" state welfare.

The case for "strengthening" and "extending" state welfare seems to be enhanced as the arguments are "thickened" (based on a more "embedded, relational" analysis) as in, for example, "the old welfare theory" of Beveridge and Titmuss on the limitations of the legal system and voluntary insurance. Our sociolegal perspectives confirm the significance of such an "embedded, relational" approach in legitimizing the boundaries between needs that should be met and those that may remain unmet. The reasoning used to adjudicate in the resulting disputes being "thick reasoning," the arguments deployed being clearly contextual.

While others have identified the "thin" and "thick" definitions of need as points on a continuum (Drover and Kerans 1993, 11), Gough (and Doyal) seem to have locked themselves into a dichotomous either–or approach. There are two competing alternatives; either an objective, universalist, generalizable, and useful concept of need, or a concept of need that is subjective, useless, and might for all practical purposes be "banished from our vocabulary" (Doyal and Gough 1984, 6)—the latter phrasing revealing something of the "inherent totalitarianism" (Soper 1993, 71) of "common, objective, universalist human needs." Yet their own substantive "objectivist" theory apparently needs to be "complemented by a procedural theory" (Gough 1997, 84). Why do they need a "procedural theory?" Obviously because there are "endless disagreement and debates over the strategies, satisfiers and policies which best contribute to overall need satisfaction" (Gough 1997, 84). It seems that even within a "universalist ethical and conceptual framework," the concept of human needs will continue to be "continually if confusingly used at the level of social welfare practice, by the most varied groups" (Doyal and Gough 1984, 8). The implication is that the "thin" definition will require a good deal of "thickening" if it is to provide a viable rationale for developing and operationalizing "strong, extensive" state welfare programs.

The "collapse into subjectivism" represents no more than an observation made long ago that "the situation in which different kinds of need arise and are recognised as 'needs' has changed and will continue to do so" (Titmuss 1958, 40). It is a recognition of the nature of social change, in which societies, or more accurately, pressure groups, political parties, administrators, professionals, legislators, and others, construct and reconstruct various (and often competing) concepts of need in response to, for example, changing normative relationships between individuals and changing views on the restrictions or abundance of resources. It may be that we should be looking for those needs on the margins of boundaries that have defined acceptable needs, and ask the simple question: Are marginal needs to be brought within legitimate boundaries? Whatever the answer, the justification of denial or satisfaction could be examined as a method of assessing new needs and those which it is no longer necessary for public authorities to meet.

So "not only are the 'needs' and 'situations' different but they are differently seen," as Titmuss reminded us all those years ago (Titmuss 1958, 40). The different views can be sustained and coexist, at least in part, through the social division of welfare. They are also capable of being resolved in certain respects at certain points in time, as we have illustrated by one dimension of that social division—the role of the courts. Here of course there is a strong connection with Gough's case. It is the very significantly subjective component of a key concept like human need that provides the rationale for his preconditions for optimization (civil and political freedom and political participation). These preconditions also provide the means by which we can live with and work with the subjective concept of human need. We cannot of course rule out the possibility that we will use these freedoms to participate in a redefinition of human need and become less socially responsible for those needs in a way that we (and Ian Gough) would find less acceptable than the welfare arrangements with which we are currently familiar. But there is much empirical evidence—both contemporary and historical—to suggest that such a "nongolden age of welfare" will not readily or simply come into existence. For those that wish to avoid such a situation, there may be more productive activities to undertake than pursuing the chimera of "truly universal human needs" and "universalist ethics" (Gough 1997, 82) as the basis for such practical, working social institutions as for example a universal national health service.

There is no doubt that the problematic, subjective constituents of many concepts of human need provide immense scope for potential conflicts and would appear to have the potential to paralyze, if not destroy, the operationalization of the concept in the service of state welfare programs—and therefore in a sense to imperil the future of "the welfare state." On the other hand, a substantial state welfare institution like the National Health Service has survived half a century, despite being beset by such conflicts. Perhaps this is because "millions of ordinary people" have learned pragmatically how to reconcile the "diversity of their needs" as well as reconciling "the diversity of their principles, desires, and interests." The latter reconciliation being attributable not to any espousal of "the methods of unitary system-builders or rational-choice theorists but . . . (a reliance) . . . on a mixture of reason, sentiment and habit and the lessons of experience" (Pinker 1995, 85).

On this reading, concepts that are "socially, historically and culturally specific" are not so much "vulnerable" (Gough 1997, 82) as viable. Indeed the concept of need is resilient (along with associated welfare institutions) precisely because it is used, however "confusingly" and "loosely," in "everyday discourse." Furthermore, the real conflict we experience in making sense of needs and related welfare activities may simply be a part of something that is a necessary component of freedom and democracy (Pinker 1995, 87). If we examine "modern welfare states" from the beginning of this century, we would have to say that their origins were invariably conflictual, and their key components—health, social security, housing, and education—have continued to be the focus of conflict for most of their history—punctuated by relatively brief periods of "near consensus." Notions of "need," like those of obligation and entitlement and of rights and responsibilities "are complex and not fully understood by experts, which is to be expected, given that they are part of people's private lives" (Pinker 1992, 282).

In conclusion, our response to Gough's paper has been based in particular on four themes. First, we believe the link established by Gough between the moral case and the consequentialist aftermath of need-based decisions is an innovative framework and well worth adopting in the analysis of need-meeting practices. It clarifies the conceptual, value-based, and intellectual origins of need and allows practitioners to "price" their resulting decisions. Second, "old welfare theory" can be utilized within this innovative framework and indeed remains an essential element in arguments for more than minimal, residual state welfare. Third, the concept of need as used in social policy debates and in practice remains viable, despite associated confusions and conflicts. Fourth, our sociolegal examples of real life situations indicate that in practice, administrative welfare state disputes between claimants and providers leads to "thick" decision making, because these disputes take place within the specific context of scarce resources. This uncomfortable utilitarian position may go against the Kantian idealism of the "thin" definition. Nevertheless, "thickness" is likely to be the definition, the ethic, and the consequences most viable for practitioners, claimants, and academics in the foreseeable future.

"History is now and England" was one poet's conclusion (T. S. Eliot, "Little Gidding") and we would say the same of both "the concept of need" and of the arguments for a "strong, extensive welfare state." This is not suggesting the superiority of a Western, culturally superior definition of "need" or "welfare state" by which all others can be measured. Rather it is a recognition that the administration and understanding of these concepts has at least a "history" in the United Kingdom. This particular history informs what we say now about both "need" and "the welfare state"; and while what we say may have a relevance in some way beyond "now and England," we cannot escape the conclusion that as we move away from this particular location in time and space, some of what we say may lose some of its relevance. In this sense, the moral and consequentialist case for a "strong, extensive welfare state" needs to be continually revisited, reexamined, and reconstructed.

REFERENCES

Atkinson, A. B. 1995. *The Welfare State and Economic Performance*. Welfare State Programme Discussion Paper 109, STICERD, London School of Economics, May.

Barnett, C. 1986. *The Audit of War: The Illusion and Reality of Britain as a Great Nation*. London: Macmillan.

Beveridge, William. 1942. *Social Insurance and Allied Services*. Cmd. 6404. London: HMSO.

Calabresi, G., and Bobbitt, P. 1978. *Tragic Choices*. New York: Norton.

Carrier, J., and Kendall, I. 1986. "Categories, Categorization and the Political Economy of Welfare." *Journal of Social Policy* 15: 315–335.

———. 1998. *Health and the National Health Service*. London: Athlone Press.

Doyal, L., and Gough, I. 1984. "A Theory of Human Needs." *Critical Social Policy* 10 (1): 6–38.

———. 1991. *A Theory of Human Need*. London: Macmillan.

Drover, G., and Kerans, P. 1993. "New Approaches to Welfare Theory: Foundations." In *New Approaches to Welfare Theory*, ed. G. Drover and P. Kerans. Aldershot, U.K.: Edward Elgar.

Esping-Anderson, G. 1994. "Welfare States and the Economy." In *The Handbook of Economic Sociology*, ed. N. J. Smelser and R. Swedberg. Princeton, N.J.: Princeton University Press.

Fraser, N. 1989. *Unruly Practices: Power, Discourse and Gender in Contemporary Social Theory*. London: Polity Press.

Gough, I. 1994. "Economic Institutions and the Satisfaction of Human Needs." *Journal of Economic Issues* 28 (1): 25–65.

———. 1997. "Social Aspects of the European Model and Its Economic Consequences." In *The Social Quality of Europe*, ed. W. Beck, L. van der Maesen, and A. Walker. The Hague: Kluwer Law International.

———. 2000. "Normative and Consequentialist Arguments for the Welfare State." In *Into the Promised Land: Issues Facing the Welfare State*, ed. A. Ben-Arieh and J. Gal. Westport, Conn.: Praeger.

Harris, J. 1990. "Enterprise and Welfare States: A Comparative Perspective." *Transactions of the Royal Historical Society*, ser. 5, vol. 40: 175–196.

Ignatieff, M. 1984. *The Needs of Strangers*. London: Chatto and Windus.

In re Payatt (Law Report, The Times, 4 May 1998).

Le Grand, J. 1997. Afterword to *The Gift Relationship*, ed. R. Titmuss, with new chapters edited by A. Oakley and J. Ashton. London: London School of Economics.

Martlew, V. 1997. "Transfusion Medicine towards the Millennium." In *The Gift Relationship*, ed. R. Titmuss, with new chapters edited by A. Oakley and J. Ashton. London: London School of Economics.

Pfaller, A., Gough, I., and Therborn, G., eds. 1991. *Can the Welfare State Compete? A Comparative Study of Five Advanced Capitalist Countries*. London: Macmillan.

Pinker, R. 1992. "Making Sense of the Mixed Economy of Welfare." *Social Policy and Administration* 26 (4): 273–284.

———. 1995. "Golden Ages and Welfare Alchemists." *Social Policy and Administration* 29 (2): 78–90.

Polanyi, K. 1959. *The Great Transformation*. New York: Rinehart.

Polonski v Lloyd's Bank Mortgages Ltd. 1997. Law Report, *The Times*, 6 May.

R v Cambridge Health Authority, ex parte B. 1995. *The Weekly Law Reports*, 16 June, 898–907.

R v East Sussex County Council, ex parte Tandy. 1998a. Law Report, *The Times*, 21 May.

———. 1998b. *All England Law Reports*, 3 June, 769–777 (N.B.: East Sussex is wrongly transposed to Essex in the titles–subtitles but not in the text).

———. 1998c. *The Weekly Law Reports*, 5 June, 884–892.

R v Gloucestershire County Council and another, ex parte Barry. 1987. Law Report, *The Times*, 21 March, 34.

R v North Derbyshire Health Authority, ex parte Fisher. 1997. Law Report, *The Times*, 3 September.

R v Sefton Metropolitan Borough Council, ex parte Help the Aged and others. 1997. Law Report, *The Times*, 27 April, 36.

Soper, K. 1993. "The Thick and Thin of Human Needing." In *New Approaches to Welfare Theory*, ed. G. Drover and P. Kerans. Aldershot, U.K.: Edward Elgar.

Titmuss, R. M. 1958. *Essays on the Welfare State*. London: Allen and Unwin.

———. 1968. *Commitment to Welfare*. London: Allen and Unwin.

———. 1974. *Social Policy: An Introduction*. London: Allen and Unwin.

Turnbull, M. 1973. "Attitude of Government and Administration towards the 'Hunger Marches' of the 1920s and 1930s." *Journal of Social Policy* 2 (2): 131–142.

Walzer, M. 1983. *Spheres of Justice : A Defence of Pluralism and Equality*. Oxford: Blackwell.

FURTHER READING

Abel-Smith, B., and Titmuss, K. 1987. *The Philosophy of Welfare: Selected Writings of Richard M. Titmuss*. London: George Allen and Unwin.

Beveridge, William. 1942. *Social Insurance and Allied Services*. Cmd. 6404. London: HMSO. Esp. Part 1, "Introduction and Summary," ¶1–10; Part 5, "Plan for Social Security," ¶310–319.

Foster, P. 1983. *Access to Welfare: An Introduction to Welfare Rationing*. London: Macmillan.

Ware, A., and Goodin, R. E., eds. 1990. *Needs and Welfare*. London: Sage.

3

Representation of Gender Equality Issues in Liberal Welfare States

Julia S. O'Connor

Over the past decade there has been a considerable amount of research on social policy frameworks, within and across several countries, in terms of their gender logic and how this logic has changed over time. There has been relatively little attention, however, to how gender equality issues have been politically represented. In particular, there has been little attention to the mobilization and orientation of gender equality movements in the context of national and historically specific institutional structures. This is the concern of this chapter, which outlines a framework directed to exploring how gender equality issues are represented. This framework is outlined in the next section and is then followed by its application to an analysis of the representation of gender equality issues in the United States and Australia over the past two decades. Restructuring of welfare states is an integral part of the context within which the representation of gender equality issues in the political system, and the associated gender policy logics, are being played out in all OECD countries, including the two considered here. The implications of this are the focus of the third section.

THE REPRESENTATION OF GENDER EQUALITY ISSUES: A FRAMEWORK FOR ANALYSIS

Much welfare state analysis has concentrated on the role of political parties and trade unions in influencing policy outcomes. These are essential elements of any explanation but they provide only part of the explanation in relation to gender equality issues. The framework proposed here involves five elements: social movement mobilization and orientation, mobilization of antifeminist movements, political party configuration, the political opportunity structure, and the institutional context and legacy.

Social Movement Mobilization and Orientation

Social movement orientation refers to the political strategy pursued by gender equality movements, in particular, with regard to the state. The term "gender equality movement" is used here to refer to the movements for women's equality in the sense of gender equality, which are widely identified as the feminist movement. There is no single movement in any country. In using the term "feminist movement," we recognize that the term "feminism" has a broad range of connotations. Similarly, the women's movement in all countries encompasses a range of movements with shared but also diverse emphases. The term "feminism" is used here to refer to analysts and/ or activists who recognize gender as a fundamental structuring mechanism in contemporary societies. There is no single feminist analysis of the welfare state, and significant differences in emphases and in policy prescriptions are evident in published analyses. Liberal, socialist, and radical perspectives, the two former paralleling long-standing analytical and political approaches in Western countries, identify the major traditions in feminism from the 1960s to the present. The concern here is not with establishing definitive designations; rather it is with identifying key strands of the women's movement that have had resonance within the United States and Australia since the 1960s. While all feminist analyses give primacy to gender and the achievement of gender equality, they differ significantly in their explanations of the source of gender inequality and in the proposed solutions; and there are also differences in emphases within schools (Dale and Foster 1986; Williams 1989). Two key questions are of particular significance in relation to gender equality movements' orientation to the state: Is the state perceived as inherently oppressive of women or is it a potential resource? If the state is a resource, is participation in state institutions in the development and implementation of policy the most effective approach, or is change more effectively achieved through external pressure?

Mobilization of Antifeminist Movements

While such movements are often characterized as against equality in their orientation, they invariably stress equality in their programs—the emphasis is on equality, but within the context of difference and traditional gender roles, including a traditional gender division of labor.

Political Party Configuration

This term is used to refer to the relative strength of left, center, and right parties. This configuration is likely to influence the representation of gender equality issues, both directly in terms of party positions and more importantly in terms of its influence on the context within which social movements and groups represent these issues. There is considerable evidence that parties on the left of the left–right political spectrum—social democratic and labor parties—are more favorably disposed to gender equality issues than parties on the right of the political spectrum, with central parties occupying an intermediate position. This is borne out in analyses of these and several other countries (Lovenduski 1986; Randall 1987; Lovenduski and Randall 1993; Kaplan 1992; Katzenstein and Mueller 1987). Yet there is cross-national variation in the commitment to gender equality of parties of the same political hue and over-time variation in the commitment of individual parties. It is also important to recognize that the same label does not imply the same orientation. Liberal parties are often categorized as center parties, but the Australian Liberal Party is more appropriately categorized as a moderate-right conservative party. This fact is reflected in its consistent coalescing with the Country Party, which is on the far right of the political spectrum by cross-national standards (Castles and Mair 1984). A caveat must also be entered in relation to the Australian Labor Party (ALP), which is affiliated with the Socialist International and is characterized in cross-national classifications as a moderate-left party, but is on the center side of this designation relative to other moderate-left parties. In relation to the U.S. Republican and Democratic Parties, there is general agreement on their right and center-right designations in terms of U.S. politics (Castles and Mair 1984). Yet it must be recognized that these parties are coalitions of relatively diverse interests, and this diversity is often reflected in intraparty divisions on gender equality issues. While acknowledging this complexity we argue that the political party configuration is crucial to the character of the political opportunity structure within which gender equality advocates operate.

The Political Opportunity Structure

We are using this concept, as developed by Sydney Tarrow, to refer to access to state institutions, the stability of political alignments, and the relationship to allies and support groups (1983, 28–34). We are particularly concerned with the political opportunity structure confronting the gender equality and antifeminist movements.

The Institutional Context and Legacy

Examples of this are the unitary or federal structure of government, the centralization of government, the potential for bureaucratic policy machinery, and the industrial relations framework.

THE REPRESENTATION OF GENDER EQUALITY ISSUES IN LIBERAL WELFARE STATE REGIMES

We now use this framework to analyze the representation of gender equality issues in the United States and Australia over the past two decades. There is overwhelming evidence of liberal influences on the origins and development of these welfare states (Esping-Andersen 1990; O'Connor, Orloff, and Shaver 1999). In liberal welfare state regimes, state intervention is clearly subordinate to the market in social provision and there is a strong emphasis on income and/or means testing for access to benefits. This contrasts with the typical social democratic welfare state, as exemplified by the Nordic countries, which is characterized by universalism in social rights, a strong role for the state, and the integration of social and economic policy. A gendered division between public and private is a central feature of liberal ideology. While all welfare states display some elements of a split between the family, on the one hand, and the state and the market, on the other, the sharpness of this split varies across welfare states, and a strong division is identified as characteristic of liberal welfare states. Consistent with their liberal policy orientation, the United States and Australia have been characterized by recognition of gender difference and/or a public–private division, which was a gender division in practice (Orloff 1991; Jenson 1986; Shaver 1987). However, each has also been characterized by its own variant of this policy logic and in the contemporary period, movement away from it, or at least its modification.

There has been a shift in thinking away from policy formation based on gender difference since the 1960s, to some extent, in both countries, but the character of the change is very different. For example, the analysis of income maintenance, labor market participation, related legislative and social provision, and reproductive rights indicates a commitment in the United States to gender sameness by the 1990s. This treats women, like men, as workers, but based on a traditional male worker model; that is, the recognition of gender sameness is not paralleled by a mechanism to compensate for difference in conditions such as differences in responsibility for caring for dependent people. Australia has also moved from the treatment of women as dependents of men to one of formal gender neutrality, within which women are treated as independent citizens but care giving is still a basis for claims. Despite a considerable increase over the past two decades, female labor force participation is considerably lower, considerably more likely to be part-time, and more likely to enjoy publicly supported child care than is the case in the United States. Labor market equality gains in the two countries differ: while the United States has been relatively successful in reducing gender-based occupational segregation, Australia has been relatively successful in reducing gender-based pay differentials. The benefits of the former tend to be greater for those at the upper end of the occupational spectrum, while those of the latter tend to be spread more widely (O'Connor, Orloff, and Shaver 1999).

THE UNITED STATES: THE WOMEN'S MOVEMENT AS A "SOPHISTICATED INTEREST GROUP"

Where does the United States fit in terms of the five-point framework outlined earlier? It has both a strong gender equality movement and a strong antifeminist movement. The National Organization of Women (NOW) was formed in 1966, at least in part, out of frustration at failure to implement gender equality policy following federal and state commission and task force reports. The failure of the Equal Employment Opportunity Commission (EEOC) to enforce the 1964 Civil Rights Act gender provisions was particularly significant. NOW concentrated much of its energies on fighting sexual discrimination in employment through legal action. The women's movement in the United States is one of the highest profile movements in the world, yet the gender equality policy outcomes have been less encompassing than in several countries with weaker movements. On the other hand, civil citizenship rights in the United States are as strong as, or stronger than, elsewhere in the OECD, and the decrease in occupational segregation over the past three decades has been among the best in the OECD. This does not preclude marked gender-based pay differentials and the existence of a glass ceiling which limits the percentage of women in the most senior positions. These apparent contradictions give rise to a question about the compatibility of mass and elite strategies. Before considering this, we must consider the role of the counterequality movement and the shifting fortunes of it, and the equality movement over time, depending on political party configuration; also associated with this, the political opportunity structure.

The counterequality movement was particularly active during the Equal Rights Amendment ratification process from 1972 to 1982, through the Stop ERA and the Eagle Forum organizations. It continues to be active not only with regard to abortion issues but also regarding the role of the state vis-à-vis the family. For example, one of its elements—Concerned Action for America—actively campaigned against the Family and Medical Leave Act until it was passed in 1993. Throughout the Reagan–Bush period, the counterequality movement enjoyed a favorable political opportunity structure relative to the gender equality movement. In contrast, the Clinton administration has provided a relatively positive opportunity structure for the women's equality movement, at least in terms of equal opportunity and access to positions of influence. The most obvious manifestation of this is women in Cabinet positions and in senior administrative positions. In view of the length of presidential office holding by the Republican Party over the past twenty-five years, it must be asked whether the absence of reliance on the government as a mechanism for achieving gender equality, identified by Marian Sawer (1990) in her comparison with Australia, is an inherent characteristic of the U.S. women's movement or a realistic response to the political opportunity structure.

The U.S. gender equality movement has never been monolithic, and the dominant orientation has varied over time (Costain and Douglas 1987; Davis 1991), although liberal feminism has always been the core of U.S. women's mobilization. The primary focus of liberal feminism is on inequalities associated with sex discrimination and associated attitudes. This leads to an emphasis on antidiscrimination and equal opportunity policies directed toward increasing the representation of women in politics and in public and private institutions, especially at senior levels. Since the mid-1980s, there has been more diversity in the U.S. movement and in its organizational locus. This is reflected in enduring and widespread grassroots activities (e.g., rape crisis centers and women's bookstores) along with more mainstream political activity; in addition, there has been a proliferation of women's caucuses in professions and the growth of specific-issue organizations around abortion rights, peace, and nuclear disarmament (Harder 1990; McGlen and O'Connor 1995, 300–301). The diversity is also reflected in an identifiable feminism on the right of the political spectrum, distinctly different from any of the traditional feminist orientations in professing a libertarian and promarket orientation (Klatch 1990).

As in several other countries, there has been a persistent tension between those who wished to pursue formal legal equality versus those who favored protective legislation which recognized differences in conditions (Freeman 1987). This difference is captured in the opposing positions on the Equal Rights Amendment (ERA), which was passed by Congress in 1972 but which did not gain the support of sufficient states to ensure ratification by 1982, and thus failed to be incorporated in the constitution. The division among gender equity proponents on the ERA illustrates the complexity of the issues related to equality versus difference. It was opposed by some equality proponents who feared it would negate protective legislation. Support for the ERA is consistent with the U.S. focus on civil citizenship over social citizenship rights. Despite the failure to ratify the ERA, the thinking on which it is based—gender sameness—is now the taken-for-granted framework for public policy in the United States.

After the defeat of the ERA in 1982, the focus of the women's equality movement became more diverse. The 1980s also saw increasing mobilization around political representation. The objective of getting more women elected to political office was not crowned by early success. Yet the proportion of women officeholders at state and national levels increased from 4.3 percent in the 1981 to 1983 period to 10.3 percent in the 1993 to 1995 period (Center for the American Woman and Politics 1993).

Costain and Douglas (1987) identify three periods in terms of the dominant approach to attaining political influence by the contemporary U.S. women's movement, as represented by NOW and the Women's Equity Action League (WEAL) (formed as a breakaway from NOW in 1968). During the formative period of 1966 to 1972, the movement concentrated on protest and working through political elites. In the routinizing period of 1972 to 1977, a range of tactics was used, including constitutional amendment, legislative lobbying, and political protest. During the institutionalizing period from 1978 onward, legislative lobbying has been the preferred tactic together with an emphasis on electoral politics, especially since 1980. Writing in the mid-1980s, Costain and Douglas concluded that political parties had been largely tangential to the successes and failures of the women's movement. They argue that the characteristics of the American political system, especially its highly decentralized decision-making structure, the highly decentralized organization of political parties, and the diversity of their policy preferences, frustrate social movement efforts to change policy (1987, 208–209), and that the successes achieved by the women's movement came largely through "sophisticated interest group" behavior, the legitimacy of which was based on the demonstration of strong grassroots support for the positions advocated. As a tactic this affords access to policy makers in Washington. Parallel to this, many of the most significant equality achievements by the U.S. women's movement were achieved through the courts—for example, abortion rights, antidiscrimination, and equal opportunities decisions.

While not doubting the importance of legal action and lobbying, it is important to recognize that the political party in power has influenced considerably the scope and possibilities for gender equality activity. This is reflected not only through the composition of the Supreme Court and other senior appointments, but also by its support, or lack thereof, for the limited bureaucratic policy agencies that exist in the United States, such as the Women's Bureau (Stetson 1995) and the Equal Employment Opportunities Commission. The Reagan–Bush period was one of constraint on all of these grounds for the women's equality movement, whereas it was relatively favorable to the counterequality movement, coinciding with the identification of the Republican Party with antifeminism. These developments reinforced the shift of the women's movement towards lobbying the Congress, which was controlled by the Democrats. The emergence of the gender gap in party identification and voting in favor of the Democratic Party was associated with considerable activity by gender equality activists within that party. This is reflected in recent electoral outcomes.

The dominant orientation and strategy of the U.S. women's equality movement has been consistently liberal feminist, and while this has had little success in achieving mass economic gains, it has been relatively successful in the equal opportunity and antidiscrimination domain, which has been of particular benefit to better educated women, and in the strengthening of civil citizenship rights. These gains would appear to be relatively secure, since they are consistent with the overall policy framework and tradition, although they are not unchallenged, as is evidenced by abortion. In terms of its lack of success in relation to mass equality issues, such as pay equity, it is noteworthy that the highly decentralized industrial relations framework provided institutional barriers, and the weak and declining labor union movement meant that allies were sparse. In contrast, the rights orientation finds a fertile context not only in the policy tradition but also in the existence of numerous supportive rights organizations.

AUSTRALIA: AN ALLIANCE BETWEEN THE AUSTRALIAN LABOR PARTY GOVERNMENT, THE WOMEN'S MOVEMENT, AND THE LABOR MOVEMENT

In contrast to the United States, Australia did not have a strong counterequality movement. For an extended period from the early 1970s to the early 1990s, its gender equality movement enjoyed a relatively favorable political environment. The contemporary women's equality movement in Australia has three main elements:

grassroots organizations, women in the labor movement, and the Women's Electoral Lobby (WEL). The latter organization, which was founded in 1972, was nonparty and focused on bringing women's equality issues—child care, equal pay, equal opportunity, and reproductive rights—onto the political agenda. It gained immediate prominence because of its very effective election strategy in the same year. This election brought the Labor Party back into power after twenty-three years of Liberal–Country Party coalition government. Since the new government was strongly committed to women's equality issues, some of the demands made by WEL enjoyed almost immediate success—in particular its demands for greater representation of women in the government and bureaucracy (Sawer 1995). While WEL has received considerable attention because of its high profile success, it is important to acknowledge that much of the success of the Australian women's equality movement, especially in terms of achievements such as pay equity, which benefited the mass of women, is a story of the concerted action of diverse strands. It involved not only elected women and feminists in the bureaucracy—the "femocrats"—but also the successful organization of women in the trade union movement and the pressure on and criticism of the feminists in the bureaucracy by grassroots movements.

Australia is not unique in having a relatively strong labor party and union movement; there are some key elements, however, especially institutional structures which, combined with the political party configuration over the 1970s and 1980s, made the Australian situation favorable to the achievement of mass equality gains. The Whitlam government in the 1972 to 1975 period was the first labor government in almost a quarter century. Its concern with gender equality issues was consistent with the acknowledgement by social democratic and labor parties cross-nationally at this period of the importance of gender equality in the context of their broader commitment to equality. The U.S. civil rights movement helped to raise the profile of equality issues throughout the Western world at this period. The concern with gender equality issues by the Whitlam government was also a reflection of electoral concerns—the ALP had traditionally fared relatively poorly among women voters. These concerns were heightened by the activities of WEL.

Considerable gains were made during the Whitlam government's tenure both in relation to social programs in general and specifically relating to the institutionalization of a concern with women's issues in government and in the federal bureaucracy. This was reflected in the establishment of policy machinery and the recruitment of several feminist activists to the bureaucracy, both of which were maintained, although with varying levels of support, throughout the coalition governments which followed (Watson 1990; Sawer 1991). Much of this was replicated at the state level, with the result that Australia has an extensive array of gender-related bureaucratic policy machinery. Some of these measures were strengthened in the period from 1983 to 1996, during which time the ALP again held office at the federal level. The Women's Budget Program introduced in 1984 and 1985 (from 1987 on entitled the Women's Budget Statement), is particularly noteworthy. This required Commonwealth departments and agencies "to provide a detailed account of the impact of their activities on women for a document circulated by the Prime Minister on budget night." This enhanced the effectiveness of the requirement introduced in 1983 that all Cabinet submissions must include a statement of their impact on women (Sawer 1990, 228). The Women's Budget Statement had a significant educative role in sensitizing bureaucrats and the public on the gender impact of apparently gender-neutral programs. Rather than asserting neutrality, departments were obliged to provide a gender disaggregated analysis of programs—for example, labor market programs and taxation measures (Sawer 1990, 229–231). This program was abolished by the Liberal–Country coalition in 1996.

The accord between the ALP and the Australian Council of Trade Unions (ACTU), which came into effect in 1983, included a commitment to protect social security incomes and those of low wage earners from the effects of structural change. Despite early criticism that the accord had institutionalized gender pay inequality, the period of the accord until 1993 saw significant decreases in the gender wage gap. It was also associated with other gender equality gains.

In analyzing the relative success of the Australian women's movement in effecting change in government policies over the 1970s and 1980s, Marian Sawer (1991, 260) argues that four factors make the Australian situation unique: (1) the Australian political tradition whereby radical social movements automatically looked to government to satisfy their demands; (2) the window of opportunity provided by the election of reformist governments at national and state levels at a time when the political energy of the Australian women's movement was at its height; (3) the lack of effective opposition—antifeminist organizations did not win the credibility with mainstream political organizations that they achieved elsewhere, most notably in the United States; and (4) the existence of a centralized wage-fixing system.

What makes the Australian situation unusual throughout most of the 1970 to 1990 period is the simultaneous occurrence of these four factors. This created a relatively favorable political opportunity structure for the women's equality movement, although it is important to recognize that this was more consistently true in some areas than in others. While the gender equity bureaucratic policy machinery remained intact during the government tenure of the ALP, the centralized bargaining system, which was the source of the mass gender equality gains, was effectively ended in October 1991. Enterprise bargaining was introduced at the end of 1991, despite an earlier statement by the Industrial Relations Commission that it "places at a relative disadvantage those sections of the labour force where women predominate" (IRC 1991, 56, quoted in Lee 1994, 190). In recognition of this, an award system was retained to provide a safety net to protect those unable to make workable agreements with employers and to ensure compliance with ILO conventions concerning minimum pay, equal pay for work of equal value, and redundancy (Lee 1994, 190). Despite these commitments by the Labor government, considerable concern was expressed by gender equality advocates. Much of this centered on the government commitment to increase labor market flexibility and the fear that this would take primacy over equality issues. Economic policy emphasized fiscal restraint and increased labor market flexibility as key imperatives of national policy to the exclusion of other considerations (Pusey 1991). This was the rationale for enterprise bargaining.

While the ALP had already seriously compromised the successful model through the introduction of enterprise bargaining, some of the other gains of the 1970s and 1980s came under challenge almost immediately with the election of the Conservative coalition in 1996. For example, the Women's Budget Statement was abolished, and the Office for the Status of Women budget was cut significantly and the scope of its mandate lessened. At least one analyst detected a shift back to elements of a male breadwinner model in the early action of the coalition (Mitchell 1997). She cites action such as the introduction of a family tax rebate paid to the primary breadwinner, in its first budget, and commitments to abolish parts of the child care support structure and to cut back on others.

These changes suggest that the gains associated with the relative success of the Australian women's movement identified by Marian Sawer are under serious challenge. They also suggest that when gender equality gains conflict with government economic objectives, gender equality takes second place. This occurs despite the existence of a range of gender equality bureaucratic policy units and the increased representation of gender equality advocates in the bureaucracy and parliament. While the changes during the

1970s and 1980s in gender-related issues suggest the possibility of a "woman friendly" policy scenario in Australia, a longer-term view suggests that the institutionalization of these successes cannot be taken for granted. This longer-term view suggests that the orientation of the women's movement of looking to government to satisfy its demands yields significant gains only in the context of a favorable political and economic opportunity structure.

SOCIAL MOVEMENT MOBILIZATION AND ORIENTATION IN THE CONTEXT OF RESTRUCTURING

It is noteworthy that the most recent change of government in Australia has made a marked difference in several policy areas, including gender equality. This contrasts with the transition from Labor to the coalition (that is, from the Whitlam to the Fraser government) in 1975 which did not result in a direct attack on the changes made by Labor in the gender equality area, although it made a significant reversal in relation to the national health system, Medibank, and other social services (Mishra 1990, 79–80). While these changes undoubtedly made an impact, the specific gender equality changes made by Labor were not challenged. That change reflected a Liberal–Country replacement of a Labor government which had been in power for only three years, while the 1996 change followed a Labor government that had been in power since 1983. Consequently, the argument of institutionalization of the changes in the earlier period does not carry weight as an explanation of the different behaviour of the Liberal–Country Party coalition in the two periods. Is the difference due to the greater impact of restructuring in the 1990s, in particular its influence on the political context? While Mishra's (1990) account of restructuring in Australia in the 1980s points to the persisting social democratic influence as a mitigator of the more blatant restructuring experienced in the United States under Reagan and in Britain under Thatcher, this influence was considerably lessened in the 1990s. The Australian Labor Party had already adopted a significant range of policies in response to restructuring by the late 1980s and early 1990s (Pusey 1991).

Restructuring is evident in a whole series of developments, none of which are unique to this period, but all of which are more acutely evident throughout the 1980s and 1990s (e.g., rapid technological change, growth of nonstandard employment, high government deficits, falling rates of productivity growth, stagnating real incomes, and in Australia, high unemployment, especially long-term unemployment). By the mid-1980s, both Australia and the United States had begun to respond to these issues, and this was reflected in policy output, including the restructuring of social programs. Fiscally restrictive policies were often justified by reference to globalization, in particular the threat posed to employment by the increasing competitiveness of the globalized economy and globalized financial markets. The emphasis on globalized financial markets was associated in some countries, including Australia, with considerable emphasis on credit ratings and their influence on the cost of repaying foreign debt and on currency stability. These arguments were marshalled to support arguments for the absence of choice in domestic policy.

The configuration of these influences identified—especially the preoccupation with fiscal rectitude—has fostered an environment which is not favorable to responding to new needs through the expansion of programs. Yet the economic and, in particular, labor market restructuring which characterized the 1980s and 1990s gave rise to new needs that changed the traditional state–market–family balance. Female labor force participation continued to increase, and this was reflected in the increase in dual-earner and single-earner households. But the labor market in which many of these women were participating is very different in character than that which faced the traditional male industrial worker.

Despite these changes in the composition of the labor force, a compensating change in the social policy framework was constrained by the new political and economic context. The combination of the challenge to the Keynesian paradigm from conservative and new-right analysts, the apparent failure of the welfare states to solve certain problems, the changing global context, and the associated claim of the ineffectiveness of national solutions were associated with a loss of confidence in collective solutions. This had an impact on retrenchment, but a more forceful impact on expansion. What we are concerned with in gender equality areas is neither traditional program expansion nor retrenchment, but expansion and refocusing of social policy frameworks in an era of retrenchment. Many of the relevant policies would involve a restructuring of the state–market–family relationship, but this was precisely the area which deficit politics was targeting for cuts. The policies being advocated by gender equality proponents had a dual focus, which made their adoption particularly problematic in the context of deficit politics. This was exacerbated in some countries by political conservatism. These policies had not only a redistributive element, they also had a redefinition element. This redefinition has a number of dimensions: redefinition of the scope of public policy, which involves the recognition of the care of dependent people as a public issue, which was formerly considered private–family responsibilities. Associated with this is the redefinition of "worker" from the male breadwinner without caring responsibilities to the earner with caring responsibilities. In summary, it involves a redefinition of the state–market–family division of responsibility. This process is ongoing and contested to varying degrees across countries and over time.

CONCLUSION

As welfare states with strong liberal influences, the United States and Australia provide fruitful sites for exploring the usefulness of the framework outlined for analysis of the representation of gender equality issues. The clear indications from this review of developments since the 1970s is that all five elements of the framework are essential to a rounded analysis. In terms of social movement mobilization and orientation, we find contrasting orientations: The American movement functioned as an influential and effective interest group outside the political system, whereas the Australian movement strove to influence the political and public policy system through participation in an alliance with the Labor Party in government and with the labor movement. This is not to suggest that the gender equality movement in either country was, or is, monolithic, but to recognize the dominant strategy chosen. Although influenced by the U.S. women's liberation movement in the 1960s, the Australian movement adapted its strategy of mobilization to the uniqueness of the Australian situation, which included the simultaneous occurrence of the four factors identified by Sawer (1991) relating to the orientation and strength of the movement in the context of the election of reformist governments, the lack of effective opposition, and the existence of the centralized wage-fixing system. The American movement also adapted to its opportunity structure, which included a highly decentralized industrial relations system, a weak union movement, and a relatively hostile political environment during the Nixon, Ford, Reagan, and Bush presidencies. These presidencies were not only hostile to the gender equality movement but favorable to the counterequality movement—this was particularly true during the Reagan–Bush era.

Given the very different strategies pursued by the gender equality movements in the two countries, it is appropriate to ask if one of these strategies is more successful than the other in effecting change in government policy on gender equality and in the long-term enhancement of citizenship rights. The success of the Australian movement in effecting change in gender-related issues over the 1970s and 1980s suggests considerable merit in the strategy chosen. But some of the gains, in particular the wage gains, came under threat during the later years of the Labor government's period in office because of the introduction of enterprise bargaining. A concerted reversal of more explicit gender equality policies is evident under the coalition government that was elected in 1996. This highlights the fact that political party in power matters, and also the fact that none of these changes had become institutionalized as taken-for-granted citizenship rights. When the economic context changed and/or when the party in government changed, these policy initiatives were expendable. In contrast to Australia, the U.S. movement concentrated to a considerable extent on enhancing civil citizenship rights through court action and lobbying from outside political parties. Not only are civil citizenship rights more difficult to reverse, in that change entails legal challenge, but, while they challenge the existing policy framework, they run with the grain of the dominant ideology of liberalism and the individual rights orientation of the U.S. policy framework. Another difference between Australia and the United States is the mass and elite orientation of the gains made. This is, of course, not a clear-cut division, but a comparison of pay equity and employment equity–affirmative action points to a significant difference between them. The former benefits people throughout the occupational spectrum, while equality of treatment among men and women, for example in hiring and promotion, is more readily relevant to those at the upper end of the occupational spectrum. It may well be that elite gains are more stable and more difficult to challenge due to the constituency which they predominantly advantage.

While this chapter confined its analysis to two welfare states where there is evidence of strong liberal influences both historically and in the contemporary period, it is equally applicable to the analysis of the representation of issues in other regimes and other types of issues. The analysis illustrates marked variation in the representation of gender equality issues across the two countries, despite strong historical and contemporary liberal influences. In analyzing the process of redefining of the state–market–family division of responsibility and its contestation, political party mobilization is only one influence. Social movement mobilization may be of considerable importance but must be analyzed within a multidimensional approach that recognizes not only political party structure, mobilization, and influence, but the political opportunity structure and the constraints and/or opportunities associated with institutional structures and policy response patterns. These are in turn influenced by economic context.

NOTE

This chapter draws on a larger project on gender and social policy in liberal welfare states by Julia S. O'Connor, Ann Shola Orloff, and Sheila Shaver entitled *States, Markets, Families: Gender, Liberalism and Social Policy in Australia, Canada, Great Britain and the United States* (1999).

REFERENCES

Castles, F., and Mair, P. 1984. "Left–Right Political Scales: Some 'Expert' Judgements." *European Journal of Political Research* 12 (1): 73–88.

Center for the American Woman and Politics. 1993. *Fact Sheet*. November.

Costain, A. N., and Douglas, W. C. 1987. "Strategies and Tactics of the Women's Movement in the United States: The Role of Political Parties." In *The Women's Movements of the United States and Western Europe: Consciousness, Political Opportunity, and Public Policy*, ed. M. F. Katzenstein and C. M. Mueller. Philadelphia: Temple University Press.

Dale, J., and Foster, P. 1986. *Feminists and State Welfare*. London: Routledge and Kegan Paul.

Davis, F. 1991. *Moving the Mountain: The Women's Movement in America since 1960*. New York: Simon and Schuster.

Esping-Andersen, G., ed. 1990. *The Three Worlds of Welfare Capitalism*. Princeton, N.J.: Princeton University Press.

Freeman, J. 1987. *The Politics of Women's Liberation*. New York: McKay.

Harder, S. 1990. "Flourishing in the Mainstream: The U.S. Women's Movement Today." In *The American Woman: 1990–1991*, ed. S. E. Rix. New York: Norton.

Jenson, J. 1986. "Gender and Reproduction: Or, Babies and the State." *Studies in Political Economy* 20: 9–45.

Kaplan, G. 1992. *Contemporary Western European Feminism*. London: Allen and Unwin.

Katzenstein, M. F., and Mueller, C. M., eds. 1987. *The Women's Movements of the United States and Western Europe: Consciousness, Political Opportunity, and Public Policy*. Philadelphia: Temple University Press.

Klatch, R. 1990. "The Two Worlds of Women of the New Right." In *Women, Politics and Change*, ed. L. Tilly and P. Gurin. New York: Russell Sage.

Lee, J. 1994. "Women and Enterprise Bargaining: The Corset of the 1990s?" *Australian Journal of Public Administration* 53 (2): 189–200.

Lovenduski, J. 1986. *Women and European Politics: Contemporary Feminism and Public Policy*. Amherst: University of Massachusetts Press.

Lovenduski, J., and Randall, V. 1993. *Contemporary Feminist Politics: Women and Power in Britain*. Oxford: Oxford University Press.

McGlen, N. E., and O'Connor, K. 1995. *Women, Politics, and American Society*. Englewood Cliffs, N.J.: Prentice Hall.

Mishra, R. 1990. *The Welfare State in Capitalist Society, Policy, Retrench-ment and Maintenance in Europe, North America and Australia.* Toronto: University of Toronto Press.

Mitchell, D. 1997. "Family Policy in Australia: A Review of Recent Devel-opments." Discussion Paper No. 50, Graduate Program in Public Policy, Australian National University.

O'Connor, J. S., Orloff, A. S., and Shaver, S. 1999. *States, Markets, Fami-lies: Gender, Liberalism and Social Policy in Australia, Canada, Great Britain and the United States.* Cambridge: Cambridge University Press.

Orloff, A. S. 1991. "Gender in Early U.S. Social Policy." *Journal of Policy History* 3: 249–281.

Pusey, M. 1991. *Economic Rationalism in Canberra.* Melbourne: Cambridge University Press.

Randall, V. 1987. *Women and Politics: An International Perspective.* Chi-cago: University of Chicago Press.

Sawer, M. 1990. *Sisters in Suits, Women and Public Policy in Australia.* Sydney: Allen and Unwin.

———. 1991. "Why Has the Women's Movement Had More Influence in Australia than Elsewhere?" In *Australia Compared: People, Policies and Politics*, ed. F. Castles. Sydney: Allen and Unwin.

———. 1995. "Femocrats in Glass Towers? The Office of the Status of Women in Australia." In *Comparative State Feminism*, ed. D. S. McBride and A. Mazur. London: Sage.

Shaver, S. 1987. "Design for a Welfare State: The Joint Parliamentary Committee on Social Security." *Historical Studies* 22 (8): 411–431.

Stetson, D. M. 1995. "The Oldest Women's Policy Agency: The Women's Bureau in the United States." In *Comparative State Feminism*, ed. D. M. Stetson and A. Mazur. London: Sage.

Tarrow, S. 1983. "Struggling to Reform: Social Movements and Policy Changes during Cycles of Protest." Western Societies Occasional Paper No. 15, Center for International Studies, Ithaca, New York.

Watson, S. 1990. "The State of Play: An Introduction." In *Playing the State: Australian Feminist Interventions*, ed. Sophie Watson. London: Verso.

Williams, F. 1989. *Social Policy, A Critical Introduction: Issues of Race, Gender, and Class.* Cambridge, U.K.: Polity Press.

FURTHER READING

Bryson, L. 1992. *Welfare and the State.* London: Macmillan.

Burton, C. 1991. *The Promise and the Price: The Struggle for Equal Oppor-tunity in Women's Employment.* Sydney: Allen and Unwin.

Cass, B. 1994. "Citizenship, Work and Welfare: The Dilemma for Austra-lian Women." *Social Politics* 1 (1): 106–124.

Castles, F., ed. 1993. *Families of Nations: Patterns of Public Policy in West-ern Democracies.* Aldershot, U.K.: Dartmouth.

Edwards, A., and Margarey, S., eds. 1995. *Women in a Restructuring Australia*. St. Leonards, Australia: N.S.W., George Allen and Unwin.

Esping-Andersen, G., ed. 1996. *Welfare States in Transition: National Adaptations in Global Economic*. London: Sage.

Langan, M., and Ilona, O. 1995. "Gender and Welfare: Toward a Comparative Framework." In *Toward a European Welfare State?*, ed. G. Room. Bristol: School for Advanced Urban Studies.

Leibfried, S., and Pierson, P., eds. 1995. *European Social Policy*. Washington, D.C.: The Brookings Institution.

Leira, A. 1992. *Welfare States and Working Mothers*. Cambridge: Cambridge University Press.

Lewis, J. 1993. *Women and Social Policies in Europe: Work, Family and the State*. Aldershot, U.K.: Edward Elgar.

————. 1997. "Gender and Welfare Regimes: Further Thoughts." *Social Politics* 4: 160–177.

Mitchell, D., and Geoffrey, G. 1996. "Women and the Welfare State in the Era of Global Markets." *Social Politics* 3: 85–94.

O'Connor, J. S., Orloff, A. S., and Shaver, S. 1999. *States, Markets, Families, Gender, Liberalism and Social Policy in Australia, Canada, Great Britain and the United States*. Cambridge, U.K.: Cambridge University Press.

Pierson, P. 1996. "The New Politics of the Welfare State." *World Politics* 48: 143–179.

Quadagno, J. 1994. *The Color of Welfare: How Racism Undermined the War on Poverty*. New York: Oxford University Press.

Sainsbury, D. 1996. *Gender, Equality and Welfare States*. Cambridge: Cambridge University Press.

Whitehouse, G. 1996. "Legislation and Labour Market Gender Inequality: An Analysis of OECD Countries." *Work, Employment and Society* 6 (1): 65–68.

4

Social Exclusion, Solidarity, and the Challenge of Globalization

Graham Room

The 1990s have seen increasing concern about the growth of poverty and social exclusion. That is true of Israel: Our colleague Abraham Doron warned in a paper last year of "the widening gaps between the different population groups, the increase of economic and personal insecurity in general and among weak population groups in particular, resulting in considerable harm to integration and cohesiveness" (Doron 1997). It is no less true of western Europe, associated with fears about the resurgence of high unemployment, and in central and eastern Europe, amidst the stresses of the transition to a market economy.

This growing concern has been evident in debates at the level of the European Union (EU): first, within the narrow realm of DGV (the Directorate General for Employment, Industrial Relations and Social Affairs), with its antipoverty programs, research studies, and efforts at statistical harmonization (Room 1993); second, in DGXII (the Directorate General for Science, Research and Development), which included social exclusion within its Fourth Framework Research Program; and finally, in the incorporation of social exclusion into the Maastricht and Amsterdam Treaties and the objectives of the Structural Funds. Alongside these initiatives by the EU institutions, the Council of Europe has also been commissioning studies of social exclusion, focused on the wider range of European countries which make up its membership and informed by its specific interest in human rights (Duffy 1995).

During the 1970s and 1980s, the European Commission embraced the language of "poverty" when championing its research studies and action projects concerned with disadvantage, despite the displeasure of some governments, notably the British and German. During the 1990s, in contrast, under the inspiration of Jacques Delors and the French political debate, the European Commission adopted the language of "social exclusion." The Council of Ministers passed a resolution in 1989 calling for action to combat social exclusion, and in 1990, the commission set up a research network, a so-called "observatory," to monitor national trends and policies in this field (the author was until the end of 1993 coordinator of this observatory: Room 1992).

Until recently, researchers and policy makers in Britain tended to regard "social exclusion" as rather unhelpful, combining as it did the imprecision of the French social philosophical debates with the echoes of earlier, discredited right-wing accounts of the "underclass." The election of the new Labour government in May 1997 changed all that. The prime minister has established in Downing Street itself a policy unit concerned with social exclusion; the ESRC has established at the London Shool of Economics a high-profile Centre for the Analysis of Social Exclusion; and "social exclusion" recurs throughout a wide range of government policy documents as a central point of reference.

This chapter has two aims. The first is to clarify the conceptual relationship between poverty and social exclusion: Is the difference merely semantic, or does "social exclusion" offer the basis for new insights into disadvantage and new guidance for policy makers? The second is to analyze social exclusion in relation to the globalization of our market societies and to highlight the policy dilemmas that this poses.

SOCIAL EXCLUSION: FIVE STEPS BEYOND POVERTY

Until recent years it was commonplace in poverty research—in particular, cross-national studies within Europe—to focus on the disposable income (or expenditure) of an individual or household at a moment in time. This was the basis for most of the estimates of the overall poverty rate in the EU that have appeared during the last decade and a half (see, for example, O'Higgins and Jenkins 1987). The reason for this narrow focus was, at least in part, because of the limited data that were available on a cross-nationally comparable basis: Eurostat had secured some consistency of national household budget surveys, but other data sources remained disparate.

Recent years have seen growing acknowledgement that this focus is too narrow (Room 1995). In part because of this awareness and in part under the influence of the proponents of "social exclusion," the research debate has changed significantly during the 1990s. There are five main elements in this reconfiguration of the debate.

From Financial to Multidimensional Disadvantage

Financial resources are, of course, of enormous importance for the whole range of life chances which a person can enjoy. Nevertheless, financial indicators such as low income are insufficiently reliable as proxies for general hardship: Multidimensional indicators are needed. It is moreover important for policy and for explanatory purposes to disentangle different elements of hardship and to identify their interrelationships.

During the 1990s, the European Commission in its work on disadvantage has shown growing interest in this multidimensionality (Whelan and Whelan 1995). Eurostat has been developing new statistical tools, centred on the European Community Household Survey, launched in 1995, which collect information on multiple disadvantage from a multinational panel.

Those who use the language of social exclusion have also been prominent in these efforts. However, they risk overlooking the fact that many of the classic studies of poverty during the 1970s and 1980s were already well aware of this multidimensionality: Examples include Townsend's various studies, Mack and Lansley's survey of "Breadline Britain" (Mack and Lansley 1985), and Ringen's analysis of direct (consumption) and indirect (money) measures of deprivation (Ringen 1988). Many of the cross-national studies and pilot projects sponsored by the European Commission itself had this same multidimensional notion of disadvantage (Room 1993). Only the early, crude, cross-national comparisons of poverty rates can be fairly accused of a narrow concern with financial resources alone, and even then the paucity of comparable data provide an excuse. In short, the move to an appreciation of the multidimensionality of disadvantage hardly suffices to justify the excitement which the new language of social exclusion has been generating.

From a Static to a Dynamic Analysis

A second feature of recent analyses of disadvantage has been the concern with the dynamics and processes involved. As Robert Walker (1995) has written, "Far from time simply being the medium in which poverty occurs, it helps to forge different experiences." It is not enough to count the numbers and describe the characteristics of those who are disadvantaged; it is also necessary to identify the factors which can trigger entry or exit from this situation and to understand how the *duration* of disadvantage helps to shape how it is experienced and what its consequences are. As Walker again writes, "There is growing evidence that the events which trigger poverty are widespread but that poverty is a comparatively rare outcome." To explain the circumstances under which particular trigger events do result in poverty is an important research priority.

There is a growing number of national panel surveys that can provide insights into these dynamics. Some focus on those who fall below a particular poverty line (Muffels 1992) or within the lowest section of the income distribution (Goodman, Johnson, and Webb 1997); others on the recipients of minimum benefits (Leibfried 1995). They find that most poverty is short term: There is plenty of income mobility, although many of those who escape from poverty remain on its margins and may subsequently descend into it once more. These panel studies can also identify those most at risk of falling into poverty and staying there: people who are poorly educated, are unemployed or disabled, and single mothers. Factors related to employability are crucial in determining who escapes. These national panel studies will soon be enriched by the findings emerging from the new European Community Household Panel, with annual waves from 1995 onwards (see also Leisering and Walker 1998).

Many of those who use the language of social exclusion place this dynamic analysis at the center of their own work and appear to believe that this is the major step forward from which the notion of social exclusion involves (Atkinson and Hills 1998). Again, however, this risks overstating the situation. Many of the classic studies of poverty were already well aware of this dynamic or temporal dimension, even if they were not equipped with the technical possibilities that panel studies offer. Studies of disadvantaged local communities—for example, Coates and Silburn's study (1970) of the St. Anne's district of Nottingham—explored the dynamics of change over a period of years; and during the 1970s the alleged processes of intergenerational transmission of poverty were at the heart of the ESRC's research program on transmitted deprivation (Rutter and Madge 1976). Again, therefore, while the move to an appreciation of the dynamic aspects of disadvantage is important, of itself it hardly suffices to justify the excitement which the new language of social exclusion has been generating.

From the Individual or Household to the Local Neighborhood

As I have argued, many of the conventional cross-national comparisons of poverty rates take as their focus the *financial resources* which are held at a *particular moment*: held, that is, by an *individual or household*. This focus on the individual or household has come under attack from two directions: first, from feminist writers who wish to direct attention to the processes of unequal access to resources inside the household unit (Glendinning and Millar 1992); and second, from writers who point to the resources which are available or lacking within the local community, which affect the extent to which a household or individual is able to manage in times of adversity. It is on the second of these that I focus here.

Deprivation is caused not only by lack of personal resources but also by insufficient or unsatisfactory community facilities, such as dilapidated schools, remotely sited shops, and poor public transport networks. Such an environment tends to reinforce and perpetuate household poverty. Household surveys and panel studies need to include questions on the availability or nonavailability of these local community resources if we are to understand the differential vulnerability of different individuals and households to social exclusion and disadvantage. No less important are local traditions of mutual aid, self-help organizations, and other elements of development potential; and, more negatively, local subcultures which may limit and undermine the capacity of local people to take up opportunities and to take control of their lives.

This is of obvious relevance for policy makers, who must consider what actions they will take to invest in these local community resources, alongside policies which are targeted on particular individuals and households. In many countries, poverty alleviation measures include pinpointed resource allocation to run-down localities, such as derelict inner urban city centers or areas of industrial decline.

Again, while the recent debates in terms of social exclusion have encouraged attention to this local community dimension, this is not an invention of the 1990s. First, there is a long tradition of studies of disadvantaged local communities and of the interplay between individual and community resources. In the United Kingdom, an obvious example is provided by the studies coming out of the Institute of Community Studies in the 1950s and 1960s and out of the Community Development Project in the 1970s (Home Office 1977). Second, but in a different tradition, governments have used indicators of disadvantage of local areas in their programs of resource allocation. In the United Kingdom, the Department of the Environment has been using its so-called z-scores for many years for this purpose. The most recent updating of these indicators, undertaken by Professor Brian Robson (1995) in Liverpool, uses the 1991 census data collected from households, but marries these with data pertaining to the local area as a whole. Finally, and in a different vein again, William Julius Wilson (1987) in Chicago has investigated the processes of community erosion and isolation which affect the black and Hispanic inner-city areas of the northern United States and compound the experience of disadvantage for individual households in those neighborhoods. His research, although in one sense admitting the existence of an underclass, aims to explain that underclass by reference to the collapse of employment opportunities, the lack of good quality public services, the exit of the black middle class and the counterattractions of a delinquent subculture of crime and drugs in neighborhoods where there are no "legitimate" opportunities.

From a Distributional to a Relational Focus

There is a fourth element in the shift from poverty to social exclusion which is, if anything, more fundamental still. The notion of poverty is primarily focused upon *distributional* issues: the lack of resources at the disposal of an individual or a household. In contrast, notions such as social exclusion focus primarily on *relational* issues: in other words, inadequate social participation, lack of social integration, and lack of power.

These two sets of concepts can be related to the different intellectual traditions from which they derive. Research into poverty, in its modern scientific form, is primarily an Anglo Saxon—more specifically a British—product of the nineteenth century (Rowntree 1901; Townsend 1979). It is closely associated with the liberal vision of society, under which society was seen by the relevant intellectual and political elites as a mass of atomized individuals engaged in competition within the marketplace. The goal of social policy is then to ensure to each person sufficient resources to be able to survive in this competitive arena. I acknowledge that Peter Townsend, as the most prominent contemporary heir of this tradition, judges the sufficiency of the resources at the disposal of an individual or households by whether the person is able to "participate" in the activities customary in their society. He thus makes an effort to break out of the limitations of the Anglo Saxon legacy and to include relational elements also. Nevertheless, with his focus on the resources which individuals need to have at their command, it is still distributional issues that are at the heart of his definition (Townsend 1979).

In contrast, notions of social exclusion are part of a continental— and perhaps more particularly, a French—tradition of social analysis. Society is seen by intellectual and political elites as a status hierarchy or as a number of collectives, bound together by sets of mutual rights and obligations which are rooted in some broader moral order. Social exclusion is the process of becoming detached from this moral order (Castels 1995). The task of social policy is to reinsert or reintegrate people into society.

At first glance, to operationalize this relational notion of social exclusion for purposes of empirical investigation is not as easy as measuring the financial resources at the disposal of an individual or household. There are several recent studies, however, which can be seen as offering such an operationalization (whether this is how they see themselves is unknown).

Paugam (1995) uses cross-sectional survey data in France to explore the relationship between a person's detachment from the occupational community and his or her detachment from the extended family. By comparing individuals categorized according to the security or fragility of their employment situation and examining the proportions of such individuals who lack links with their extended families, Paugam is able to show that the two forms of detachment tend to go together. This is especially the case for men: Women, when their occupational integration weakens, seem to be able to maintain their family links to a much greater extent. Paugam goes on in a subsequent study to consider cross-national variations in the strength of these occupational and family relationships (Paugam 1996). He shows using national data sets—albeit imperfectly comparable—that the French experience is mirrored in the other large urban industrial societies of northern Europe, the United Kingdom, and Germany; in Spain and Italy, however, as separation from the occupational community worsens, the extended family seems to play a stronger role, as our stereotypes of the southern European family might indeed lead us to expect.

A second, although rather different, approach to these relational aspects of social exclusion is provided by Perri 6, the former research director of the Demos think tank, which has been highly influential in shaping the new Labour government's social policy (1996, 6). Perri 6 distinguishes two sorts of social bonds: those that link us to people in the same position as ourselves—our family members, people in the local neighborhood, our immediate colleagues at work—and those that link us to people in very different positions from ourselves, especially those people who are in contact with opportunities which they can bring to our attention, but of which we are unlikely to be able to avail ourselves without their help.

Perri 6 proceeds to argue that our social policies typically concentrate disadvantaged people together with people like themselves, instead of helping them to make the second type of link: with people who are in touch with opportunities in the wider society, people who can therefore provide ladders for them to move out of their disadvantaged positions. We concentrate low income families into the same housing estates; we put the young unemployed together onto separate training programs; we neglect low cost public transport that could enable low income families to maintain and develop contacts and networks in the wider society. An appreciation of the importance of the relational dimension of social exclusion should, Perri 6 argues, prompt policy makers to reexamine some of these practices.

Continuity or Catastrophe

There is one final element in moving from poverty to social exclusion. The most common estimates of the proportion of people who are poor, especially for the purpose of cross-national comparison, make use of a fairly arbitrary poverty line defined in financial terms. One of the most commonly used poverty lines is drawn at 50 percent of the mean or median disposable income (or expenditure) in each of the societies being compared. But recognizing that 50 percent is indeed arbitrary, estimates are then often also produced based on 40 percent or 60 percent lines as well.

In a famous debate with David Piachaud, Peter Townsend argued that as one moved down the income hierarchy, at a certain point the consequences of income deprivation had a disproportionately great effect on the capacity of a household to join in the activities customary in their society. This discontinuity or "kink" provided an objective indicator of what it was plausible to call the poverty line. Piachaud (1981) disagreed. No evidence of such a discontinuity could be found in Townsend's data: To define poverty, and to distinguish the poor from the nonpoor, required an arbitrary value judgement, from which the empirical data could not provide an escape.

Whatever the outcome of this debate in reference to Townsend's own data, I suggest that when we speak of social exclusion, the concept carries with it the connotation of separation and permanence: a catastrophic discontinuity in relationships with the rest of society. This is very evident in Wilson's depiction of the underclass of Chicago. It may or may not be true of other groups of the population suffering disadvantage. To use the notion of social exclusion carries the implication that we are speaking of people who are suffering such a degree of multidimensional disadvantage, of such duration, and reinforced by such material and cultural degradation of the neighborhoods in which they live, that their relational links with the wider society are ruptured to a degree which is in some considerable degree irreversible. We may sometimes choose to use the notion of social exclusion in a more general sense than this, but here is its core. And if it is to be useful to us as an analytical concept and as a point of reference for policy design, it may be better to use this core notion as the basis for discussing "social exclusion," rather than to use the term as no more than a synonym of "disadvantaged."

SOLIDARITY AND THE CHALLENGE OF GLOBALIZATION

As stated, the notion of social exclusion consolidates and integrates five key elements in the definition and study of disadvantage. None of these elements is sufficient by itself to justify the research and political interest that the notion of social exclusion has generated, although together they probably can. None is so novel as to render irrelevant previous research into poverty. Nor does the notion of social exclusion provide some wondrous new approach as far as policy is concerned: We need to learn from past efforts to combat disadvantage, examining what worked as well as what did not. Not the least role of the academic researcher is to oppose any tendencies to collective amnesia.

While the new notion of social exclusion provides illumination, it also holds certain perils. For example, it may encourage us to conceive of society as a moral community (albeit hierarchical) with networks of mutual support: Social casualties lose touch with these networks and the task of social policy is to reintegrate them. This is a form of neofunctionalist social theory. The counterview is that society is a battleground of different social groups (based on factors such as social background, ethnicity, economic interest, gender, and age), seeking to maintain and extend their power and influence in a zero-sum struggle with other groups whom they seek to exclude. "Exclusion" is the result of this struggle, rather than it being a label that we attach to the casualties of some impersonal process of urban-industrial change. Social exclusion is a normal and integral part of the power dynamics of modern society.

This suggests a further agenda of questions for empirical research. First, in what ways are the actions of more advantaged groups shaping the processes of exclusion which were discussed earlier? Second, in what ways are these same groups shaping the policies for inclusion that governments are pursuing? Are these policies—for example, the welfare to work programs that many governments are now pursuing, in one form or another—providing stepping stones back into mainstream society, or are they condemning disadvantaged people to eking out low skill, low paid jobs on the margins of society? Third, how ready are these same groups to support more vigorous inclusionary policies? Peter Golding (1995) at Loughborough University has used Eurobarometer data to analyze the perceptions of the disadvantaged held by more advantaged groups: he finds little evidence of substantial support for such policies.

Earlier I mentioned Perri 6's work. He calls for policies which will promote social mixing—in our local communities, in our schools, in our vocational training schemes—in order to create contacts and networks of mutual support between more and less advantaged people in our societies. But this begs the question: One can see what the poor might get out of such contacts, but what will the middle classes get? Will they not always face the temptation to retreat into their fortresses? Perhaps more seriously still, if the more capable among the disadvantaged are creamed off in the way that Perri 6 proposes, what of those who are left behind, lacking now those most capable of providing leadership for disadvantaged local communities? This is precisely the situation described by Wilson in his account of inner-city Chicago. The prospects of these communities becoming the beneficiaries of more vigorous policies aimed at their inclusion would seem more remote than ever.

In the aftermath of World War II, T. H. Marshall (1950) offered his famous account of social citizenship, set within the context of universalist welfare services. Titmuss continued the argument, pointing out that with such an infrastructure of universalist services, one could hope that the more prosperous sections of the population would feel sufficiently the mutual obligations of a shared citizenship, that they would—to return to the vocabularly used by Perri 6—be ready to establish ties with people distant from themselves. At least in the United Kingdom, however, the 1980s saw growing inequality (Hills 1998) and polarization, coupled with the curtailment of this infrastructure of common citizenship institutions.

The globalization of our economies can only make this worse—and not just in the United Kingdom. One of the most obvious expressions of this is the way that, in the upper reaches of the income hierarchy, it is the global, rather than the national, market for top managers that shapes the scale of their rewards. Within the United Kingdom, the chief executive of SmithKline Beecham, the pharmaceuticals company, commands an annual remuneration package which includes £60 million in share options, which his chairman justifies by reference to the global market in managers (*Guardian*, 29 April 1998). This is at a time when the mass of the working population receive pay increases which do little more than preserve their real standard of living; while those who depend on social benefits are lucky if they get even this. The consequent elongation of the rewards hierarchy—something which individual national governments are fearful of challenging, lest capital make use of its mobility to exit to other countries—erodes all sense that we live in a single national society with shared criteria for the distribution of rewards.

This is not all. Once someone is part of this small circle of highly privileged people, it is not at all easy to leave it. Managers of large corporations who fail, instead of receiving their just desserts, often receive golden handshakes on a scale of which most of us can only dream. Nor is it only the financial failures who find that failure is sweet. The unprecedented slaughter of conservative members of Parliament in May 1997 in the British General Election did not produce a surge in the ranks of social benefit recipients; it has been more common for them to find themselves appointed to lucrative directorships (*Guardian*, 28 April 1998). They have no lack of the sort of ties of which Perri 6 speaks, that is, acquaintances who are ready and able to find alternative sources of income and standing when existing employment suddenly terminates. This is not a situation of *catastrophe*, in the sense I spoke of earlier, but one of what we might term *bliss*. (The state of bliss is less researched than that of social exclusion; this may spring from the reluctance of the affluent to give up the privacy surrounding their dealings, at least as far as academic researchers are concerned. See, however, Gregg, Machin, and Manning 1994) Their coexistence in the same society belies the notion that we share a common citizenship. This matters. As Titmuss always insisted, we cannot separate the way that our economy functions from the way in which we organize our common institutions and define our common citizenship.

"Who is my stranger?" asks Titmuss (1973) in his book *The Gift Relationship*, cleverly reworking the New Testament question, "Who is my neighbor?" Titmuss was concerned with the way that we perceive our fellow men and women, within the anonymity of the market society, and the extent to which, encouraged by universalist welfare institutions, we treat every stranger as our neighbor. In a world where the global market overrides the boundaries and identities of local and national communities, this question is particularly poignant. Universalist welfare institutions will be able to transcend the divisions of the marketplace only if they too have a global dimension: only if they are universalist in a double sense.

The International Labor Organization (ILO), the World Health Organization (WHO), and some arms of the United Nations Organization represent partial and fragmentary steps towards establishing a global framework for welfare. So also does Jubilee 2000 campaign by Aid Charities for the cancellation of the debts of the poorest countries. When compared with the progress of the World Trade Organization, however, their scope is sadly limited. Along with what they are doing, actions can also be traced within the various regional blocks, notably the European Union, to establish a social framework for economic activities and to ensure that social policy objectives are met on a transnational basis. But even here, progress is pitifully limited. As we enter the twenty-first century, this surely stands alongside and equal to the environmental challenge as the major political choice that our people and politicians face. It must involve efforts to establish a common moral basis for the distribution of rewards; to ensure a basic minimum for all citizens; and to reassert the social responsibility of business, against the amoral anonymity of the global marketplace.

NOTE

An earlier version of this chapter appeared in *International Journal of Social Welfare*.

REFERENCES

Atkinson, A. B., and Hills, J. 1998. *Exclusion, Employment and Opportunity*. London: London School of Economics and Political Science.

Castels, R. 1995. *Les Metamorphoses de la Question Sociale*. Paris: Fayard.

Coates, K., and Silburn, R. 1970. *Poverty the Forgotten Englishmen*. Harmondsworth, U.K.: Penguin.

Doran, A. 1997. "The Contradicting Trends in the Israeli Welfare State: Poverty, Retrenchment and Marginalization." Paper presented at the ISA Research Committee on Poverty and Social Policy, 19th meeting, Copenhagen, 21–24 August.

Duffy, K. 1995. *Social Exclusion and Human Dignity in Europe*. Strasbourg, France: Council of Europe.

Glendinning, C., and Millar, J. 1992. *Women and Poverty in Britain: The 1990s*. Hemel Hempstead, U.K.: Harvester Wheatsheaf.

Golding, P. 1995. "Public Attitudes to Social Exclusion." In *Beyond the Threshold: The Measurement and Analysis of Social Exclusion*, ed. G. Room. Bristol: The Policy Press.

Goodman, A., Johnson, P., and Webb, S. 1997. *Inequality in the UK*. Oxford: Oxford University Press.

Gregg, P., Machin, S., and Manning, A. 1994. "High Pay, Low Pay and Labour Market Efficiency." In *Paying for Inequality*, ed. A. Glyn and D. Miliband. London: Rivers Oram Press.

Hills, J. 1998. *Income and Wealth: The Latest Evidence.* York, U.K.: Joseph Rowntree Foundation.

Home Office. 1977. *The Costs of Industrial Change.* London.

Leibfried, S. 1995. "What a Difference a Day Makes: The Significance for Social Policy of the Duration of Social Assistance Receipt." In *Beyond the Threshold: The Measurement and Analysis of Social Exclusion,* ed. G. Room. Bristol: The Policy Press.

Leisering, L., and Walker, R., eds. 1998. *The Dynamics of Modern Society.* Bristol: The Policy Press.

Mack, J., and Lansley, S. 1985. *Poor Britain.* London: George Allen and Unwin.

Marshall, T. H. 1950. *Citizenship and Social Class.* Cambridge: Cambridge University Press.

Muffels, R. 1992. "A Multi-Method Approach to Monitor the Evolution of Poverty." *Journal of European Social Policy* 2 (3): 193–214.

O'Higgins, M., and Jenkins, C. 1987. *Poverty in Europe.* Bath: University of Bath.

Paugam, S. 1995. "The Spiral of Precariousness." In *Beyond the Threshold: The Measurement and Analysis of Social Exclusion,* ed. G. Room. Bristol: The Policy Press.

———. 1996. "Poverty and Social Disqualification: A Comparative Analysis of Cumulative Disadvantage in Europe." *Journal of European Social Policy* 6 (4): 287–304.

Piachaud, D. 1981. "Peter Townsend and the Holy Grail." *New Society* (10 September): 419–421.

Ringen, S. 1988. "Direct and Indirect Measures of Poverty." *Journal of Social Policy* 17 (3): 351–365.

Robson, B. 1995. "The Development of the 1991 Local Deprivation Index." In *Beyond the Threshold: The Measurement and Analysis of Social Exclusion,* ed. G. Room. Bristol: The Policy Press.

Room, G. 1992. *National Policies to Combat Social Exclusion* (Second Annual Report of the EC Observatory on Policies to Combat Social Exclusion). Brussels: European Commission.

———. 1993. *Anti-Poverty Action–Research in Europe.* Bristol: SAUS.

Room, G., ed. 1995. *Beyond the Threshold: The Measurement and Analysis of Social Exclusion.* Bristol: The Policy Press.

Rowntree, B. S. 1901. *Poverty: A Study of Town Life.* London: Macmillan.

Rutter, M., and Madge, M. 1976. *Cycles of Disadvantage.* London: Heinemann.

6, Perri. 1996. *Escaping Poverty.* London: Demos.

Titmuss, R. 1973. *The Gift Relationship.* Hardmondsworth, U.K.: Penguin.

Townsend, P. 1979. *Poverty in the United Kingdom.* Harmondsworth, U.K.: Penguin.

Walker, R. 1995. "The Dynamics of Poverty and Social Exclusion." In *Beyond the Threshold: The Measurement and Analysis of Social Exclusion,* ed. G. Room. Bristol: The Policy Press.

Whelan, B. J., and Whelan C. T. 1995. "In What Sense Is Poverty Multi-Dimensional?" In *Beyond the Threshold: The Measurement and Analysis of Social Exclusion,* ed. G. Room. Bristol: The Policy Press.

Wilson, W. J. 1987. *The Truly Disadvantaged*. Chicago: University of Chicago Press.

FURTHER READING

Leisering, L., and Walker, R., eds. 1998. *The Dynamics of Modern Society*. Bristol: The Policy Press.

Levitas, R. 1996. "The Concept of Social Exclusion and the New Durkheimian Hegemony." *Critical Social Policy* 16 (1): 1–20.

Paugam, S. 1996. "Poverty and Social Disqualification: A Comparative Analysis of Cumulative Disadvantage in Europe." *Journal of European Social Policy* 6 (4): 287–304.

Room, G., ed. 1995. *Beyond the Threshold: The Measurement and Analysis of Social Exclusion*. Bristol: The Policy Press.

5

Fifty Years of Social Security in the Making: A Participant's Journey

Abraham Doron

This chapter seeks to describe the journey in social policy I have participated in over my career. I began working and studying in the field of social policy in the early 1950s. At that time I had a somewhat childish and naive yearning for a better world and a belief that this could be achieved by means of progressive social policies. Nearly fifty years have passed since then. I am thankful for the opportunity given to me to observe the struggles, conflicts, compromises, and what actually happened by way of implementation in the field. It is thus a privilege for me today to recall some of the major developments and events that took place in the evolution of the welfare state in general, and in Israel in particular, during this period.

Looking back at these events, I can see the struggles that accompanied these developments, the successes and failures, the enormous changes, and the improvement of the conditions of life that took place during these years in all of our societies. But having experienced these changes I am also very much aware of their mutability and of the constant swings of the pendulum from one extreme to another in setting the development course and the outlines of social welfare in our societies.

The changes in social policies that took place, and especially those that have taken place in recent years, will shape the face of our societies in the twenty-first century. We have all seen the radical shift from the mostly consensual support for the launching and expanding of the welfare state in the 1950s and 1960s to the coun-terrevolution against it in the 1980s and 1990s. We have moved away from the support of universality and nonmeans testing of our collective arrangements in social security, health, education, and the personal social services, to selectivity, targeting, and the in-creased use of means and income testing.

Looking at public attitudes and the general mood, it is clear that we have moved away from the optimism and belief that by active interventionist policies of governments and social engineering, we can make our societies better places to live in and thus enhance the well being of the entire population, and have moved toward the almost total mistrust of governments and their capacities to deal effectively with the social problems that we are facing. The shift that occurred was from what we used to call the "revolution of ris-ing expectations" that we experienced in the heyday of the welfare state to the current pessimism, declining expectations, and even growing apprehension about what the future holds. The prophe-cies of doom seem to have taken over the belief in progress and a better future.

In the political arena the transmutation was from class politics and the controversies associated with it, which were central in shap-ing the post–World War II settlement, the establishment of the welfare state, and the strengthening of the social dimension of the status of citizenship. Alongside the declining powers of the social democratic labor movement, the move was a return to politics based on ethnicity, traditional status, religious privileges, and more re-cently on gender differences.

Moreover, in terms of class politics, the newly dominant busi-ness classes succeeded in reasserting their position of power and brought to an end the modus vivendi established earlier with the labor unions. Using the free market rhetoric of the right of manage-ment to manage, they returned to a more aggressive, authoritarian, and paternalistic role of management. As a result, growing numbers of working people are left in jobs increasingly insecure, with little protection against the harsh behavior of many employers.

In contrast to earlier periods when the increased affluence cre-ated by social and economic development raised the level of living of all, the more recent periods of sustained economic growth did not bring about a moderation of economic differences and patterns of inequality, but in fact led to the widening of the already existing gross inequalities in the distribution of income, status, and power. These periods also brought about steep increases in the extent of poverty and an exacerbation of the living conditions of the popula-tion groups suffering from economic hardships.

In the realm of the organization of social protection, in the post-war period, the dominant paradigm was to embrace the social insurance model as the cornersone of modern welfare. The basis of the social insurance paradigm was not insurance in itself but an underlying conception of social solidarity. The idea was to provide benefits to all, workers and middle classes alike, without means or income testing at the point of use. The intention here was more than to merely provide universal social protection, but also to achieve other important social objectives, such as promoting social solidarity, strengthening social cohesion, and bringing about the integration of the underprivileged classes into the mainstream of societal life.

The shift we are facing here is a growing questioning of the viability of the social insurance model and a return to the more traditional model of social protection based on need-conditioned assistance benefits and the widespread use of means and income testing (Clasen 1997).

It seems that the more recent policy changes point to a direction in which the social insurance model will play a decreasing role in providing social protection. The prevailing trends lead to a residualization of the existing social insurance programs by the withering of the insurance principle within them and by their permeation with means and income testing. The important social invention of social insurance that emerged towards the end of the nineteenth century as a novel design for providing social protection to all, on the basis of tripartite participation of governments, employers, and employees, and without recourse to the stigmatizing effect of limiting its benefits to the needy and poor only, seems to have had its time (Erskine 1997).

These obvious retreats from the postwar thinking on social security and social welfare, and the mostly consensual settlements that were established as a result of these beliefs, seem to be at least in part a result of the success of these settlements, as well as a result of the clear failure of some of the more important postwar arrangements which I will try to examine more closely.

SOCIAL SECURITY: THE VICTIM OF ITS SUCCESS

The comprehensive social protection systems established in the postwar period succeeded in extending their coverage to the entire population and in providing a floor of income to all. These systems were grounded upon a mixture of social insurance principles and the progressive evolution of social rights of citizenship. Eventually they produced among the population as a whole a sense of material security as important psychologically as it was materially. In contrast to the interwar period, the new social arrangements prevented a return to the unrestrained free market economics and lack of social protection that caused so much hardship to the working population, whether at work or out of work, during that period, and especially during the years of the Great Depression in the 1930s (Logue 1979).

The generation that experienced these hardships during that period was thus able to appreciate the achievement of the welfare state and of the working of the new universal systems of social protection. The fact that people were no longer left at the mercy of the vicissitudes of market forces and that they enjoyed a greater degree of equality in their capacity as consumers was considered a major achievement by this generation. The belief that they could now depend on the collective provision of a basic income in times of need, without having to apply for help to the poor law authorities or other public assistance bodies, became a source of pride to them.

The very success, however, in providing greater economic security and also, at least in part, material deprivation has also changed the political agenda and brought about a reduction in support for the welfare state. The generation born into the improved social security arrangements found the material needs that were paramount to the earlier generation much less pressing. They found it hard to appreciate the relative affluence and economic security that the welfare state provided. It was therefore much easier for them to turn to different issues on their political agenda with little regard to the welfare state.

SOCIAL SECURITY: THE VICTIM OF ITS FAILURE

Along with the very success of the welfare state in providing greater economic security and abolishing, at least in part, material deprivation, one has also to bear in mind some of its significant failures. The main failure of welfare state politics and policies was that it left almost without change the distribution of wealth and power in capitalist societies. Essentially, it left almost untouched the existing inegalitarian pattern of distribution of incomes and subsequently left unchanged the economic status quo and the political power base of the forces opposed to the postwar compromise settlement that was instrumental in the creation of the welfare state.

Although these forces never completely accepted the social changes that resulted from the postwar welfare settlement, they went along with it as long as the rapid economic growth, and the increased national prosperity of the 1950s and the 1960s, enabled them to maintain their relative position of wealth. The fruits of accelerated economic growth of the period made it possible to redistribute the surplus wealth created by it to larger parts of the population without making any financial imposition on the privileged position of the well-to-do.

All this came to an end with the economic crises of the 1970s and 1980s. For the first time in the postwar period, the economic stagnation of these years required, in order to continue to maintain the newly established social protection systems, an impingement on the relatively privileged circumstances of the rich. One has to seek the origins of the current counterrevolution against the welfare state in the original sin of its failure to change the distribution of wealth and power in capitalist societies when it could do so. As soon as circumstances arose, as they did in the last decade, the forces opposed to the welfare state did not hesitate to use their established positions of power to turn the clock back and return to the traditional pattern of reducing welfare expenditures and to a pattern of minimal social protection on the line of the prewar, need-based and means tested, poor law traditions.

In the immediate postwar years, it was thought that such a counterrevolution would be rather unlikely. The assumption was that it would be impossible to undo the changes that were set in motion in the sphere of social welfare and social protection. Moves to restore the past, whether in theory or in practice, seemed unthinkable because of the new social framework created by the welfare state (Crosland 1963). Even as late as in the 1980s, it was thought that the welfare state was an irreversible major institution of advanced capitalist societies and had become an integral part of their structures (Therborn and Roebroek 1986).

The main achievements of the welfare state as envisaged in its heyday are however quickly being eroded. What we are experiencing is the increasing subjection of most spheres of life to market influences, the domination of the profit motive, growing gaps in the distribution of incomes, a rapidly increasing degree of class stratification, and the active involvement of governments in giving support to the promotion of these policy trends (see also Hattersley 1996).

Another major failure of the welfare state lies in its incapacity to eradicate poverty in its basic form of assuring an adequate income for all and also in its more subtle and varied forms of individual and family life. The most powerful argument in support of the welfare state was its goal to eliminate poverty. Its promise was to eradicate poverty entirely from the advanced industrial societies, or at least to reduce the extent of poverty to a bare minimum. In spite of the welfare state's success in providing greater economic security, poverty has nevertheless remained a major problem in most of the advanced welfare states.

The Luxembourg Income Survey (LIS) data indicate that there has been an increase in povety rates in almost all countries during the years from the late 1970s till the early 1990s. A comparison of twenty industrialized countries shows that on average about 14 percent of households in these countries lived in poverty, that is, with an equivalent income below a 50 percent average after social security benefits and direct taxation. In some countries like the United States and the United Kingdom, these poverty rates reached the level of somewhat higher than 23 percent (Bradshaw and Chen 1997). The results of a study of twenty European Union states using subjective measures indicate that the net increase in the number of poor people in these countries over the last decade was on average 43 percent (Heikkila and Sihvo 1997).

Employing both objective and subjective measures, the available data show not only the persistence of poverty, but that poverty has also been on the increase in the advanced welfare states. The data are certainly worrying as they draw the attention to the inability of the welfare states to fulfill their major goal of preventing poverty and providing an adequate income to all. Moreover, the existing trends seem to indicate that there are no indications that poverty rates are going to be diminished in the years to come.

There has also been a serious failure in capturing the changing mood of the population, especially among the young, in mobilizing their support for a more humane and eventually more equal society which is an integral part of the welfare state. The social democratic political forces in support of the welfare state somehow lost their confidence in face of the neoconservative onslaught on the welfare state. Instead of counterattacking the simplistic ideas preached by its opponents that a return to unrestrained free market policies will solve the social and economic problems of our societies, the supporters of the welfare state mostly accepted the conservative agenda.

In order to prevent further increases in poverty and inequality, it is essential to continue with interventionist welfare state policies. In the absence of such policies, the danger looming ahead is a return to the unjust prewar conditions of a highly stratified and unequal class society. Among the younger groups of the population, and indeed large segments of the general population, there seems to prevail a basic desire to promote a more equal society. The trouble is, however, that in the current circumstances, the struggle for a better society seemed to have lost its way. It is in this context that the welfare state has failed in its bid for the "hearts and minds" of the people.

THE ISRAELI EXPERIENCE

The evolution of the welfare state in Israel started immediately after gaining independence. During the initial period of statehood in the 1950s and 1960s, it was mostly a consensual process, whether as part of nation building or as a response to the increasing demands for social protection in the context of the insecurity of a rapidly growing industrial society. In later years, broader areas of social need were recognized as proper fields of government intervention and new social programs were established to deal with them. Subsequently, a broad network of social services in the field of health care, education, housing, social security, and the personal–social services was established. By the mid 1970s, Israel has acquired the basic features of a modern welfare state.

The leadership of the major political forces in Israel at the time was dominated by a Labour Zionist ideology that stressed the values of collective responsibility, mutual aid, and egalitarianism. The Beveridge model of social reforms introduced by the then in power Labour government in Britain as part of the process of social reconstruction greatly influenced the thinking of the Israeli leadership. As a result of these influences, a short time after independence, an interministerial committee was established and given responsibility to develop a social insurance program for the country. The report produced by the committee recommended the gradual establishment of a comprehensive system of social protection, with the social insurance paradigm as its cornerstone.

The report was published in 1950 during an extremely difficult economic situation and in conditions of inordinate austerity stemming from the aftermath of the protracted war of independence, the influx of mass immigration, and the continuous threat to national security. In spite of these difficult circumstances, the report was accepted by large parts of the population with great optimism and the belief that it was a major step to the building of a better and more secure future. I myself, at the time a student of social work in Jerusalem, well remember that Dr. G. Lotan, our social policy teacher and himself deeply involved in preparing the report, took great pride in the report and claimed that its implementation will eventually solve most of the social problems Israel was then facing. Our somewhat naive yearning for a better world led us to believe in that grand promise.

Certainly, it took some years until the comprehensive social protection system envisaged by the report was implemented in full. The main achievements of the fully developed system in the 1970s were its progressive extension to a wide range of programs to cover the entire population against most risks of loss of income. The effect of the established protection system was to strengthen the feelings of personal security and to improve the quality of life for the majority of Israelis. It also brought about some redistribution of incomes and a change in the existing pattern of inequality. All this was accomplished within a mostly universal system that consciously moved away from the traditional utilization of means and income testing.

As in other countries, the political process that lead to the establishment of this protection system and making it the main core of the welfare state was, at least in part, a result of class politics led by the Israeli labor movement. This does not imply that many steps in the evolution of the system were not accompanied by fierce political debates and controversies; but these were mostly about practical details of the programs involved and not against their essence. Although there was some opposition by the middle classes to some programs, overall there was a basic consensus about the interventionist role of government in providing a broad floor of social protection for all. These achievements of the welfare state brought about a transformation of life in Israeli society.

THE ISRAELI WELFARE STATE: VICTIM OF ITS SUCCESS

The achievements of the welfare state in Israel and its rather comprehensive system of social protection have over the years lost much of their significance to large parts of Israeli society. The fact that the system has succeeded in assuring a guaranteed minimum level of income to all and that people are no longer left without protection at times of need, as was the case in the not so distant past, does not seem to impress even those population groups who are mostly dependent on these collective social protection arrangements.

The rapid economic growth and the relative affluence brought with it to most people in Israel have made these welfare state achievements less relevant to the aspirations and desires of a large number of groups composing Israeli society. The younger population groups born into this relatively affluent society and its welfare state take the existing system of social protection for granted. It is hard for them to grasp that its very existence is of very short duration and that it was possible for a society to function properly without it. Thus they find it difficult to appreciate the meaning it had to the earlier generation. They also find it difficult to understand that these achievements are mutable and can be reversed, disappear, and seriously affect their own circumstances.

The low income population groups who benefited the most from the established system of social protection seem also to lend little support for it. Although the universal system of social security benefits led the way to their increased integration into the mainstream of societal life, their rather successful integration left them oblivious to the fact that it is the welfare state and its social protection system that was instrumental in facilitating this development.

It is these groups that have the most to lose from the cuts in social security spending or from the current policies intended to partly or fully dismantle the hard-fought-for protection systems. The very success of the welfare state, however, seems to have brought to an end the support of these groups for class politics that made its establishment possible. It is among these groups that support for the universalistic welfare state is increasingly being replaced by involvement in and support for narrowly defined particularistic politics of ethnical identity, religious fundamentalism, or nationalistic directions.

THE ISRAELI WELFARE STATE: VICTIM OF ITS FAILURE

As in many other countries, it is important to look at the failures of the Israeli welfare state. In contrast to other countries, the failure of Israel's politics and policies was not in leaving unchanged the existing distribution of wealth and power, but in actually creating and increasing the power base of a new capitalist class. Israel was not an egalitarian society at the time of its inception. Its capitalist class was rather small and poorly organized. The main levers of political and economic power rested in the hands of the various organizations of the labor movement and the Histadrut— or, the Trade Union Federation. It was claimed then that the distribution of incomes in the country was highly egalitarian, though there are some doubts whether there was much factual support for this claim.

It was the labor-controlled political leadership of the country during the last forty years that consciously and deliberately led to the creation of the current power base of the new capitalist class (Rosenfeld and Carmi 1976). This new class is at present using its recently acquired positions of power to turn the clock back and cut back the country's social security system, established after prolonged struggles in the period between the 1950s and the 1970s.

Over the last decade, the new capitalist class and its supporters led the counterrevolution which eventually brought about the downfall of the Israeli labor movement from its position of power and to the collapse of the Histadrut. It is also the refusal of this capitalist class to bear the burden of the welfare state that is behind the strategy of reducing welfare expenditures and the return to a pattern of minimum protection based on means and income tests that is being introduced under the guise of targeting.

The achievements of the Israeli welfare state, most of which were achieved in the pre–Yom Kippur War period, are at present in the danger of being eroded. More spheres of life are being rapidly subjected to the control of market forces. The unequal pattern of distribution of incomes has reached unprecedented heights. Once considered one of the more egalitarian societies, Israel is now one of the most unequal. Its pattern of income distribution is at present more unequal than the pattern existing in virtually all other advanced Western capitalist societies, with the exception of the United States.

The more affluent middle class groups and stronger groups within the employee population seem to be more and more inclined to denigrate the universal protection system which no longer satisfies their increased expectations. The low level floor of protection provided to all by the universal welfare state system led these groups to create for themselves separate systems of protection. At first these additional system were designed to augment the meager universal systems. Over time, however, these separate systems of protection, or private welfare states, have made the universal welfare state seem unnecessary for these groups.

The Israeli welfare state has also done rather poorly in its goal to eliminate poverty. Although the welfare state has broadened the field of social protection, one cannot ignore the limits of the achievements in this field. Its main success has been in eliminating absolute poverty by guaranteeing a minimum level of income to all. It has, however, failed to reduce the extent of relative poverty that has been steadily on the increase in the last two decades. In 1969, 11 percent of Israeli families were living in poverty (Roter and Shamay 1971). By 1990 the poverty rate among Israeli families had risen to 14.3 percent, and it reached the rate of 16 percent in 1996 (*National Insurance Institute Annual Survey* 1996/97). Part of this trend can possibly be explained by the rapidly changing political and economic circumstances of Israeli society. Nevertheless, the fact is that the country's welfare state policies failed to restrain and redirect market forces in their unsettling drive to increase poverty. Similarly, the social protection system (social security payments and direct taxes) was able to assist no more than half of families in poverty to reach income levels above the poverty line.

Doubtless, the continuing persistence of poverty and its increasing rates and the growth of inequality both seem to have contributed to the disillusionment with the welfare state. The unfulfilled promises and hopes connected with it inevitably had an important impact on the changing mood of the population and the undermining of support for the welfare state among political parties and groups that were its traditional supporters. The simplistic claims of the neoconservative forces made significant inroads on this support.

Judging from the electoral outcomes in recent years in Israel, it seems that the conservative agenda of attacking the welfare state has been gaining increasing support, despite the deplorable effects these policies have on the conditions of life of low income population groups. It may sound paradoxical, but in a democratic society such as Israel, Former Prime Minister Netanyahu could promise a Thatcherite revolution and still gain the political support of the majority of the underprivileged population groups in Israeli society.

THE CRUCIAL ISSUES STILL WITH US

History tends to play a painful game with our beliefs. Almost fifty years ago, when I started my journey with social security policy, most of us, including myself, believed in progress. We were convinced that the pattern of change set in motion at that time would lead toward improvement in our social affairs. Moreover, we believed that the changes in social policy and social protection would continue to move only in one general direction and would be irreversible (Pollard 1968). The last two decades have shown us how erroneous we were in this belief.

As things stand at the present, we cannot assume that there will not be a further relapse and retrenchment in our welfare state and social protection policies. At the same time we should not assume that further progress and improvements in the state of our social affairs is impossible. The ground seemingly lost in the present can be regained in the future. It is important to bear in mind that all changes, whether for good or worse, are mutable. The sense of social responsibility that dominated the thought of social thinkers and policy makers in the not-so-distant past can be secured again. We need to believe that this is not beyond our capabilities, but lies in the realm of the possible.

REFERENCES

Bradshaw. J., and Chen, J. 1997. "Poverty in the UK: A Comparison with Nineteen Other Countries." *Benefits* 13: 13–17.

Clasen, J. 1997. "Social Insurance: An Outmoded Concept of Social Protection?" In *Social Insurance in Europe*, ed. J. Clasen. Bristol: The Policy Press.

Crosland, C.A.R. 1963. *The Future of Socialism*. New York: Schocken.

Erskine, A. 1997. "The Withering of Social Insurance in Britain." In *Social Insurance in Europe*, ed. J. Clasen. Bristol: The Policy Press.

Gray, J. 1998. "The Best-Laid Plans." *The New York Times Book Review*, 19 April.

Hattersley, R. 1996. "Back to the Future." *The Guardian*, 28 September.

Heikkila, M., and Sihvo, T. 1997. "Concepts of Poverty and Exclusion in Europe." *Scandinavian Journal of Social Welfare* 6: 119–126.

Logue, J. 1979. "The Welfare State: Victim of Its Success." *Daedalus* 108 (4): 69–88.

National Insurance Institute Annual Survey 1996/97 (in Hebrew; English summary). 1997. Jerusalem: National Insurance Institute, Research and Planning Administation.

Pollard, S. 1968. *The Idea of Progress, History and Society*. London: C. A. Watts.

Rosenfeld, H., and Carmi, S. 1976. "The Privatization of Public Means, The State-Made Middle Class, and the Realization of Family Values in Israel." In *Kinship and Modernization in Mediterranean Society*, ed. J. G. Peristiany. Rome: The Center for Mediterranean Studies, American Universities Field Staff.

Roter, R., and Shamay, N. 1971. "The Distribution of Personal Income in Israel: Trends in the 1960s" (in Hebrew). *Social Security* 1: 55–62.

Therborn, G., and Roebroek, J. 1986. "The Irreversible Welfare State: Its Recent Maturation, Its Encounter with the Economic Crisis, and Its Future Prospects." *International Journal of Health Services* 16 (3): 319–338.

FURTHER READING

Bryson, L. 1992. *Welfare and the State: Who Benefits?* London: Macmillan.

Donnison, D. 1998. *Policies for a Just Society*. London: Macmillan.

Esping-Anderson, G., ed. 1996. *Welfare States in Transition: National Adaptations in Global Economies*. London: Sage.

Pierson, P. 1996. *Dismantling the Welfare State? Reagan, Thatcher and the Politics of Retrenchment*. Cambridge: Cambridge University Press.

PART II

ISSUES IN THE STUDY OF
THE ISRAELI WELFARE STATE

6

Issues and Developments in the Israeli Welfare State

Jack Habib

In examining the Israeli welfare state, it is necessary to ask ourselves what are the key principles of the welfare state and the criteria by which to evaluate and analyze its development. The key elements of the welfare state as it has developed include:

1. A commitment to social goals of assuring a minimal access to resources and of promoting a reasonable degree of equality, equality of opportunity, and horizontal equity.
2. A belief that society should intervene in the degree to which individuals insure themselves against social contingencies.
3. An emphasis on the importance of social services in the overall basket of societal consumption and the role of public decisions in influencing the level of expenditures on these commodities based on considerations of externalities and investment in human capital (Castles 2000; Center for Social Policy Studies 1998).

These concerns in turn lead to

1. Programs to redistribute income—transfer payments and progressive taxes.
2. Programs to impose compulsory social insurance.
3. Programs to publicly finance and subsidize basic social services so as to assure access and influence the level of consumption of these goods.
4. Programs to publicly provide social services so as to ensure equality of access and standards.

In implementing these programs, a number of strategic issues that relate to how we implement these principles arise including

1. Selective versus universal approaches.
2. Entitlements versus budgeted benefits.
3. More or less competition in the provision of services.
4. More or less emphasis on users' charges to control costs and on incentives to avoid inappropriate utilization.
5. More or less emphasis on the government as the provider of services as opposed to the voluntary or for profit sector (privatization) (Commission on Tax Reform 1975; Doron 1991).

This leads us to alternative approaches to evaluating the welfare state. We can distinguish between efforts to evaluate the welfare state from three perspectives:

1. The degree to which these various programmatic approaches and strategies are pursued.
2. The total resources devoted to social welfare programs, as reflected in public budgets and national resources in relation to the GNP.
3. The achievement of desired outcomes.

Some general comparison across countries of social welfare expenditures in relationship to GNP are included in the chapter by Professor Castles in this book (Doron 1991; Doron and Kramer 1991). Comparisons at this level, however, can be misleading:

1. They do not allow for differences in needs, as most directly reflected in differences in the age structure, but as also reflected in differences in unemployment, family structure, or pretax-transfer poverty and inequality. Israel, for example, has a much younger age structure, which influences its need for overall social spending.
2. Of note is what is included in social expenditures when making these comparisons and whether it includes the full range of income support, health, education, and social services. In Israel, expenditures on education are relatively high, and are lower in other areas.
3. Also the relative role of public versus work-related provisions for social insurance and health insurance needs to be taken into account. In Israel, work-related social insurance measures, as well as payments for health insurance, play an important role.
4. The age of systems and their maturity must also be noted. In Israel, as a young country, pension schemes, for example, have not yet reached maturity, which keeps the level of expenditures low even though the potential pension benefits are high.

Unfortunately there has not been a serious analysis of relative expenditure levels that tried to address these different factors for some time in Israel. The evaluation of the welfare state based on outcomes is also complex. The degree to which goals are achieved is not only an outcome of the resources allocated but is also determined by them in the ongoing social and political dialectic. Thus the extent to which societies monitor social outputs and the processes by which images of outcomes are generated has an important role in explaining its development.

The failure to achieve desired outcomes can lead to two alternative interpretations that can have contrasting impacts:

1. More resources are required in order to meet the goals.
2. Resources are being ineffectively utilized, and therefore expenditures should be cut back.

Moreover, in comparing countries, differences in outcomes need to be related to differences in underlying needs and conditions about which data are often not available. In addition, social outputs need to be evaluated in relation to economic outputs. Economic conditions will affect the ability and the will to invest in social goals.

FORCES AFFECTING THE WELFARE STATE

We now turn to an analysis of the social structure in Israel and how this has affected the particular challenges facing the welfare state in Israel.

The Social Structure of Israel

Israel is at a crossroads of four major social challenges that are becoming increasingly important in all modern societies, but have had very significant dimensions in Israel:

- Massive rates of immigration.
- Tremendous cultural and social heterogeneity among the population.
- Relationships between Israel's Jewish majority and its large Arab minority against the background of different national aspirations.
- Dramatic differences among the ethnic and national groups in education, family size, and women's labor force participation, creating inequalities among ethnic groups and in the society as a whole.

These factors have had a number of implications:

1. The need at various periods to allocate exceptional resources to immigrant integration and the creation of an ongoing issue of resource allocation between immigrants and nonimmigrants.

2. The significance of equality among ethnic groups, along with the tension between the melting pot versus the multicultural approach to ethnic differences.

3. The generation of high levels of poverty and inequality due to the large variance in social capital and family size in the population. This was exacerbated by the fact that segments of the population received reparations from Germany while other refugee groups did not.

4. The creation of a complex dynamic between the Arab and Jewish populations and tensions around equality between the Arab minority and the Jewish majority. This has been complicated by the ongoing conflict between Israel and its neighbors, with the Arab minority torn between the two sides. The fact that the Arab minority for obvious reasons was not required to serve in the army, and generally does not, also led to complex issues of differential entitlements based on compensation for military services.

From Socialism to the Welfare State

A second major factor influencing the development of the welfare state has been Israel's socialist origins. The ideology of the leading figures in the founding of the State of Israel had strong socialist origins. Indeed Israel defined itself as a socialist state, and the labor party, which dominated Israeli politics for the first several decades, defined itself as a socialist party. This has had important influences on the development of the welfare state, but in conflicting ways.

The socialist origins of the state contributed to a commitment to principles of equality and to collective action on behalf of these goals. It also contributed to the development of social solidarity as a social value. These principles found expression in high levels of intervention and influence over the market economy.

The socialist origins, however, also had more negative impacts on the welfare state. One of these was to serve to disguise existing social problems. By definition, in a socialist state, there had to be low rates of poverty and highly equal income distribution. And, indeed, this was the image that Israel had of itself for most of its first two decades.

With the undermining of socialist ideology in the world and the growing emphasis on the market economy, socialist ideology has lost most of its adherents in Israel and become more and more the subject of criticism (and even ridicule) as a major negative factor in

Israel's economic development. At the same time a distinction has not been adequately made between socialism as an economic regime and the social goals of socialism. This has led to the failure to carefully distinguish between socialism and the welfare state and to place an emotional and intellectual block to the more reasoned examination of the role of the state in addressing social goals within an economic system based on market principles. The level of the public understanding of these distinctions is very limited, and many policy makers share this confusion. The failure to make these distinctions more vigorously has meant that the backlash against socialism has also spilled over into a backlash against the welfare state.

ACHIEVEMENTS AND PROBLEMS

Against this background, we can raise the question as to what the Israeli welfare state has achieved. In broad terms, despite the very significant challenges, Israel has managed to avoid some of the more extreme forms of social deterioration that have characterized many developed societies with relatively low rates of deviance and a strong family structure. This has been possible in large measure due to Israel's social welfare policies:

- The provision of a basic safety net that has served to prevent some of the more severe forms of deprivation, such as homelessness.
- The development of a social security system that provides basic protection against the major contingencies.
- The assurance of broad access to health care services.
- The availability of generic social welfare services covering the full range of needs at the local level.
- An educational system which is common to all social classes rather than the stratified systems that have been developing in many countries.
- The development of a strong and dynamic voluntary sector.

On the other hand, the most significant blemish on Israel's social map is the high rate of inequality and poverty. Thus Israel has not been able to overcome the large differences in educational levels and in family size, which are the sources of these gaps, or to sufficiently reduce the gaps between ethnic groups and between Arabs and Jews.

Second, there is a great deal of concern in Israel today that the degree of social deviance and the degree of violence in the family, the schools, and the broader society has increased in the last decade and that processes of social disintegration have accelerated.

Although Israel has succeeded in entering the ranks of the developed world with a thriving high-tech sector, it suffered economic stagnation throughout the 1980s and is again today in a period of stagnation. Market forces have been producing more inequality and less job security.

Highlights of Social Policy Development since 1970

I shall now comment on patterns in the development of social policy and relate to various critical periods (Bruno and Habib 1976; Doron 1993; Esping-Andersen 1990).

The decade of the 1970s represented a major turning point. During this period a major shift occurred in the social consciousness of Israel. This was brought about by a combination of two events: the publication for the first time of data on poverty in Israel, and the emergence of a major protest movement which grew out of the ranks of the poor. The data were published by the Research Department of the National Insurance Institute, which had been established when Dr. Israel Katz became the general–director of the Institute (Gross, Rosen, and Shirom 1999). It provided a comparative perspective on the rates of poverty and inequality in Israel, which showed that, in contrast to common belief, the rates were very high and were among the highest in developed countries. Additional findings served to counteract stereotypes about the poor and the claims that they were not deserving by demonstrating the high percentage of elderly and working poor. Finally, the revelation of the particularly high rates of poverty among children considerably enhanced public concern and sympathy for the poor (Habib 1974). The protest movement that became known as the Israeli Black Panthers, borrowing the name from the United States, was to bring thousands of people to public demonstrations to protest poverty, inequality, and ethnic gaps in Israel. The combination of the voices of the poor and the statistics on poverty were very powerful and led to the decision by the prime minister of Israel at the time, Golda Meir, to establish a commission on youth and children in distress (Habib 1979). The work of the commission and the atmosphere it created of concern for Israel's social problems led to a period of major expansion in income maintenance programs and in social service programs. In the first half of the 1970s, a generous system of child allowances was introduced; general disability insurance and unemployment insurance were enacted; pension benefits were increased; and many other related measures were initiated. The upshot was to significantly reduce poverty during this period (International Social Security Association 1999).

The experience in this period points to the important role that social monitoring and information about outcomes can play in influencing the development of the welfare state. However, at the same time, it also points to the importance of paradigms by which we analyze social policy strategies. Thus, a major issue was the degree to which these issues should be addressed through universal versus selective systems. This was viewed initially as a tradeoff between economic efficiency and a broader concern for stigma and social solidarity. However, new analyses that were carried out during this period demonstrated that, when appropriately analyzed, universal systems could also prove to be economically more efficient (International Social Security Association 1999; Liebfried and Pierson 1995). This analysis was to pave the way for the enactment of the new system of child allowances, which was largely financed by the elimination of tax exemptions for children, which were much less progressive (National Insurance Institute 1981–1996).

Subsequently and after a long period of rapid economic growth, Israel entered a period of major economic stagnation, with triple-digit inflation and high unemployment, exacerbated by the fact that real wages continued to grow. This led to an increase in transfers in relation to GNP, but not relative to wages. Moreover, in response, there were efforts to reduce the levels of pensions and child allowances in relation to wages that served to unravel the improvements in poverty and inequality (OECD 1996).

During this period there emerged among the economic elite in Israel the belief that there were basic structural factors related to inflation, size of the public sector, and tax rates that prevent a dynamic of growth. This has led to a long-term interest in reducing social expenditures as part of this effort to achieve structural change. Indeed, the slowdown in growth that began at the end of the 1970s was to continue throughout the 1980s, and at the end of the decade there was 9 percent unemployment in Israel.

This debate was to be temporarily postponed during the 1990s with the initiation of massive immigration from the former Soviet Union (FSU), which began in 1989 and was to bring some 770,000 immigrants to Israel from the FSU between 1989 and 1998. The effort to address this unique challenge had two conflicting impacts. On the one hand it required the allocation of massive resources, and on the other it led to a period of rapid economic growth that pulled Israel out of a long-term period of stagnation. Unemployment rose from 9 percent in 1989 to 11 percent in 1993, but had declined to 6 percent by 1996.

Despite the preoccupation with the mass immigration, this period was one of significant developments in social policy of a somewhat paradoxical nature. On the one hand, it was a period of major new initiatives; on the other hand, of ongoing efforts to reduce social expenditures and introduce shifts in strategy. The significant new initiatives included

1. The introduction of National Health Insurance in 1995, which significantly enhanced the progressivity and equity of the health system (Prime Minister's Commission 1973).
2. Improvements in income maintenance programs focused on poverty reduction, particularly among one-parent families and the Arab population.
3. The implementation of the special education law, enacted in 1988, and the passage of a new equality of opportunity law for the disabled.
4. Major expansion in expenditures on education and, toward the end of the period, enhanced commitments to expanding the school day and extending free and universal education in the preschool years. Moreover, this was a period of major increases in the relative wages of personnel in the health, education, and social service sectors, representing a basic change in the relative wage position of these professions. On the other hand, it was a period in which there were ongoing efforts to introduce cutbacks in social expenditures. These were focused not only on the actual levels of benefits, but rather on the strategies for addressing various goals.

The strategy shifts were focused on:

1. Efforts to introduce more targeted and selective as opposed to universal benefits.
2. Efforts to prevent and reduce entitlements in favor of budget-constrained programs.
3. Efforts to expand services rather than income support.
4. Efforts to enhance the role of private provision of services and reduce public provision and related efforts to enhance the role of competition in the provision of social services.

Most of these efforts were not successful, and these initiatives, although often proposed by the government, were defeated in the Knesset. One major exception is the process of privatization of the provision of social services, which has expanded in a number of areas. A second is the major reform of the work-related pension system and the civil service pension system, with the shift from pension frameworks based on mutual subsidy among beneficiaries to pension systems based more on accrued benefit principles and individual accounts.

These efforts to reduce social services in the 1990s have been motivated by the continued concern with structural barriers to growth. However, they received additional impetus from the adoption of the principles of the "new economics," leading to a significant legal constraint on the size of the deficit and an effort to reduce inflation to "European levels" (2 to 3%), without raising taxes. This implies by definition reduction in expenditures. Moreover, the growth in the weight of social expenditures in the government budget makes them a more and more inviting target. They rose from 31.7 percent in 1980 to 45.2 percent in 1990 and 52.8 percent in 1998. During this same period, defense expenditures declined from 39.5 percent to 23 percent, and this was a facilitating factor. As a percentage of GNP, social expenditures rose from 17.7 percent in 1980 to 23.1 percent in 1998. Unfortunately consistent data are not available for the 1970s (Doron 1993). In addition, these concerns have been fueled by the fact that Israel returned, after 1996, to a period of low growth and high unemployment, which reached over 9 percent in 1999. A low rate of inflation has been achieved of close to 4 percent, but at the price of very high interest rates.

Unless Israel restores economic growth and maintains low inflation, there will be continued pressure to contain and reduce social expenditures. Thus, beyond any specific critiques of the welfare state, new economic ideologies and conditions are a major source of pressure on social expenditures. This is the case even though it is probably politically possible in Israel to raise taxes to support greater public spending. However, the concern with the impact on incentives for growth remains an important constraint to this alternative approach.

Beyond all these considerations, however, there seems to be a major underlying concern that is not often the focus of direct public discussion. This concern focuses on the question of the degree of control that society has over the trend in social expenditures. There is a very strong concern, particularly within economic circles, as to whether social expenditures are becoming more and more out of control and subject to a dynamic that will lead to constant increases. Allied with this is the belief that the degrees of freedom for expressing preferences among societal objectives is significantly reduced by this dynamic. This argument is related specifically to the rapid growth of expenditures in some of the major entitlement programs, such as disability and to the expansion of entitlement principles to more and more income support and even direct service programs.

A second factor is the increasing concern about the responsibility of the legislative process and of the decision-making processes within the government. Changes in Israel's electoral system within and between the parties have contributed to the increased independence of members of Parliament and the decline of party discipline. In addition, these changes have led to the proliferation and strengthening of small parties, which have created more complex coalition governments and more complex processes within the Knesset. One direct consequence has been the enhanced difficulty of the government to impose discipline on its own coalition and therefore implement its decisions. Second, it has contributed to the proliferation of parliamentary initiatives to expand existing and introduce new social benefits, many of which have been successful. A contributing factor as well as a consequence has been the emergence of ethnically based political factions and parties. On the one hand, these developments have contributed to the expansion of various social benefits. On the other hand, there is no overall logic to the nature or direction of this expansion, and these developments considerably enhance the concern about control.

One interesting example in which the issue of control has been central is that of the finance of the health system. The 1995 health insurance law created a clearly defined entitlement for health benefits for the first time. It also eliminated price competition among the HMO health providers. The Finance Ministry has viewed both of these developments very negatively and as leading to a dynamic of cost escalation. The reform did introduce a strategy for cost containment based on a capitation system, with the size of the cap determined in part by a formula, but in large measure by the discretion of the government with respect to allowances for population growth and technological change. The Finance Ministry has, however, doubted the effectiveness of the strategy in light of political pressures to raise the cap. Therefore, it has made continuous efforts to modify the principles of the system, which have been partly successful in an effort to establish more cost control. Thus the critical issue has not been so much the level of health expenditures, which have not increased significantly since the reforms, but rather the question of control (Roter and Shamai 1971, 20).

To some extent, there seems to be a trade-off between the willingness to allocate resources to social services and the degree to which these resources are protected from ongoing review and scrutiny in a national priority-setting process.

CONCLUSION

There is no doubt that the uncertainty about the future social development of society has increased. This is in part due to economic and social trends that seem to be exacerbating some of the underlying social problems. This is also in part due to the uncertainty with respect to social welfare policy. New economic ideologies and conditions, changing social ideologies, the absence of an informed public debate, the growing chaotic and random nature of the policy making and legislative process—all raise questions about the nature and the effectiveness of decisions that will be made with respect to social welfare policies.

In my opinion, under these circumstances we need to give priority to efforts to enhance rational decision making:

1. We need to promote education about the rationale for the welfare state, differentiating it from socialism, and to raise the sophistication of the analysis of social strategies.

2. We need to promote more broadly the fundamental question of societal goals and the trade-off between private and social consumption.

3. We need to enhance our knowledge of social trends and their underlying causes and how to influence them.

4. We need to take very seriously the critiques of the welfare state. All those who have a commitment to social goals need to address the critiques of the welfare state on their own grounds: to understand the underlying values and assumptions about the world that underlie these critiques and policy positions and to address these head on.

5. We need to do everything we can to enhance the efficiency of the social welfare system and the extent to which it is characterized by a willingness to learn from experience and to change.

6. We need to invest much more in the availability of policy analyses in relation to the key strategic issues that we face in the development of social policy. We need to address seriously the concern over the control over the dynamics and trends in social welfare expenditure—how much it is an issue and how to deal with it proactively and creatively.

7. We need to pursue an electoral and political structure that will promote responsible decision making.

At the same time, there remains, in my opinion, strong general support for the principles of the welfare state in Israel. This is evidenced, for example, by the fact that in the public debate in Israel the issue of abuse of the social services, or of their potential impact in creating dependence, has not found expression, in contrast to the important role these issues have played in the recent debate in many Western countries.

Moreover, viewed in historical perspective, there is much more recognition today in Israel of the problems of poverty and inequality and much less questioning of the reliability of the data. Similarly, there has not been serious opposition to the continued use of a relative definition of poverty that is fully adjusted for the average standard of living. Recently, more and more of the significant political figures and political parties have given recognition to the social gap as a major issue of national priority. Finally, the backlash against the effectiveness of public expenditures has not been as severe as it has been in some Western countries and has been weakened by changes in recent years in the consumer orientation of these services.

The high rates of poverty and inequality in Israel are clearly one of the major blemishes on the Israeli welfare state and represent a serious threat to the positive social development of Israeli society as well as to the reduction of gaps between ethnic groups and Arabs and Jews. The continued clarification as to why these rates are so high and of policies to reduce them needs to be a high priority. One critical question is: Why was Israel able to reduce poverty and inequality in the 1970s out of a much lower GNP and not in the 1990s out of a much higher level of GNP and social service expenditures?

The Israeli welfare state has had major successes under exceptional conditions. The challenge in the years ahead is to preserve what we have achieved and attempt to move ahead. We need in short to remember that it is not only the nature of the challenges but how well we address them that will determine our success. Social welfare is a serious business. It requires an informed and thoughtful dialogue.

REFERENCES

Bruno, M., and Habib, J. 1976. "Taxes, Family Grants and Redistribution." *Journal of Public Economics* 5: 57–59.

Castles, F. G. 2000. "Social Protection in the Postwar Era: OECD Experience." In *Into the Promised Land: Issues Facing the Welfare State*, ed. A. Ben-Arieh and J. Gal. Westport, Conn.: Praeger.

Center for Social Policy Studies. 1998. *Allocation of Social Service Resources* (in English and Hebrew). Jerusalem: Author.

Commission on Tax Reform. 1975. *Proposals for the Reform of Direct Taxes* (Ben-Shahar Report) (in Hebrew; English translation, 1976). Jerusalem: Ministry of Finance, State Revenue Administration.

Doron, A. 1991a. *The Welfare State in a Changing Society* (in Hebrew). Jerusalem: Magnes Press.

———. 1991b. "Social Security in Israel in Transition: The Effects of Changed Ideology" (in Hebrew). *Bitachon Soziali* (Social Security) 35: 15–26.

Doron, A., and Kramer, R. 1991. *The Welfare State in Israel: The Evolution of Social Security Policy and Practice.* Boulder, Colo.: Westview Press.

Esping-Andersen, G. 1990. *The Three Worlds of Welfare Capitalism*. Princeton, N.J.: Princeton University Press.

Gross, R., Rosen, B., and Shirom, A. 1999. "The Health Care System in Israel Following the Implementation of the National Health Insurance Law" (in Hebrew). *Bitachon Soziali* (Social Security) 54: 11–35.

Habib, J. 1974. *Children in Israel: Some Social, Education and Economic Perspectives*. Jerusalem: The Henrietta Szold Institute, National Institute for Research in the Behavioral Sciences.

———. 1979. *An Integrated Approach to Taxes and Transfers*. Jerusalem: The Maurice Falk Institute for Economic Research in Israel.

International Social Security Association. 1999. *Summing up the Evidence: The Impact of Incentives and Targeting in Social Security* (Conference Volume) (January): 25–28.

Liebfried, S., and Pierson, P., eds. 1995. *European Social Policy: Between Fragmentation and Integration*. Washington, D.C.: The Brookings Institution.

National Insurance Institute. 1981–1996. *Annual Survey* (in Hebrew). Jerusalem: National Insurance Institute.

OECD. 1996. *Social Expenditures Statistics of OECD Member Countries* (Provisional Version). Paris: Author.

Prime Minister's Commission. 1973. *Report on Children and Youth in Poverty* (in Hebrew). Jerusalem: Author.

Roter, R., and Shamai, N. 1971. "Patterns of Poverty in Israel: Preliminary Findings" (in Hebrew). *Bitachon Soziali* (Social Security) 1: 1–20.

7

Values, Categorical Benefits, and Categorical Legacies in Israel

John Gal

The subject of this chapter is the role of categorical benefits in the Israeli welfare state. In other words, this chapter seeks to explain why benefit programs, which do not require recipients to submit to either an assessment of their financial need or to conform to the conditions of social insurance, play a surprisingly dominant role in the Israeli social security system. Indeed, it would appear that, due to various factors, categorical benefits have achieved a far more important role in the Israeli welfare state than that which they play in other, more universal and egalitarian welfare states.

The focal point of the discussion will be upon the role that values play in the policy-making process within welfare states. The claim that values influence social policy is, of course, not an original one. Indeed, in a pioneering work written in the mid-1970s, Abraham Doron and Ralph Kramer (1976) examined the ideological context of social policy decisions in the Israeli welfare state. In many earlier studies of welfare states, the tendency was to focus upon national values as a critical variable in explaining social policy (Ashford 1986; Gronbjerg, Street, and Suttles 1978; King 1973; Rimlinger 1971). For a number of years now, however, the notion that national values influence policy making and serve to differentiate between welfare states has been quite rightly viewed with growing skepticism and has been severely undermined empirically (Skocpol 1992, 15–23). Nevertheless, here it is proposed to follow the path taken by Doron and Kramer and by a number of contemporary scholars (George and Wilding 1994; Reich 1988; Weir 1992) and to return to the examination of the role of values in the formulation of policy. Unlike the earlier usage of this variable, this paper focuses not on national values that are presumed to be traditionally characteristic of an entire society, but rather on the values and ideologies of specific decision makers seeking to define policy in a specific social and historical context. In other words, in this chapter an attempt will be made to investigate the manner in which the norms and values of the major decision makers, and the efforts of interest groups identified with these values, influenced which social security benefits were introduced, when this happened, and why these benefits took the form that they did. In particular, the nature of the policy adopted will be linked to what can be referred to as the "categorical policy legacy" of the Israel welfare state.

In order to carry out this task, the chapter will begin with some definitions, and then the findings of a quantitative study of the historical development of the social security system in Israel will be presented. Following that, the chapter focuses on one of the findings of this analysis. This finding underlines a unique characteristic of the Israeli social security system, as compared to that in other welfare states. It is the major role that nonmeans tested and noncontributory benefit programs play within the Israeli welfare state. The final part of the chapter is devoted to an attempt to explain this finding by examining the role of values in the decision-making process and the policy legacy context in which the policy was formulated.

CATEGORICAL BENEFITS IN WELFARE STATES

The subject matter of this chapter is one of the three fundamental program types found in social security systems. These three program types differ in the techniques, which they employ in order to determine eligibility for access to a program, as shown in Table 7.1. These varying methods of assessing eligibility, however, also reflect different approaches to clients, and their needs, rights, and responsibilities (Titmuss 1968). The three program types are social assistance, social insurance, and categorical benefits (Atkinson 1989). Social assistance programs are those in which eligibility is based upon an assessment of a person's need in which income and other resources are taken into account. Means or income tests are the tools through which this assessment is undertaken. Social insurance programs, by contrast, do not require any individual assessment of a person's needs as an eligibility condition. Right to benefit is conditional, however, upon financial contribution to a

Table 7.1
Common Definition of Benefit Schemes (Based on Dominant Eligibility Conditions)

	Contributory Condition	No Contributory Condition
Means Tested	-	Social Assistance (*Income Support*)
Not Means Tested	Social Insurance (*Old-Age Pensions)*	Categorical Benefits (*Child Benefits)*

social insurance fund. Only those individuals who have a proven contributory history of a predetermined length or value will be eligible for benefits (ILO 1984). Finally, the third type, categorical benefits, differs from the other two types of social security programs in that programs of this nature require neither an individual assessment of financial need nor a contribution record as a condition for eligibility. Right to benefit is determined primarily upon the individual's belonging to a socially defined category.

This chapter concentrates on the third type of social security programs. In the literature, categorical benefits appear under different titles. Among the more common are demogrants, universal benefits, social allowances, basic incomes, universal benefits, contingency benefits, citizenship benefits, and categorical entitlements. Doron (1987, 71–72) has described these benefits as "statutory benefits," thereby seeking to emphasize the underlying principle of these programs—that the unique status of the recipients of these benefits grants them rights that are guaranteed by legislation. Regardless of the term employed, all refer to a variety of nonmeans tested and noncontributory social security programs to be found in many welfare states that include child benefits, universal basic pensions, disability benefits, war pensions, maternity grants, industrial injury benefits, and burial grants.

In more formal terms, "Categorical benefits are state-administered cash benefits paid to individuals who belong to socially-defined categories, regardless of their specific income status or prior contribution to a social insurance system" (Gal 1998, 77). This definition seeks to emphasize that categorical benefits are always dependent upon an individual's membership in a specific category of people that has been socially defined (Stone 1984). This qualification is intended to stress the fact that the decision as to which individuals should be granted a portion of the common wealth without actually earning it through their own efforts, or without their having insured themselves against specific contingencies, is a social decision. This decision generally includes at least two stages. The first is a political decision in which a "deserving" category of individuals is established. This decision is typically undertaken, in the last instance, by policy makers within the political arena and hinges upon the way in which they identify "deserving" categories. A second stage takes place within the bureaucratic arena (though it usually needs to be approved by political policy makers). During this stage, administratively defined slots are created, thereby prescribing the specific characteristics according to which an individual belonging to the previously established category can be clearly identified.

A second element worthy of emphasis in this definition is the issue of conditionality. While categorical benefits seek to target individual's needs, these needs are not based upon an assessment of an individual's specific *financial* situation but, for different reasons, the assumption is that, on average, anyone belonging to the deserving category is likely to have financial needs linked directly to the characteristics that enable them to belong to this category. This, however, should not be seen to imply a lack of conditionality. Conditions that define one's membership of a specific category of people deserving benefits can be very diverse and often include more than one condition. While these do not include a means test or an examination of contributory history, they can include proof of one's age, parenthood, place of residence in a country for a predetermined length of time, an assessment of one's ability to function in the labor market (as is the case for industrial injury benefits), disability benefits and invalid care benefits, or, as in the case of maternity grants in Israel, both the criterion of giving birth and that of doing so in a hospital (as opposed to in the home). In short, categorical benefits are always conditional, though *not* upon contributional history or financial means.

As noted, categorical benefits take diverse forms in different welfare states, and they seek to address a wide variety of needs and risks. Nevertheless, it would appear that it is possible to differentiate between three different functions which are served by categorical benefits, and to distinguish between three categorical benefit types that can be identified according to the function which they fulfill. The three functions are

1. A compensatory function. *Compensatory categorical benefits* seek to provide compensation for individuals in the case of job loss, death, or loss of faculty. These benefits are unique in that they are linked to specific circumstances (such as military service or work) under which the loss occurred. Individuals suffering loss in these circumstances are perceived as particularly deserving of compensation by society (Bolderson 1974). As a result, benefits of this type are typically either

relatively high flat rated, graduated, or earnings related. Inability to work due to injury incurred at the workplace or loss of faculty resulting from military service or injuries as a result of hostile actions take this form in most welfare states.

2. An income maintenance function. *Income maintenance categorical benefits* provide a minimum income to those individuals who, for a variety of reasons, are unable to support themselves through paid work. However, unlike compensatory categorical benefits, this inability is not due to circumstances that are regarded as justifying compensation. As these benefits are intended to serve primarily a safety net function they typically adhere to the "least eligibility" principle by which the support offered is lower than the amount earned by the lowest waged employee. The benefits then tend to be low flat-rated benefits and are often linked to a formal assessment of the recipient's ability to work for a living. The General Disability benefit is an example of this kind of categorical benefit in the Israeli welfare state.

3. An income supplement function. *Income supplement categorical benefits* cover the expenses incurred by specific groups within the population who are regarded as having additional needs and expenses. The most common example of this kind of benefit is, of course, child benefits or family benefits, which can be found in virtually all welfare states. Maternity grants, burial grants, and single parent benefits are additional examples of this type of benefit that can be found in various welfare states. Being intended to supplement income received either through work or through other social security programs, income supplement categorical benefits tend to be small.

Most welfare states include within their social security systems programs that are based upon all three of the fundamental types of social security programs (i.e., social insurance, social assistance, and categorical benefits) and indeed often include programs that contain elements of more than one of the three types. Various welfare states, however, can be differentiated according to the relative role that each of the three types fulfills within their social security system. In other words, one can identify the predominant guiding principles in the specific social security programs in a welfare state, categorize them by program type, and assess the relative role of each of the types within the system as a whole. Figure 7.1 presents a comparison of the role of categorical benefits in a number of welfare states, clearly indicating the very different role that these benefits can play. As can be seen from the figure, the role of categorical benefits fluctuates greatly in different welfare state settings. While in the Swedish welfare state categorical benefits comprise more than one-third of all expenditure on social security, in the German and the Australian systems, these benefits play a peripheral role

Figure 7.1
Expenditure on Categorical Benefits as Percentage of Total Social Security
Expenditure, 1994–1995

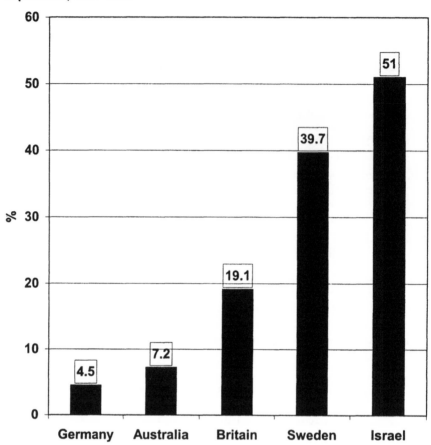

Sources: Data for Australia from Australian Bureau of Statistics, *1997 Year Book Australia* (Canberra: Australian Bureau of Statistics, 1997); Data for Britain from Department of Social Security, *The Government's Expenditure Plans* (London: Department of Social Security, 1996); Data for Germany from Federal Statistical Office, *Statistical Yearbook 1996* (Wiesbaden: Federal Statistical Office, 1996); Data for Israel from annual reports and budgets published by the State Comptroller, Treasury, Ministry for Immigrant Absorption, Ministry of Defense, National Insurance Institute, Central Bureau of Statistics, Ministry of Labour and Social Affairs. Other sources include Y. Moav, *The Social Security System in Israel 1976–1980* (in Hebrew) (Jerusalem: National Insurance Institute, 1982); M. Zinmon, *Social Security for Workers in Israel* (in Hebrew) (Jerusalem: Tarbut VeHinuch, 1964); Data for Sweden from NOSOSCO, *Social Security in the Nordic Countries* (Copenhagen: Nordic Social Statistical Committee, 1995).

in social security coverage, comprising well less than one-tenth of all spending. Nonmeans tested and noncontributory benefits in the British welfare state have, by contrast, a more central role. One in every five pounds spent on benefits in Britain is devoted to benefits of this type. Yet, in comparison to all these welfare states, categorical benefits play a far more significant role in the Israeli social security system. Slightly more than one-half of all social security spending goes to benefits that do not require either an assessment of financial need or prior contribution to the social security fund.

The overt explanation for the very significant difference in the relative role of categorical benefits in most of the welfare states in the diagram is relatively straightforward. The limited role of these programs in the German welfare state can be linked to the overriding Bismarkian principle of social insurance that characterize this case (Clasen 1997). In other words, eligibility for virtually all the benefit programs in the German social security system is contingent upon one's having been previously insured by the state and having a satisfactory contributory record (Bonoli 1997). In the Australian case, the explanation is also relatively simple—while the contributory issue is irrelevant in this welfare state, means testing is not. Indeed, this is a welfare state which has traditionally emphasized the wide use of means testing in order to determine eligibility for benefits. As a result, eligibility for very few social security programs is determined solely by belonging to a socially defined category. In the Swedish case, by contrast, the social democratic nature of the welfare state translates into a marked preference for universal benefit programs that are categorical benefits, universal old age pensions being a prime example. While there are also many income-related programs in the Swedish system, in which prior contribution is a primary determinant of eligibility, much of the expenditure upon social security is devoted to benefits that are categorical (Castles 1994).

The findings regarding the Israeli case however are more puzzling. The Israeli welfare state combines an adherence to the Beveridge social insurance model with an emphasis on social assistance provision for the poor. Benefit levels are relatively low and, like Britain, Israel places great emphasis upon the provision of social insurance through free market mechanisms, particularly through the widespread existence of occupational pensions for the elderly, with state programs intended to serve as a safety net and top-up (Doron and Kramer 1991; Evans 1998). While the Israeli welfare state was clearly modeled on the Beveridge model when it was first established during the 1950s, it moved closer to the social democratic model during the 1970s with the introduction of more

wage-related benefits, wider coverage of needs, and better index-
ing of benefit levels (Doron 1994). Nevertheless, it would appear to
be closer to the liberal welfare state ideal type than any of the other
welfare state regimes in the Esping-Andersen (1990) typology.
Moreover, decision makers in Israel during the last decade and a half
have been publicly committed to cutting welfare expenditure and to
placing emphasis upon individual provision of needs through the
market (Gal 1994a). In other words, unlike the social democratic welfare state model, which can be expected to adopt categorical benefit
programs that conform with its universalistic goals, there is little outward reason for categorical benefits to play a major role in the Israeli
welfare state. However, our findings indicate that the role that categorical benefits play in the Israeli case is a far greater one than
that they fulfill in the welfare state upon which it was modeled—
the British welfare state. Indeed, the role of categorical benefits in
Israel is even greater than that of these benefits in the archetypal
social democratic Swedish welfare state. Clearly, this emphasis upon
categorical benefits in Israel requires an explanation.

THE CHANGING ROLE OF CATEGORICAL BENEFITS
IN THE ISRAELI WELFARE STATE

In order to make some sense of the role of categorical benefits in
the Israeli welfare state, the role of these benefits since the establishment of social security system in the mid-1950s has been calculated. In Figure 7.2, the proportion of expenditure devoted to each
of the three types of programs within the Israeli social security
system over a forty-year period is portrayed. Unlike most studies
of the social security system in Israel, the figures here refer to the
percentage of overall expenditure on social security by the various
government ministries and by the National Insurance Institute.
Our interest is not in benefits that are formally defined as social
security programs solely because they are provided by the National
Insurance Institute, but in any benefit that seeks to fulfill the function of providing social security to Israeli residents. Clearly, this function need not be, and is not, the sole domain of National Insurance
Institute administered benefits. Indeed, the irrelevance of the actual
administrative body when seeking to compile data upon social security programs is illustrated by the case of the program of Military
Reserve Service benefits that provide social security for those suffering income loss while serving in the military reserves. In recent
years, responsibility for the administration of this benefit has moved
from the National Insurance Institute to the Ministry of Defense.
Its function, however, and all its other characteristics, have re-

Figure 7.2
Expenditure on Social Security in Israel 1955–1995, by Program Type

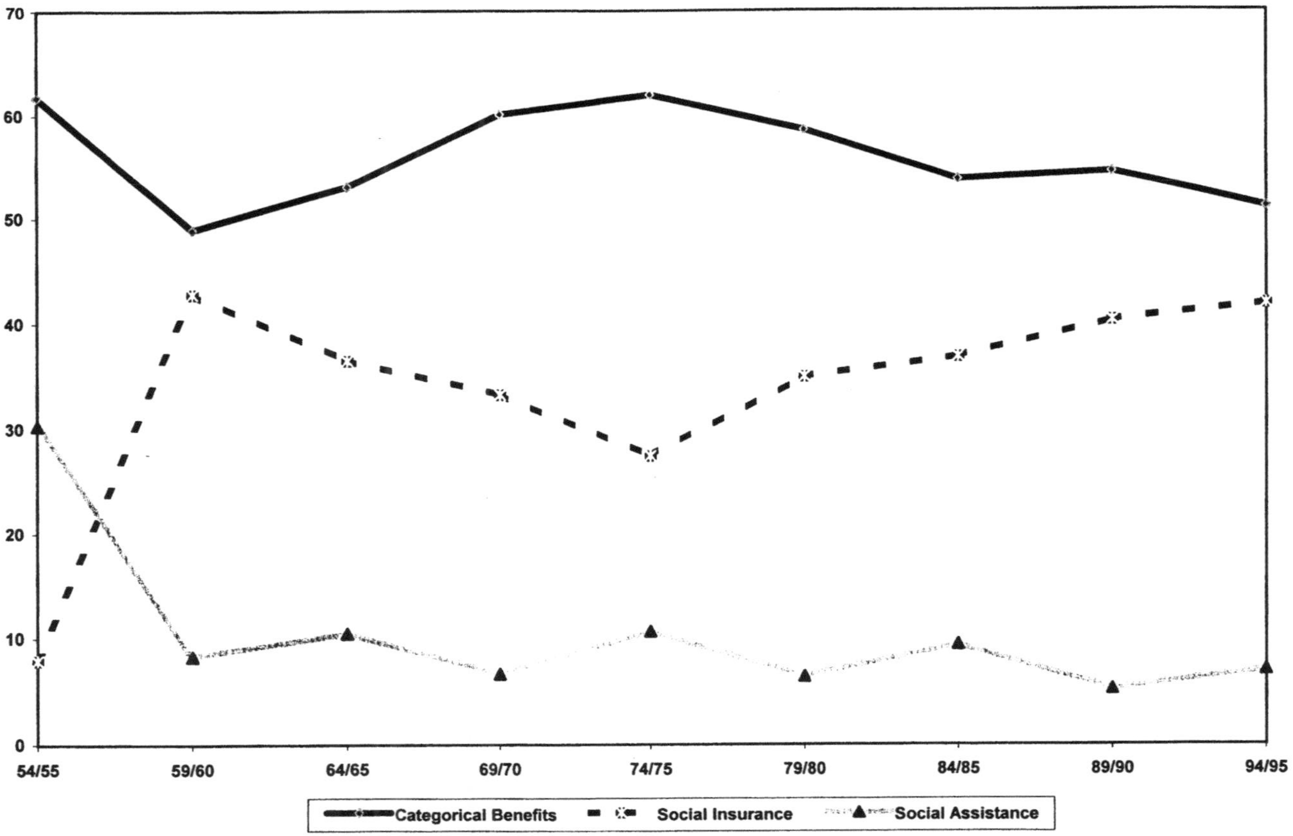

Categorical Benefits ■ Social Insurance ▲ Social Assistance

mained the same. As such, included in the categorical benefit category are all National Insurance benefits which do not require any qualification period or a means test as a condition of eligibility. In addition, there are some other benefit programs which have similar characteristics but that are provided by the Ministry of Defense, the Ministry for Immigrant Absorption, or the Treasury.

Under the title of social insurance programs are to be found benefit programs that require applicants to have paid social insurance contributions for a minimal qualification period as an eligibility condition. In the Israeli case, these include Old Age, Survivors, Unemployment, Long-Term Care, and Maternity Insurance. Social assistance benefits, by contrast, are those in which a means or income test is employed as a primary means of determining eligibility. These include Income Support (and prior to its adoption—the Welfare Payments), Income Supplement for the Elderly, and Alimony Benefits.

Figure 7.2 portrays graphically the changing roles that the three benefit types have played in the social security system in Israel. One very obvious trend is the decline in the proportion of expenditure devoted to social assistance programs over the period, from a high of nearly a third of the total expenditure to less than a tenth in 1995. By contrast, the role of social insurance programs has increased dramatically from 8 percent in 1955 to just over 40 percent in 1995. This reversal of roles is partly due to the fact that the first social security programs were legislated in 1953, only two years before the first data set in the diagram. It is also the result of the fact that over the years many beneficiaries of social assistance programs have been transferred to newly introduced social insurance programs, that changes have been made in existing programs, and that new social insurance programs, such as Unemployment Insurance and Long Term Care, have been introduced (Gal 1994b; Ben Zvi 1994). Finally, it is a reflection of the changing demography of Israeli society and, in particular, the dramatic growth in the number of the elderly eligible for old age benefits. Thus, while there were only 6,172 beneficiaries of the Old Age and Survivors benefit in 1957, by the middle of 1998 the number of beneficiaries of this benefit had reached 616,731 (National Insurance Institute 1998, 38).

Unlike the changing fortunes of the other benefit types, the proportionate role of categorical benefits has been relatively consistent over the period. Clearly, these benefits have played a major role in the Israeli social security system since its establishment. True, over time, the proportion of expenditure devoted to categorical benefits has fluctuated and indeed even dropped in recent years, but it has nevertheless remained very high, comprising more than half of all social security expenditure. An explanation of this rather remarkable finding requires us to look closer at the specific categorical benefit programs, their characteristics, and their mode of development.

In all, twenty categorical benefit programs were adopted by Israel between its establishment in 1948 and 1995. As can be seen from Table 7.2, the first programs were adopted merely a year after independence was achieved. The programs are administered by a variety of government bodies, among them the Ministries of Defense and Immigrant Absorption and the Treasury. However, the majority of the programs are provided directly by the National Insurance Institute, despite the fact that this body was originally intended to provide social insurance programs only.

Of the twenty categorical benefit programs, twelve provide compensation for either job loss or loss due to service of one kind or another. Of these, the most prominent are those provided to disabled veterans or the families of war dead and those benefits provided to the work injured. An additional six categorical benefit programs are intended to supplement the income of specific groups in the population (primarily parents with children), while two other programs, General Disability and the Absorption Package, can be best described as fulfilling an income maintenance function. The distribution of expenditure between the three types of categorical benefits over time can be seen in Figure 7.3.

In order to better understand the role of categorical benefits within the Israeli welfare state, it would appear useful to concentrate upon compensatory categorical benefits. This is because these benefits not only comprise the largest number of programs but, for much of the period, they also enjoyed the lion's share of expenditure. Indeed, while the role of this benefit type is sometimes overshadowed by the income supplement benefit type, this is due solely to the impact of child benefits during those periods when it was granted to all families with one or more children and not limited by means or categorical testing (Gordon and Eliav 1998). While categorical benefits of the income supplement variety (child benefits, in particular) are prevalent in most welfare states, the size, volume, and diversity of compensatory categorical benefits would appear to be unique to the Israeli case.

An obvious characteristic of compensatory benefits is the fact that, during the first decade or so after Israeli independence, expenditure devoted to these benefits comprised over 70 percent of all expenditure on categorical benefits and between a third and a half of the entire social security expenditure. Clearly, one explanation for this is the major role that benefits for disabled military veterans

Table 7.2
Categorical Benefits in the Israeli Welfare State

Name of Program	Type of Categorical Benefit	Administration	Year of Adoption
War Pensions (Invalids' Law; Dependents of Fallen Soldiers Law)	Compensatory	Ministry of Defense	1949
Hostile and Border Actions	Compensatory	National Insurance Institute (NII)	1949
Military Reserve Service	Compensatory	Ministry of Defense	1952
Maternity Grant	Income Supplement	NII	1954
Work Injury	Compensatory	NII	1954
Disabled Veterans of the War against the Nazis	Compensatory	Treasury	1954
Disabled Victims of Nazi Persecution	Compensatory	Treasury	1957
Child Benefits	Income Supplement	NII	1959
Family Allowance for Veterans	Compensatory	NII	1970
Prisoners of Zion	Compensatory	NII	1973
General Disability	Income Maintenance	NII	1974
Mobility	Income Supplement	NII	1975
Volunteers' Rights	Compensatory	NII	1975
Employees in case of Bankruptcy	Compensatory	NII	1975
Attendance Allowance	Income Supplement	NII	1979
Benefit to Disabled Child	Income Supplement	NII	1981
Accident Victims	Compensatory	NII	1981
Righteous Gentiles	Compensatory	NII	1986
Absorption Package	Income Maintenance	Ministry of Immigrant Absorption	1989
One Parent Benefit	Income Supplement	NII	1992

Source: Annual reports and budgets published by the Israeli State Comptroller, Treasury, Ministry for Immigrant Absorption, Ministry of Defense, National Insurance Institute, Central Bureau of Statistics, Ministry of Labour and Social Affairs.

and for the families of war dead played in expenditure on social security during this period and in later years. Undoubtedly, the proportion of social security expenditure devoted to compensatory categorical benefits in the Israeli welfare state, as compared to that in other welfare states, has been influenced by the unique military circumstances of Israeli society. Unlike other welfare states, Israel

Figure 7.3
Distribution of Expenditure on Categorical Benefits by Type, 1955–1995

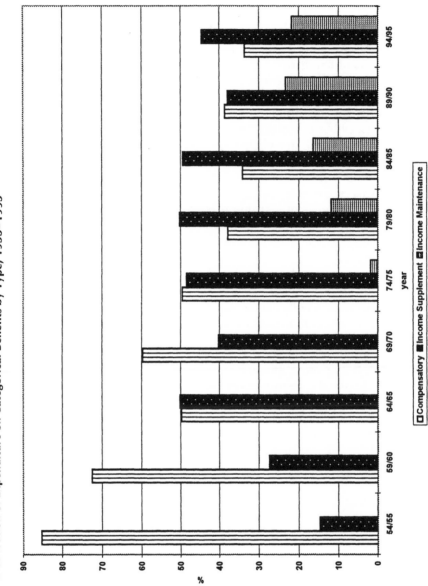

has been engaged in a continuous military conflict with its neighbors, and this has led to a growing population of disabled veterans and families of the fallen. The numbers of those receiving military pensions and disability benefits has grown from merely 6,031 in 1953 to 67,631 in 1997 (Ministry of Defense 1998, app. 1).

However, it would appear that the major role of compensatory categorical benefits in the Israeli social security system is not only a result of the growth in the number of war injured and dead. As can be seen from the data, the proportion of expenditure devoted to compensatory categorical benefits as compared to other categorical benefits has declined over the years, yet the actual number of compensatory benefit programs has continued to grow. Moreover, during this period the eligibility conditions for these benefits have become progressively more liberal, coverage has been enhanced, and benefit levels have grown. Hence, the role of this type of benefit program cannot be attributed solely to the growth in the number of recipients of a single program but also to the introduction of additional programs of this type and to the liberalization of conditions in existing programs, so that they encompass additional population groups.

The very significant role of compensatory categorical benefits within the Israeli welfare state can also be seen as reflecting a kind of "categorical policy legacy." In other words, there has been a tendency by decision makers over time to adopt the approach employed with regard to earlier needs and to choose categorical benefits as a means for dealing with the social security needs of very specific population groups. In each of these cases, when faced with the need to deal with the requirements of these social groups, Israeli decision makers have clearly made a conscious choice in favor of nonmeans-tested and noncontributory benefits. Moreover, they have generally decided to adopt the more liberal and generous type of categorical benefits—those of the compensatory variety, rather than the cheaper and more stringent income maintenance type of categorical benefit.

A careful examination of the deliberations and public activity surrounding the process of adoption of new benefit programs within the Israeli social security system and the introduction of changes within existing programs provides ample evidence of the crucial role of policy legacies. The initial decisions regarding the nature of benefit programs, the institutional frameworks that derived from these decisions, and the interest groups that were spawned by this process played vital roles in the crafting of responses to social security needs down the road (Pierson 1993; Skocpol 1992). The policy legacy associated with benefits for disabled veterans is a good example.

One such path was initiated in 1949, with the adoption of the Invalid's Law which provided disabled veterans of the War of Independence with relatively generous nonmeans tested benefits linked to civil service salaries and to degrees of injury. In addition, it included a variety of medical and occupational rehabilitation services, business and home loans, and access to personal social services and counseling. Finally, it granted special assistance to disabled veterans with no additional source of income (Nacht and Kleyff 1955, 17–25).

This decision, as to how best to deal with the needs of disabled veterans of the War of Independence, initiated a process which ultimately encompassed not only any veteran injured in military or police service after the establishment of the state but also other groups in society. These include the families of those who fell while in military service and any Jew injured in underground activities during the British Mandate while serving in the British Army during World War II or while serving in other armies that fought the Nazis. In addition, the benefits for veterans provided the basis for benefits for those civilian victims of Nazi persecution who were not eligible for reparations from Germany, for gentiles who assisted Jews during the Nazi period, for Jews persecuted for their Zionist beliefs in countries such as the Soviet Union in the postwar period, and even for families with children in which one of the family members served in the armed forces. Finally, the benefits provided disabled military veterans also served as the basis for the benefits granted to any civilians injured in terrorist attacks in Israel.

It is important to note that the rights and benefits granted these diverse groups have not always necessarily replicated those granted disabled military veterans. However, the rationale employed to justify the granting of benefits in each of these cases as well as the fundamental structure of the benefit program adopted has been explicitly linked to the disabled veterans' benefits by decision makers and lobby groups alike. Thus, for example, in 1952, public criticism of the government's proposed legislation for compensation for disabled World War II veterans who fought against the Nazis in foreign armies centered upon the differences between the proposed law and that passed in 1949, which provided compensation for the War of Independence veterans. Despite the government's claim that the proposed law was closely based upon the 1949 legislation, the differences between the two laws led to an outcry on the part of veterans' organizations and members of the Knesset and to calls for the granting of equal rights to all disabled veterans. These calls eventually led to significant changes in the law. One of the most obvious revisions was that regarding ministerial responsibility for administration of the program. While the government had originally suggested that the Ministry of Labour be responsible for implementing the law, by the time the final draft of the law was presented to the Knesset for approval, ministerial responsibility had been shifted to the Ministry of Defense, the ministry charged with administering benefits for the War of Independence disabled veterans (Nacht and Kleyff 1955). Though the resulting piece of legislation did not provide fully equal rights to the disabled veterans of the struggle against the Nazis, the structure and operating principles of the new law were similar to that of the 1949 law. In particular, the fact that responsibility for implementation of the law now lay with the Ministry of Defense provided the disabled veterans of the war against the Nazis with a sense that their standing in society was equal, at least on a formal level, to that of those disabled during the War of Independence.

A similar process occurred in 1969 during the debate over compensation for the victims of terrorist attacks (Yanay 1994). Initially, the government tabled a proposal that sought to base compensation for victims of terrorist attacks on the Work Injury Law. The implication of this was that benefits would be based upon a percentage of the victim's previous income and that administration of the program would the responsibility of the National Insurance Institute and not the Ministry of Defense. However, in the debate over the proposed law, Knesset members representing the residents of border settlements who were the majority of the victims of such attacks at the time, strongly criticized the government's position. MK Uzi Finerman claimed that "it seems to me both just and logical that the benefits granted victims of acts on the borders be equal to those of IDF casualties. We must pass legislation that prevents any unjust discrimination." By the time that the law was tabled for final approval by the Knesset, it had been changed significantly. While the National Insurance Institute was responsible for its implementation, the rights granted by the law to terrorist casualties mirrored those granted to disabled soldiers. In both the case of disabled veterans of the war against the Nazis and in the case of civilian victims of terrorist attacks, the 1949 Invalid's Law was clearly perceived as the benchmark against which the later laws were compared.

THE ROLE OF VALUES AND INTEREST GROUPS

The most obvious characteristic of all the social groups that have received compensatory categorical benefits within the Israeli welfare state over the years since independence is the fact that they have all been linked to some of the very central values dear to the elites that dominated Israeli society during this period. These values included Zionism, military defense of the state, the struggle against Nazism, and the work ethic (Eisenstadt 1967). This is particularly true of programs linked directly, or even indirectly, to military service. These reflect the perception that Israel is "a nation-in-arms" and that service in the military is a universal and vital civil duty which is crucial to the state's continued existence (Ben-Eliezer 1995). As such, anyone injured in active defense of the state or as a result of attacks against it deserves full compensation. The first prime minister, David Ben-Gurion, articulated this perception in an introduction to legislation for disabled veterans when he wrote,

I am not aware of times in the history of our people, when there were peaks of heroism and glory as those exhibited in the lives and deaths of our young men in the Jordan Valley, the Jezreal Valley, the Galilee hills, the Negev plains, the mountains of Jerusalem, in Haifa and in Tel Aviv. . . . The state has fulfilled its duty to all those who were injured during the War of Independence. Of course, there are things that the state is unable to do: Just as the state cannot bring back the lives of fallen sons to their mothers and fathers, it cannot return the lost limbs of the injured. Yet, I believe that I do not exaggerate when I say that the state has made every possible effort to rectify what can be rectified and to rehabilitate what can be rehabilitated. (Nacht and Kleyff 1955, 7)

While the needs of the social groups identified with these core values were compelling in and of themselves, the case for granting compensatory benefits has been strengthened by the fact that it has often been made by well-organized interest groups representing these groups. The lobbying activities of these groups, and the parliamentary activities of their allies in the Knesset, in the name of values so dear to decision makers, have paved the way for relatively rapid enactment of laws committing the state to provide social security benefits to meet the needs of the social groups identified with the core values. Moreover, these lobbying activities have enabled supporters of these laws to overcome government attempts to put a lid on the financial costs of these programs by limiting the scope or generosity of the laws. Not surprisingly, perhaps, in practice eligibility for these generous categorical compensation programs has been limited to Jews, while Arabs have been excluded from them.

The preference for compensatory categorical benefits rather than social insurance, means tested benefits or even more minimal income maintenance categorical benefits, as has been the case for such groups in other welfare states, appears to be related to the statist traditions that characterized Israeli society, particularly in its formative years. Unlike many central and southern European welfare states, Israel was never influenced by the Bismarkian welfare tradition, which preferred social insurance, status-preserving solutions to the needs of these groups. Similarly, the poor law tradition that has influenced decision makers in many liberal welfare states has had a limited impact on social security legislation in Israel. While the Israeli social security system has often been described as universalistic, this universalism has differed markedly, particularly in its early years, from the social democratic tradition which took root most strongly in Scandinavia.

During the mandatory period and even later, after the establishment of the state, Israeli democracy was characterized by its particularism or clientelism (Eisenstadt and Roniger 1984, 195–199). In other words, political leaders, and particularly those affiliated with the ruling Mapai party, employed the state's material resources as a means of rewarding specific groups in society for their contribution to the common good (as defined by the relevant elites) or as a means of maintaining political allegiance (Horowitz and Lissak 1978). As Shalev has noted, to a large degree, the social security system served a similar goal (Shalev 1992, 240–244). This clientelism differed significantly from the clientelism that has characterized Southern European welfare states and that takes the more blatant form of an exchange of favors for votes on an immediate or personal level (Ferrera 1996). The particularlistic social security programs in Israel were not part of direct exchanges of benefits for votes nor were they covert or illegal. Indeed, they were incorporated into the emerging universalistic structure of the Israeli social security system. The Israeli welfare state, especially during the first decades after statehood, opted for what can be best described as a form of "categorical universalism." Unlike the social democratic universalism that sought to grant equal benefits to wide sectors of society as a means of achieving greater integration, this form of universalism sought to provide universal benefits to very specific groups as a means of rewarding them for services rendered or compensating them for loss suffered due to service in the name of preferred social values. While some other groups in society were granted universal benefits during this period, access to these benefit programs was curtailed by severe eligibility conditions, particularly with regard to the minimal qualifying period during which payments were made to the social security fund, and the benefit levels were usually very low. Meanwhile, groups in society, which suffered from other needs, such as the unemployed and destitute elderly, or from losses similar to those receiving the compensatory categorical benefits but due to other causes, such as the regular disabled, were virtually ignored or subjected to stringent means or work tests, or they received particularly low benefits.

It was only much later on, mainly in the 1970s, that notions of nonparticularistic universalism successfully permeated into the decision-making process and resulted in the establishment of a more universal, equitable social security system.

CONCLUSION

Social security regimes within welfare states can be differentiated according to the dominant types of social security programs within them. In the case of the Israeli welfare state, it is clearly characterized by the fact that social security programs of the categorical benefit type play a major role within it. This is reflected in the portion of expenditure that has been devoted to these benefit programs over the forty years since the establishment of the social security system in Israel. It can also be discerned from the proliferation of programs which do not include means testing or an assessment of the contributory history of applicants as a condition of eligibility over this period.

An explanation for this unique characteristic of the Israeli welfare state has been presented in this paper. It has been suggested that policy legacies, elite values, and interests have had a major impact upon the decision to prefer social security programs based upon the categorical benefit format as a means of meeting the needs of certain population groups. From 1949 onward, categorical benefit programs, particularly those that provide more generous benefits as a means of compensating recipients, have been granted to members of groups which have been identified with core values of the decision-making elites in Israeli society. By following the path of one such policy legacy we have shown how the cherished value of military service for the country has served as the basis for the introduction of generous categorical benefit programs to those who have suffered in the name of this value. A major role in the process of adoption of these benefit programs was played by interest groups, which were identified with this value, and were able to claim compensation on the basis of previously adopted compensatory categorical benefit programs. In the specific case of military service, the 1949 Invalid's Law, which provided compensatory categorical benefits to disabled veterans of the War of Independence, served as the benchmark for subsequent debates over social security legislation.

The tendency of decision makers, particularly in the first decades after Israeli statehood, to introduce categorical benefit programs should be seen in the context of the particularistic nature of the Israeli political system during this period. As was the case in other fields of government activity, the social security system was perceived as a venue for clientelistic policies, according to which "deserving" groups in society were compensated for services rendered in the name of values dear to the elite. The result was the establishment of a social security system that can be described as having been based upon the notion of "categorical universalism." Thus, relatively generous categorical benefits were granted to anyone belonging to a "deserving" group while individuals with other needs were generally either ignored or able to receive only very minimal benefits that were conditional upon stringent eligibility conditions. While changes in the Israeli welfare state in more recent decades have led to the adoption of additional programs, more liberal eligibility conditions and higher levels of benefits, the impact of the categorical universalism of the earlier years can still be clearly identified within the social security system and continues to differentiate between the Israeli welfare state and other welfare states.

REFERENCES

Ashford, D. E. 1986. *The Emergence of the Welfare States*. Oxford: Basil Blackwell.

Atkinson, A. B. 1989. "Social Insurance and Income Maintenance." In *Poverty and Social Security*, ed. A. B. Atkinson. New York: Harvester Wheatsheaf.

Ben-Eliezer, U. 1995. "A Nation in Arms: State, Nation, and Militarism in Israel's First Years." *Comparative Studies in Society and History* 37: 264–285.

Ben Zvi, B. 1994. "The Long-Term Care Law: Achievements and Unforeseen Implications for its Implementation." *Social Security* (English Edition) 3: 84–100.

Bolderson, H. 1974. "Compensation for Disability." *Journal of Social Policy* 3 (3): 193–211.

Bonoli, G. 1997. "Classifying Welfare States: A Two-Dimensional Approach." *Journal of Social Policy* 26 (3): 351–372.

Castles, F. G. 1994. "Comparing the Australian and Scandinavian Welfare States." *Scandinanvian Political Studies* 17 (1): 31–46.

Clasen, J. 1997. "Social Insurance in Germany: Dismantling or Reconstruction?" In *Social Insurance in Europe*, ed. J. Clasen. Bristol: Policy Press.

Doron, A. 1987. *The Welfare State in an Age of Change*. Jerusalem: Magnes.

———. 1994. "The Effectiveness of the Beveridge Model at Different Stages of Socio-Economic Development: The Israeli Experience." In *Beveridge and Social Security*, ed. J. Hills, J. Ditch, and H. Glennerster. Oxford: Clarendon Press.

Doron, A., and Kramer, R. M. 1976. "Ideology, Programme and Organizational Factors in Public Assistance: The Case of Israel." *Journal of Social Policy* 5 (2): 131–149.

————. 1991. *The Welfare State in Israel*. Boulder, Colo.: Westview.

Eisenstadt, S. N. 1967. *Israeli Society*. London: Weidenfeld & Nicolson.

Eisenstadt, S. N., and Roniger, L. 1984. *Patrons, Clients and Friends*. Cambridge: Cambridge University Press.

Esping-Andersen, G. 1990. *The Three Worlds of Welfare Capitalism*. Cambridge: Polity Press.

Evans, M. 1998. "Social Security: Dismantling the Pyramids?" In *The State of Welfare*, ed. H. Glennerster and J. Hills. Oxford: Oxford University Press.

Ferrera, M. 1996. "The 'Southern Model' of Welfare in Southern Europe." *Journal of European Social Policy* 6 (1): 17–37.

Gal, J. 1994a. "Commodification of the Welfare State and Privatization: Implications for Israel" (in Hebrew). *Hevra veRevahah* 15 (1): 7–24.

————. 1994b. "The Development of Unemployment Insurance in Israel." *Social Security* (English Edition) 3: 117–136.

————. 1998. "Categorical Benefits in Welfare States: Findings from Great Britain and Israel." *International Social Security Review* 51 (1): 73–102.

George, V., and Wilding, P. 1994. *Welfare and Ideology*. New York: Harvester Wheatsheaf.

Gordon, D., and Eliav, T. 1998. "Universality vs. Selectivity in Child Allowances." *Social Security* (English Edition) 5: 115–126.

Gronbjerg, K., Street, D., and Suttles, G. D. 1978. *Poverty and Social Change*. Chicago: University of Chicago Press.

Horowitz, D., and Lissak, M. 1978. *The Origins of the Israeli Polity: Palestine under the Mandate*. Chicago: University of Chicago Press.

ILO. 1984. *Introduction to Social Security*. Geneva: International Labour Office.

King, A. 1973. "Ideas, Institutions and the Policies of Governments: A Comparative Analysis, Part III." *British Journal of Political Science* 3: 409–423.

Ministry of Defense. 1998. *50 Years of Rehabilitation* (in Hebrew). Tel Aviv: Ministry of Defense.

Nacht, M., and Kleyff, M. 1955. *Rehabilitation Laws* (in Hebrew). Tel Aviv: The Company for Law Books.

National Insurance Institute. 1998. *Quarterly Statistics* (in Hebrew). Jerusalem: National Insurance Institute.

Pierson, P. 1993. "When Effect Becomes Cause: Policy Feedback and Political Change." *World Politics* 45: 598–628.

Reich, R. B. 1988. Introduction to *The Power of Public Ideas*, ed. R. B. Reich. Cambridge, Mass.: Ballinger.

Rimlinger, G. V. 1971. *Welfare Policy and Industrialization in Europe, America and Russia*. New York: Wiley.

Shalev, M. 1992. *Labour and the Political Economy in Israel*. Oxford: Oxford University Press.

Skocpol, T. 1992. *Protecting Soldiers and Mothers: The Political Origins of Social Policy in the United States*. Cambridge: Belknap Press of Harvard University Press.

Stone, D. A. 1984. *The Disabled State*. Philadelphia: Temple University Press.

Titmuss, R. M. 1968. "Universal and Selective Social Services." In *Commitment to Welfare*, ed. R. M. Titmuss. London: George Allen and Unwin.

Weir, M. 1992. *Politics and Jobs*. Princeton, N.J.: Princeton University Press.

Yanay, U. 1994. "Assistance to Civilian Casualties of Hostile Action." *Social Security* (English Edition) 3: 137–163.

FURTHER READING

Clasen, J. 1997. *Social Insurance in Europe*. Bristol: The Policy Press.

Doron, A., and Kramer, R. M. 1991. *The Welfare State in Israel*. Boulder, Colo.: Westview.

Esping-Anderson, G. 1990. *The Three Worlds of Welfare Capitalism*. Cambridge: Polity Press.

8

Does the Knesset Matter?
The Influence of Members of
the 13th Knesset on
Social Policy in Israel

Asher Ben-Arieh

Political research deals with political activity. Most often, it seeks to examine the influences on political activity and how these activities shape policy. Similarly, a large part of social policy research attempts to learn how policy is shaped and designed and what its results are.

Most democratic governments, Israel among them, are parliamentary democracies. Indeed, despite often made claims that parliament is losing its importance and influence, it continues to have a major influence on policy design. The role of the parliament is dependent on several factors: party activity and the activities of interest groups, lobbies, and individual members of parliament. In recent years, in Israel as well, there has been an increase in the activity of parliament members, activity which does not necessarily occur within the framework of the official actions of the party to which they are affiliated. Thus, the influence of parliament and its members is significant in a number of areas. Not the least of them is in the making of social policy.

This chapter reports on the findings of a study which concentrated on the influence of the members of the 13th Israeli Knesset (1992–1996) on social welfare policy. The study addresses questions such as: Which types of activities had greater impact upon social policy design, and what background and positional variables contribute most to the influence of Knesset members? Most studies dealing with the influence of parliamentary activity on policy in general and on social welfare policy in particular focus on the formal activities of members of parliament (MPs). That is, the activities that take place in the plenary and its committees and according to what is defined in the parliament's bylaws. Following Kornberg and Mishler's lead (1976), the study sought to learn something of the influence of the informal activities of members of Knesset (MKs), either within the Knesset or outside of it (e.g., lobbying activity, correspondence, informal meetings with ministers, and advocacy).

HOW CAN WE MEASURE MKs' INFLUENCE?

Oppenheimer (1985) presents a good summary of various methods that are used to measure parliament and MPs' influence on public policy. The first is the case study method where, by studying a specific event, legislation, or issues, we can learn about the process of shaping policy, the role of parliament and the MPs' contribution to the process. The literature points to two types of case studies. The first type has used the story of a single piece or several pieces of legislation to depict how the parliament works (Reid 1980; Levine and Wexler 1981). From these we derive a richer feel for the parliamentary process and for its policy influence, but we lose some of the potential to generalize our conclusions from the particular case study to parliament's overall influence on policy. A second type of case study analyzes a particular policy issue or issue area. These studies see parliamentary influence as just one of the forces that structure public policy. Thus we have studies on social security (Derthick 1979) and Medicare (Marmor 1970), among many others. The advantage in using such case studies is in their potential for learning about the role of parliament in shaping policy in relation to other institutions and forces. The disadvantage lies in the loss of in-depth knowledge about what happens within parliament in the process of influencing policy.

A second method of research is process studies (Fenno 1966; Whiteman 1995). These studies focus not on the outcome—the policy—but rather on the process that shaped the policy. By studying the process of shaping policy, we can differentiate between activities that do and do not contribute to the formulating of policy. Such studies also enable us to estimate the relative importance of various activities within parliament in influencing policy.

Roll call analysis is another method for studying the influence of parliament on policy (Peabody 1981). Especially interesting is the study of party influence on the way MPs vote and on policy. Some studies have focused on the relationship between government and parliament as a tool for understanding the role of parliament and its influence on policy. The issue of the struggle between government officials and MPs has been dealt with in various studies (Dodd 1977; Sundquist 1981). This approach contributes to the understanding of parliament's role and its influence both in relation to the government and independently.

Oppenheimer (1985) suggests a fourth method for studying the influence of parliament on policy, by studying parliamentary rules and procedures. The importance of rules and procedures in affecting policy outputs appears throughout the literature. This importance is underscored by Forman's (1967) observation that rules and procedures are not neutral, and that they exert a considerable conservative bias, favoring the opponents rather than the proponents of policy change.

The study reported here sought to integrate the use of the various methods mentioned. By virtue of dealing with a specific social issue only, it engaged in a case study. But it also dealt with the issue of social policy at large and not with a specific piece of legislation, and thus using the type of case study that analyzes a policy issue. The study has also concentrated on the study of the process within parliament and the roll call of individual MKs. Finally, the study reported in this paper also involved an in depth study of Knesset rules and procedures.

But choosing the right method of research is not enough. Another no less important question is whether the influence of the various activities of MPs and that of the parliaments at large on policy can be measured. When undertaking a specific case study, one can attempt an analysis of all the forces involved in the process of shaping policy. But this seems inappropriate when trying to study a broad issue or area of policy, as is the case when we concentrate on social policy. This becomes even more complicated when the study aims at identifying the influence of an individual MK on the shaping of social policy. As Bochel states, "The variety of sources of pressure, and the often hidden influences that these exert upon policy, make it difficult to quantify or otherwise assess with any great precision the influences of specific participants in the process" (1992, 98).

The solution that some researchers suggest is to conduct a series of interviews with a large sample of MPs from all parties in which their perception of the MPs influence on policy will be sought (Bochel 1992; Kornberg and Mishler 1976; Marsh 1988). Nevertheless, there are few examples where the literature has taken this approach. Bochel's (1992) study of the British parliament and welfare policy is probably the only work that dealt directly with the issue of MPs influence on welfare policy. Even with regard to studies of the general influence of MPs on policy, those of Kornberg and Mishler stand almost alone (Kornberg 1967; Kornberg and Mishler 1976).

This study adopted the method of interviewing Knesset members as a means of learning about their perceptions of the influence they have on social policy in Israel. Apart from the sixty-seven MKs who were interviewed, this research added a unique angle of studying MKs influence on social policy by also including the perception of thirty-one senior government officials and ministers from social ministries on the issue. Of those, twenty-four answered a mailed questionnaire and seven ministers and general directors were interviewed in person.

DOES THE ACTIVITY OF MKs INFLUENCE SOCIAL POLICY?

Examining the issue of MKs' influence on social policy was the first and most critical step in the study. If it was found that there was no such influence, then the rationale for the study would have been lost. The data presented in Table 8.1 seeks to answer this specific question through the use of self-reported replies of MKs and government officials.

The fact that there are differences between the MKs' perceptions and those of the government officials is not surprising. The differences are probably due both to an overestimation by the MKs of their influence as well as to an underestimation by the government officials due to their need (even if latent) to emphasize the role of government in shaping policy. Nevertheless the fact that 71 percent of the government officials attribute at least some influence to MKs in the process of shaping policy leads us, together with the MKs perceptions, to the conclusion that MKs do influence the shaping of social policy in Israel.

Table 8.1
The Perceived Influence of MKs on Social Policy by Respondents Groups

| | | Split by percentage | | |
The respondents	N	Major influence	Little influence	No influence
MKs	62	85.5	12.9	1.6
Government officials	28	39.3	32.1	28.6

DOES FORMAL ACTIVITY MAKE A DIFFERENCE?

Knowing that MKs activity influences the making of policy, the study asked what kind of activities make the difference. As mentioned in the introduction, the overall activities of MKs can be divided into formal and informal types. Table 8.2 presents the research findings regarding the effectiveness of a variety of formal activities in influencing social policy.

As was the case regarding responses to the overall influence of MKs activity on social policy, it is not surprising to find variation between the answers of the two respondent groups. As a whole, one can see that government officials tend to perceive the MKs activity as less effective in influencing policy than do the MKs themselves.

When looking at the inner order of the responses of each of the groups, we can see that the MKs' perceive committee work as the most influential and legislation as the second most influential form of activity. The remainder of the formal activities are listed in the following order: regular motions, urgent motions, oral questions, questions, and speeches. The government officials regard legislation as the most influential form of MK activity and then, in the following order, committee work, questions, oral questions, urgent motions, speeches, and regular motions. It is therefore evident that both groups perceive committee and legislation activity as the most influential on social policy making.

When trying to analyze the differences between the two groups' answers, one cannot avoid the conclusion that the order of effectiveness as perceived by the government officials is correlated with the degree of their exposure to the various activities. It is especially evident when looking at the differences between the two groups' perceptions of the effectiveness of motions. This parliamentary tool is not aimed, at least not directly, at the government, and thus it does not require the government officials' involvement. This in turn leads to a lack of knowledge regarding the tool, its targets, and its effectiveness. Even more, by employing motions, MKs try to raise an issue into the public agenda. In many cases the effectiveness of the tool is indicated by influencing the parliament agenda and, by doing so, initiating a process of change and influencing policy that in many cases bypasses the government officials themselves. Consequently this is one more possible reason for the government officials not to have a high perception of the use of this tool.

To sum up, it seems plausible to suggest that the formal activity of MKs does make a difference. But at the same time, one must be aware that different activities have a different influence. Two types of activity stand out as the most influential according to both MKs

Table 8.2
The Perceived Effectiveness of Various Formal Activities by MKs in Influencing Social Policy by Type of Activity and Respondents Groups

			Split by percentage		
Type of activity	**Respondents**	**N**	**Very effective or effective**	**Little effectiveness**	**Almost no effectiveness**
Committee work	MKs	63	96.8	3.2	--
	Government officials	31	58.1	12.9	29.1
Legislation	MKs	63	88.9	3.2	8.0
	Government officials	31	80.6	6.5	12.9
Regular motions	MKs	63	77.7	19.0	3.2
	Government officials	28	25.0	25.0	50.0
Urgent motions	MKs	63	71.4	20.6	7.9
	Government officials	25	36.0	20.0	44.0
Oral questions	MKs	63	68.3	--	17.4
	Government officials	25	40.0	8.0	52.0
Questions	MKs	63	63.5	15.9	20.7
	Government officials	28	50.0	17.9	32.1
Speeches	MKs	63	60.3	20.6	19.1
	Government officials	27	33.3	14.8	51.8

and government officials. Legislative activity seems a natural choice, if only because it is one of parliament's main tasks. By adopting laws, parliament shapes the norms of the society. Committee work on the other hand, is not such a natural choice, although there is ample evidence in the literature of the importance of committee work in contributing to specific pieces of social legislation. The contribution of this study is in a generalized conclusion that committee work did make a difference in the process of shaping social policy in its broad sense, in the 13th Israeli Knesset.

DOES INFORMAL ACTIVITY MAKE A DIFFERENCE?

After studying the formal activity of MKs and before comparing formal and informal activity, it is timely to look at the perceived effectiveness of various informal activities. This data are presented in Table 8.3.

Just as in the case of formal activity, the government officials respondent group tended to perceive informal activity as less influential on social policy. Further, in regard to the informal activities the difference between the two respondent groups is greater than that regarding the formal activities.

Analysis of the answers indicates that direct approaches to ministers is perceived as very effective by both respondent groups (it is first on the MKs' list and second on the government officials'). A consensus also exists regarding the notion that the direct approach to government officials is less effective than approaching ministers.

Differences between responses of the two groups is especially evident when looking at activities such as helping citizens in distress, negotiating, or demonstrating. It is difficult to suggest an optimal explanation for these differences. It appears that the government officials do not acknowledge the contribution of MKs' "pure" informal activities. This is especially so if those activities involve direct contact between the MKs and the public, without the mediation of the professional government officials. Sometimes it even leads to a confrontation between the government officials and the MKs.

A tendency suggested by the data is that MKs seem to regard highly activities that are important to their personal career, even if they are not necessarily effective in influencing policy. This is probably the reason that the MKs perceive the effectiveness of activities such as appearance in the media and party activity as much more important than do the government officials, which are more "objective."

Even when taking all this into consideration, some activities are perceived similarly by both groups. Cooperation with NGOs is one example. It is possible that the work of both is becoming more and more contingent on cooperation with experts and interest groups and that this leads them to similar perceptions regarding the effectiveness of such activity.

Last, one should note the phenomenon of MKs lobbies as a type of activity. During the life of the 13th Knesset, this phenomenon grew dramatically, and many new MKs lobbies emerged. Thus, it is surprising to discover that both the MKs and the government officials perceive the effectiveness of this activity as limited. This leads us to the conclusion that the reason for the blossoming of the

Table 8.3
The Perceived Effectiveness of Various MKs' Informal Activities in Influencing Social Policy by Type of Activity and Respondents Groups

Type of activity	Respondents	N	Split by percentage		
			Very effective or effective	Little effectiveness	Almost no effectiveness
Direct approach to ministers	MKs	63	93.7	4.8	1.6
	Government officials	30	53.4	33.3	13.4
Helping citizens in distress	MKs	63	93.7	4.8	1.6
	Government officials	27	29.6	18.5	51.8
Negotiating	MKs	63	82.5	4.8	12.7
	Government officials	24	12.5	29.2	58.3
Appearing in the media	MKs	63	80.9	11.1	7.9
	Government officials	29	44.8	24.1	31.0
Direct approach to officials	MKs	63	77.7	12.7	9.5
	Government officials	29	48.3	31.0	20.7
Cooperation with NGOs	MKs	63	74.6	15.9	9.6
	Government officials	26	65.4	3.8	30.8
Party activity	MKs	63	69.9	11.1	19.0
	Government officials	19	31.6	15.8	52.7
Demonstrations	MKs	62	67.7	14.5	17.8
	Government officials	27	14.8	18.5	66.6
MK's Lobbies	MKs	63	60.3	20.6	19.1
	Government officials	29	48.2	20.7	31.0
Writing articles in newspapers	MKs	63	51.6	21.0	27.4
	Government officials	27	29.6	14.8	55.5
Using social contacts	MKs	63	46.0	27.0	25.4
	Government officials	26	30.8	11.5	57.7

phenomenon has more to do with fashion and acceptability than with effectiveness. Alternatively, MKs' lobbies may be especially beneficial to their chairpersons, who usually establish these lobbies, though they are less effective in influencing social policy.

THE PERCEIVED RELATIVE EFFECTIVENESS OF VARIOUS ACTIVITIES BY MKs AND GOVERNMENT OFFICIALS

What we have seen up until now is that MKs tend to regard their activities as more influential than do government officials, and some possible explanations have been offered. But another question should be asked: Is there a similarity in the relative perceived influence of the various activities? In other words, is there an agreement between the two respondent groups as to the order of importance of the different activities? It would also be important to ask if the type of activity (e.g., formal or informal) has any influence on how it is perceived. Expressed somewhat differently, is there a kind of activity that is usually perceived as more effective in influencing social policy than the other? A partial answer to these questions can be derived from the data presented in Table 8.4.

Table 8.4
The Five Activities Perceived as the Most Effective in Influencing Social Policy by the Type of Activity and the Respondent Group

| | Members of Knesset | | | Government officials | |
The activity	N	Percentage who said it is effective	The activity	N	Percentage who said it is effective
Committee work	63	96.8	Legislation	31	80.6
Direct approach to			Cooperation with NGOs		
ministers	63	93.7		26	65.4
Helping citizens in distress	63	93.7	Committee Work	31	58.1
			Direct approach to		
Legislation	63	88.9	ministers	30	53.4
Keeping contact with the					
public	63	87.3	Questions	28	50.0

We can see that the MKs' list includes three informal activities
and two formal ones. The government officials' list includes three
formal activities and two informal ones. Therefore it is probably
safe to conclude that both kinds of activity, formal and informal,
are perceived as effective in influencing social policy by the two
respondent groups.

As to the second question (i.e., possible agreement between the
two respondent groups as to the order of importance of the different activities), three types of activity are found in both lists. They
are committee work, legislation, and direct approaches to ministers. One can then conclude that there is a consensus regarding
the perceived effectiveness of the three activities in influencing
social policy. As mentioned earlier with regard to legislation, this
finding comes as no surprise. But for committee work and direct
approaches to ministers, the findings are not so obvious. Committee work is usually less evident to the public eye, and therefore
some degree of surprise is understandable. The findings in regard
to direct approaches to ministers is even more surprising, especially since government officials also listed it as a very effective
form of activity, and despite the fact that in many cases the direct
approach to ministers in effect bypasses government officials.

PERCEPTIONS OF EFFECTIVENESS REGARDING VARIOUS ACTIVITIES OF MKs AND OTHER MPs

The findings of this study indicate that MKs' activity has an influence on social policy in Israel. This influence differs according to
the various types of MKs' activity. A difference was also found in
the perceived influence of MKs' activity between the MKs and the
government officials. Nevertheless, one can point to a few activities about which there is no question with regard to their influence
on social policy.

We now turn to a deeper examination of these three activities by
comparing the study findings with some international data. Thus,
we can check if the Israeli MKs' perceptions regarding the effectiveness of their activities in influencing social policy is similar to
that of MPs in other countries. Of course one cannot avoid the fact
that different parliaments have different rules and procedures. It
is also obvious that in different countries there are different traditions, political frameworks, and social structures. In sum, any such
comparison will neccessarily be complicated and problematic (Oppenheimer 1985).

Nevertheless, as Patzelt (1994) has noted, comparative parliamentary research can facilitate mutual understanding and learn-

ing. Table 8.5 presents the perceptions of parliament members in different national settings on the effectiveness of various activities in influencing social policy or policy at large. All findings are based on MPs' self reports as obtained by personal interviews.

The most interesting finding from Table 8.5 is that regardless of the time difference, differences in the parliamentary system, the social and political contexts and the traditions, and bylaws, as well as many other differences, MPs in each of the three parliaments all share the perception that committee work and direct approaches to ministers are very effective tools for influencing policy.

More than 76 percent of Canadian MPs reported many direct approaches to ministers every month. Interestingly, most direct approaches were to ministers of social ministries, and this tool was perceived by them as the second most effective after party activity. In fact, 79 percent of the Canadian MPs said they usually got what they wanted after approaching the ministers (Kornberg and Mishler 1976, 181–182). Bochel found that members of the ruling party tended to perceive the tool of direct approaches to ministers as more effective than their colleagues from the opposition. But in any case

Table 8.5
The Five Most Effective Activities in Influencing Policy as Perceived by Members of Different Parliaments

The 13th Israeli Knesset 1992-1996	The British Parliament 1986-1987	The Canadian Parliament 1968-1972
N=63	N=53	N=187
committee work	raising debate	party activity
direct approach to ministers	direct approach to ministers	direct approach to ministers
helping citizens in distress	committee work	committee work
legislation	helping citizens in distress	questions/speeches
keeping contact with public	embarrassing the government	influencing public opinion

Sources: British parliament data are based on H. M. Bochel, *Parliament and Welfare Policy* (Aldershot, U.K.: Dartmouth, 1992), 123. Canadian parliament data are based on A. Kornberg and W. Mishler, *Influence in Parliament: Canada* (Durham, N.C.: Duke University Press, 1976), 175, 210. This research deals with policy at large and not with social policy in particular.

both of them reported that this tool is second only to raising debate in effectiveness in influencing social policy (1992, 122).

In fact, in all three studies, the direct approach to ministers was perceived by MPs as the second most effective tool for influencing policy. Norton (1982) has checked the effectiveness of correspondence between MPs and ministers and also found that it is influential in the making of policy. Finally, it should be emphasized that direct approach to ministers involves not only sending letters or even talking over the phone. In fact the approach can be carried out in a variety of ways, such as corridor talks, personal meetings, telephone, letter, party meetings, or any other desired method.

The second tool perceived by MPs of all three parliaments as one of the five most effective is committee work. Kornberg and Mishler (1976) suggest a possible explanation for this perception. Many of the activities of committees are either not seen or relatively invisible. Thus, they provide a setting in which MPs can scrutinize proposed expenditures and closely evaluate or even amend legislation without fear that their actions will be construed as either critical of cabinet policies or an indication that they publicly oppose the government. This in turn allows the government to consider suggestions from the committee without fearing that its public image will be hurt.

It is worthwhile noting that both Israeli MKs and British MPs perceived helping citizens with problems as an efficient tool for influencing social policy. The fact that this activity was not one of the five most efficient activities in the eyes of the Canadian MPs can be explained by the fact that the study dealt with policy at large. Obviously, helping people in distress refers mainly to social policy and has little to do with foreign affairs or issues of national security. Nevertheless, Canadian MPs also reported that they were very busy with requests by their constituents and that the needs and problems of their voters had a large influence on their work, mainly on the tool of direct approach to ministers (Kornberg and Mishler 1976, 184).

Finally, it should be noted that MPs from all three parliaments perceived both formal and informal activities as efficient in influencing social policy. This fact, together with the findings already discussed, leads us to the question of what kind of activity has more influence on social policy.

WHAT KIND OF ACTIVITY HAS MORE INFLUENCE ON SOCIAL POLICY?

Another major concern of this study was to identify the kind of activity that has more influence on social policy. Or, in other words, what works better—formal or informal activities?

"The corridors are the main working arena. That is where you could get the most" (interview with an MK, 19 February 1997). This sentence was repeated again and again during almost all interviews held with the sixty-seven MKs. In fact, there was not one MK who disregarded the informal activity.

"There is almost no day during which I do not receive at least one call or letter from an MK. The mere fact that an MK approaches me leads to the involvement of the director-general's office and thus procedures are speeded up" (interview with a director-general of a government ministry, 9 November 1997). Such comments were not so common among government officials, however. Some of them reported on frequent approaches of MKs while others did not. It seems that there is a considerable difference between the government officals in that regard, according to their different positions and authority.

In any case, both respondent groups were asked to relate to the frequency of MKs' formal and informal activities as well as to their perceived effectiveness in influencing policy of each kind of activity. The data are presented in Table 8.6.

Although some variation in the perceptions of the two respondent groups is evident, both respondent groups clearly associate more influence with the informal activities than with the formal ones. MKs also report higher usage of informal activities, while government officials report slightly higher usage of formal activities. A possible explanation for this difference emerges from the government officials' questionnaires. They would prefer MKs to stick with their formal activity and not to interfere with the government officials' work by using informal tools of activity.

Table 8.6
The Reported Usage and the Perceived Effectiveness in Influencing Social Policy of the Formal and Informal Activities by Kind of Activity and Respondent Group

Kind of activity	MKs N=63		Government officials N=30	
	Activity used most	Activity more efficient	Activity used most	Activity more efficient
Formal	14.3	7.9	33.3	20.0
informal	17.5	14.3	30.3	33.3
both	68.3	77.8	36.7	46.7

In order to try to clarify the picture, both respondent groups were asked to assess the perceived influence of MKs activity on social policy in two ways. The first refers to the effectiveness of the activity in regard to solving constituents' personal problems. The second refers to the influence on overall social policy. The findings are presented in Table 8.7.

Evidently both MKs and government officials perceive informal activity as more influential in solving personal problems, and formal activity in shaping overall social policy. It is also evident that a majority (64%) of government officials perceive MKs' activity as influential in solving personal problems, while only 44.8 percent perceive this activity as influential in shaping social policy. Most important, when MKs' activity is perceived as influential, the two respondent groups reported both kinds of activity as efficient.

To sum up, it seems safe to conclude that MKs' activity does make a difference and that this is evident both in terms of solving personal problems and shaping social policy. Even more, the findings of this study reveal that both kinds of MKs' activity make a difference. Informal activity is certainly more influential in solving personal problems. As for shaping general social policy, one can only conclude that both formal and informal activities make a difference, without stating which kind of activity is more influential.

CONCLUSION

The study reported in this chapter tried to deal with a number of questions in its effort to better understand whether MKs' activity

Table 8.7
The Perceived Influence of MKs' Activity on Solving Personal Problems and on Overall Social Policy by Kind of Activity and Respondent Group (in Percentage)

Kind of activity	MKs N=63		Government officials N=25	
	Solving personal problems	Shaping overall social policy	Solving personal problems	Shaping overall social policy
general	92.1	76.2	64.0	44.8
When the activity is perceived as influential:				
formal activity	23.8	88.7	50.0	100.0
informal activity	96.8	83.9	100.0	75.0

makes a difference in social policy and how. The following questions were addressed: Does MKs' activity make a difference? What is the degree of influence of the various activities? Which of the two kinds of activities, formal or informal, influence social policy more? All these perceptions of the Israeli MKs and government officials were compared with each other as well as with those of MPs from other countries.

It is important to once again emphasize that MKs' activity makes a difference! It influences personal problems solving and the shaping of social policy. The research also found that both kinds of activity influence social policy. The formal activity was perceived to be influential in shaping social policy, while the informal activity was perceived as influential in both solving personal problems and shaping social policy.

This study also found that a variety of parliamentary tools in each of the two kinds of activity (formal and informal) are effective in influencing social policy, each of them in a different way and magnitude. Thus, one can conclude that MKs have a variety of tools and activities they can use in order to influence social policy.

The difference between the MKs' and the government officials' perceptions was consistent throughout the study. This was especially evident when comparing specific activities and tools. But when taking into consideration the inner order of the various activities by their effectiveness in influencing social policy, the two respondent groups perceptions tended to support each other, thus leading to the conclusion that both kinds of MKs' activity make a difference. This conclusion was further supported by the perceptions of British and Canadian MPs as reported by Kornberg and Mishler (1976) and Bochel (1992).

REFERENCES

Bochel, H. M. 1992. *Parliament and Welfare Policy*. Aldershot, U.K.: Darmouth.

Derthick, M. 1979. *Policymaking for Social Security*. Washington D.C.: The Brookings Institution.

Dodd, L. C. 1977. "Congress and the Quest for Power." In *Congress Reconsidered*, ed. L. C. Dodd and B. I. Oppenheimer. Westport, Conn.: Praeger.

Fenno, R. F. 1966. *The Power of the Purse*. Boston: Little, Brown.

Forman, L. A. 1967. *The Congressional Process: Strategies, Rules and Procedures*. Boston: Little, Brown.

Kornberg, A. 1967. *Canadian Legislative Behavior*. Toronto: Holt, Rinehart and Winston.

Kornberg, A., and Mishler, W. 1976. *Influence in Parliament: Canada*. Durham, N.C.: Duke University Press.

Levine, E. L., and Wexler, E. M. 1981. *PL 94-142: An Act of Congress*. New York: Macmillan.

Marmor, T. R. 1970. *The Politics of Medicare*. Chicago: Aldine.

Marsh, I. 1988. "Interest Groups and Policy Making: A New Role for Select Committees?" *Parliamentary Affairs* 41 (4): 469–489.

Norton, P. 1982. "Dear Minister . . . The Importance of MP-to-Minister Correspondence." *Parliamentary Affairs* 35: 59–72.

Oppenheimer, B. 1985. "Legislative Influence on Policy and Budgets" In *Handbook of Legislative Research*, ed. G. Loewenberg, S. C. Patterson, and M. E. Jewell. Cambridge: Harvard University Press.

Peabody, R. L. 1981. "House Party Leadership in the 1970s." In *Congress Reconsidered* (2d ed.), ed. L. C. Dodd and B. I. Oppenheimer. Washington, D.C.: Congressional Quarterly Press.

Reid, T. R. 1980. *Congressional Odyssey*. San Francisco: W. H. Freeman.

Sundquist, J. L. 1981. *The Decline and Resurgence of Congress*. Washington, D.C.: The Brookings Institution.

Whiteman, D. 1995. *Communication in Congress: Members, Staff and the Search for Information*. Lawrence: University Press of Kansas.

FURTHER READING

Bochel, H. M. 1992. *Parliament and Welfare Policy*. Aldershot, U.K.: Darmouth.

Kornberg, A., and Mishler, W. 1976. *Influence in Parliament: Canada*. Durham, N.C.: Duke University Press.

Taylor-Goolby, P., and Bochel, H. M. 1988. "MPS Attitudes and the Future of Welfare." *Public Administration* 66 (3): 329–337.

———. 1988. "MPS' Influence on Welfare Policy." *Parliamentary Affairs* 41 (2): 209–217.

9

Democracy *for* the People?
Welfare Policy Making in Israel

Yael Yishai

Israel is a modern welfare state committed to the provision of basic social rights to its citizens. The welfare system in the country has evolved under two exigencies: a short time span and a continuous influx of immigrants in great need of assistance services (Doron and Kramer 1991). Consequently, Israel has adopted a pattern of welfare policy making that is highly elitist and patronizing. It is founded on the premise that democracy is *for* the people, not *by* them. This characteristic prevails despite marked changes in the economy, in the polity, and even in the value system. To demonstrate this claim this chapter will analyze two recent laws regarding health services: the National Health Insurance Law (1994) and the Patient Rights Act (1996).

An important aspect of policy making in democratic societies is the extent to which people's preferences are overridden or respected (Goodin 1993). Accordingly, policy making was analyzed in line with two basic models. The first concerned the authorities, comprising elected and nominated politicians, bureaucrats and their professional allies, as the sole, or at least the predominant, source of power. Given their mandate through periodical elections, the authorities hold the helm of the state. They are the source of initiative; they tailor policies to their own interests (Cobb and Elder 1972). The second model portrays a different picture. Here the people are predominant in the policy process. The term "people" usually refers to organized associations and social movements, rather than to the amorphous body of citizens. Admittedly, interest groups are often coopted by the elite into "iron triangles" (Heclo 1978), but in many other cases they have a marked say in shaping the political agenda and formulating policies (Polsby 1980). The two models thus differ in terms of power distribution and in the strategies of the major actors. In the elitist model, with its variations, the authorities initiate, elaborate, and implement policies. Public preferences are either unknown or remain negligible. In the pluralist model, actors external to the state abound, and their preferences properly serve as inputs into the social decision procedure. Needless to say, these two models are only approximations of reality, as the state always makes decisions, and the people are always subject to these decision. Yet the examination of case studies does show cross-country and cross-issue variation.

The two models under discussion, the elitist and the pluralist, are descriptive, portraying a certain pattern of power distribution within society. The attempt to understand their determinants elicits three factors: the external environment (Easton 1965; Hofferbert 1974), political institutions and actors (Baumgartner and Bryan 1993; Immergut 1992), and political culture (Sabatier 1991; Jacobs 1993). Each of these factors varies in line with the two models under discussion. An elitist model thrives under a centralized economy where division between state and society is blurred; pluralism is animated by the free market and decentralized society. Powerful political parties and a legal system sustaining strong government prompt elitism; a malleable state and powerful civil society galvanize pluralism. Elitism is sustained by collective and national values (Apter 1965); pluralism is nourished by norms giving precedence to individualistic needs.

The major argument of this chapter is that a shift in all three domains is readily discernible in Israel. The environment has undergone a striking change, political institutions have been altered, and norms are gradually being transformed. Surprisingly, however, these changes have failed to introduce pluralism into the Israeli polity, as the public remains detached from the policy scene, and the elite continues to act on behalf of the people as it sees fit. The reasons for the persisting elitist pattern are grounded, it is suggested here, in core values immune to change. The following first presents the two policy decisions under discussion and relates them to the policy models. Then the changes in the environment and in political institutions and culture are analyzed. The chapter concludes by offering an explanation based on core values shared by both the elite and the public.

POLICY DECISIONS

Two fundamental laws, adopted two years apart, mark contemporary legislation in health policy. The first, the National Health Insurance Law (NHI Law) (1994) regulates the allocation of health resources; the second, the Patient Rights Act (1996) relates to the rights of the people as patients. The National Health Insurance Law was adopted under the Labor government after nearly five decades of deliberation. In essence it transferred the command of the health services in the country from the health funds to the state, with the former becoming mere service providers. The collection of health insurance tax was transferred to the National Insurance Institute. The state was to determine a "health basket" out of which health services would be provided. The law was ostensibly public oriented because it stipulated that all Israelis, now mandated to join a health fund, could pick one on the basis of their own choice. Persons who prior to the law had been locked into Kupat Holim by virtue of their semicompulsory Histadrut membership were now free to move from one health fund to another.

The Patient Rights Act became law in September 1996. Its purpose was to spell out the rights of patients to receive treatment and exercise informed consent. It further stipulates the obligations of health care professionals to provide the means necessary for patients to exercise their newly protected rights. The bill had been in the legislative pipeline for more than a decade as politicians undertook a campaign to protect three fundamental patients' rights: (1) the right to universal health care; (2) the right of informed consent; and (3) the right to die with dignity, namely, the right to refuse treatment and medical intervention. Among the three, the most important was the right to informed consent, meaning that all information relevant to a patient is supplied, including diagnosis and prognosis, costs and benefits, risks, and side effects. "Consent" is achieved when the patient, after receiving the relevant information, agrees to treatment. If the patient objects, treatment may be given over the objection if an ethics committee, after hearing testimony from the patient, is convinced that the patient has received the required information, that there is an expectation that medical treatment will improve the patient's condition, and that there is a reasonable expectation that consent will follow treatment (Patient Rights Law, 1996, ¶15(2)).

ANALYSIS

The National Health Insurance Law

Although the initiators of the NHI Law emphasized its benefits to the people, it was actually designed to solve a political problem. Until the adoption of the law, health care was divided between the traditionally weak Ministry of Health, and the de facto authority wielded by the major health fund, the Histadrut's Kupat Holim. In the early years of the statehood, Kupat Holim served as a major instrument of political mobilization. Over the years its power even increased, for two reasons. First, Kupat Holim just about monopolized the provision of health care. It insured some 80 percent of the population, it operated 85 percent of the health clinics, and it owned a third of the hospital beds in the country. Second, Kupat Holim enjoyed prominent political status. It was financially and organizationally linked with the Histadrut, the giant trade movement controlled by the Labor Party. The Histadrut also enjoyed a quasi-monopoly status in organizing salaried workers in the country. As membership of the sick fund was requisitely linked with membership of the Histadrut, Kupat Holim was used as a lever for mobilization. Consequently, the Labor party granted Kupat Holim a key role in shaping health policy (Zalmanovitch 1997).

The close link between Kupat Holim and the Labor Party was strongly opposed by both Likud and members of the Young Guard in the Labor Party challenging the veteran establishment. Likud wanted to strip the Labor Party of its major instrument for mobilization. The severance of ties between the Histadrut and Kupat Holim was aimed at turning the former into a trade union with weak political clout. The actual processing of the law took place, however, under a Labor government. The health minister had in mind two goals: first, to rationalize health care in the country by vesting in the ministry the power to plan, coordinate, administer, and supervise the health services; second, and perhaps more important, to remove from office the old guard of the Histadrut and party leadership.

The major actors in the process of legislation were confined to the elite. First and foremost were the executives in the Ministry of Health, headed by the minister. Although the Ministry of Health was traditionally considered weak and vulnerable, the minister of health played a key role in initiating and pushing forward the bill. The second was the Histadrut, supported by professional health care trade unions. The Israeli Medical Association, a long-time opponent of any attempt to nationalize the health service (Yishai

1982), supported the move in the 1990s. Its acquiescence emanated from a long-time "iron duet" between policy makers and physicians, shielding policy issues from grassroots participation (Yishai 1992). The "people" were not asked, nor were they requested to voice their opinion. The nationalization of health care was not an issue in the 1992 electoral campaign. Social movements and citizens' groups failed to mobilize. According to Zalmanovitch (1997, 266), the NHI Law bestowed yet more power on Israel's already highly centralized government. The new law simply replaced one large, cumbersome bureaucracy with another. The main problem which the new law aimed to solve was the relations between Kupat Holim and the state. This issue had very little to do with the interests of the Israeli people, who continued to stand in line for scarce medical resources.

The National Health Insurance Law did give impetus to the rise, albeit limited, of grassroots participation. Since the late 1960s Israel has witnessed a striking rise in the number of civil associations and political movements (Yishai 1991, 1998). In the health domain these include also self-help groups, the common denominator of which is a chronic illness necessitating continuous consumption of health services. In 1996 there were approximately two hundred associations linked with health problems. This number, although smaller than in Western countries, indicates significant growth. One of the reasons for the expansion of public associations is loopholes in legislation. Many questions remained unanswered, such as what are the basic rights granted by the law, what are the guarantees for quality control, what are the time spans for receiving treatment, and what are the benefits of additional insurance? The uncertainty regarding these issues triggered the emergence of concerned citizens' groups. The need to coordinate efforts brought about the establishment (in 1992) of a roof organization, the Health Consumers Associations (HCA), including some seventy groups focusing on specific problems. Has the NHI Law awakened the dormant Israeli public? The answer is at best equivocal.

The formation of the HCA is a sign of fledgling civic activity. The association, however, has remained weak and ineffective. First, like many other public associations in Israel, it suffers from chronic financial shortage. It is modestly funded by scarce membership dues and contributions from the New Israel Fund, an organization soliciting money from the U.S. Jewry. Second, the HCA suffers also from weakness related to its human composition. Activists are themselves ill or take care of ill relatives and therefore lack the resources essential for prolonged organizational activity. Third, activists in the HCA find it difficult to divide their effort between the promotion of their specific health concern, on account of which they initially became active in the voluntary association, and advocacy for general purposes. Finally, strings in the HCA are pulled by the political establishment. Its offices, for example, are located in the Histadrut building. The HCA thus has no impact on the formulation of health policy. The scene remains dominated by the political authorities and their professional allies.

THE PATIENT RIGHTS ACT

Until the passage of the Patient Rights Act, patients routinely complained that health care was delivered with little sensitivity to their preferences. At face value the new law rectified this situation by providing the patients the right to know all that needs to be known about their illness and to determine whether they want the proposed treatment. Elitist strands of decision making, however, are clearly manifest in the power of the ethics committee authorized to decide on behalf of the patient. The committee, including a judge, two expert physicians, a psychologist or a social worker, and one "public delegate," is empowered to act in the courts' stead on issues relating to a patient's desire to refuse treatment. Israeli health care professionals are not very sensitive to patients' rights. They appear willing to force-feed patients unwilling or unable to feed themselves and are reluctant to withhold life support solely at a patient's request. Likewise, there is no judicial enthusiasm for patients' rights (Gross 1999). The PRA transferred paternalism from the physician to the ethics committees, by whose decision provision of information to patients and their ability to refuse treatment are determined. The ethics committees, furthermore, are to follow daily and routine medical practice, rather than provide general guidelines for medical conduct. If implemented in word and letter (which it is not), the PRA could establish another oligarchy in the health care system. Needless to say, patients' groups were not involved in the process of legislation. Their opinion was not sought, and their voice was not raised. Critics of the law claim that instead of being a document elaborating a social dialogue on the contours of medicine in a free democratic society, the law constitutes a legal document based on hierarchical models (Peri and Raz 1997).

These two laws were adopted by a state undergoing significant changes in the socioeconomic, institutional, and cultural spheres.

Changes in the Socioeconomic Environment

In the first years of Israel's existence, the economic system was highly centralized and politicized, and political parties controlled

most of the resource allocation. With the passage of time, this structure has gradually changed. The most noticeable change is the economic surge. Israel is currently numbered among the more
developed nations on the world with an annual income per capita
of nearly $17,000 (for comparison, the comparable figure in the United
Kingdom is $20,000). At the same time, the state involvement in the
economy has decreased greatly. One manifestation of this phenomenon is the size of the government budget. It grew from 36 percent of
GNP in 1965, to 80 percent in 1975. In 1977, the budget was equal to
102 percent of GNP! Since then, the ratio has steadily gone down.
Public expenditure is also declining. It reached a peak of 77.4 percent
in 1980, and declined to 56 percent in 1995 (Aharoni 1998, 132). These
macroeconomic figures reveal decentralization tendencies. Furthermore, in the past decade all Israeli governments were committed
to privatization of the giant state corporations. The postal services,
the telephone communication network, the television network, to
name just a few state-owned companies, were all transformed into
autonomic enterprises, administered by a board of governors. At
the time of writing (May 1998), economic centralization has just
been dealt a major blow with the liberalization of foreign currency.
To sum up, a process of depoliticization and decentralization has
taken place in the economic sphere.

Changes in the Political Institutions

Changes in political institutions are manifest in the power of
political parties and in the electoral system. Political parties were
the major actors on both the political and the social scene. Utilizing a
dense network of auxiliary associations parties were the major providers of social services. They controlled nominations to political office, permeated the bureaucracy, and left their imprint on the national
communication network. In fact, parties were deeply involved in most
aspects of social life. To use Akzin's term (1955), they took care of the
citizen from cradle to grave. Present-day Israel is much different
from Akzin's description. Parties have tuned into electoral machines,
using modern campaign techniques in the race for public support.
They no longer possess economic enterprises but heavily depend
on state funding for their budgeting. Welfare services are provided
by state agencies and by their proxy voluntary associations.

The second change pertained to electoral laws and practices. In
the past, the party headquarters monopolized recruitment to public office. This is no longer the case. Candidates of many parties to
the Knesset are no longer selected by closed elite committees, but
are chosen by the mass party membership. Changes swept the coun-

try at large when the Knesset adopted in 1992 the direct elections to the premiership. These practices had led to the "privatization" of the political market and to the erosion of party loyalty. They have also given rise to the expression of particularistic interests associated with religious and ethnic identities. Consequently, the two major parties lost about a third of their legislative power; the small sectional parties grew considerably. All these changes portend a shift from the elitist model to a more pluralistic one. The direct involvement of the people in selecting candidates to legislative office and in electing the prime minister might have moved the balance from the elite to the public. The rapid expansion of civil society, sustaining direct participation in politics, could have also caused a changing policy style.

Changes in Political Culture

The economic and political shifts described above were followed by (or perhaps triggered) a change of mood. Israeli society no longer resembles the pioneer society in the heyday of statehood. In its formative period Israel was dominated by strong collectivist values. Sacrificing one's own interests for the sake of the nation was a widely accepted practice. Today Israel is characterized less by a collectivist orientation and more by ideas and institutions stemming from Western societies. Self-fulfillment and conspicuous consumption have become top priority in the order of priorities. There is, for example, a noticeable reduction of motivation to serve in the combat units of the armed forces and a strong drive toward the attainment of individual benefits. Many Israelis are no longer willing "to die for the country," a sacred norm originating in the prestate era and nurtured by the enduring Arab–Israeli conflict. Instead, as a famous pop song asserts, "there is nothing worth dying for." "Lying on your back and enjoying life," as the song continues, is a much preferable objective.

These shifts are echoed in attitudes toward welfare policy in general and health policy in particular. Commentators have noted that the ideological foundations upon which social policy in Israel are based are undergoing marked changes. Doron (1991) forecasted a dismantling of the core of the social security system resulting from a drop in the government's commitment to the welfare state. The intention to cancel the universal attributes of the support system and to predicate transfer payments on economic criteria on the one hand, and the change relating to financing social services on the other, give the impression that the welfare state is dwindling, yielding to the principles of the free market. According to Doron these

changes do not only reflect fiscal strains or any inherent economically given limit, but have been caused mainly by ideological shifts.
The financial and business administrators have abandoned the
progressive social–democratic agenda and adopted instead a conservative, consumer-oriented capitalism that encourages people to look
after their own interests. Economic development and the ensuing rise
in standard of living have made collective values irksome and anach-
ronistic. Individual rights and individual achievements have become objects of intense adulation.

The shifts in the public mood are relevant for the health scene as
well. Health care in Israel was originally built on socialist values
epitomizing social solidarity and mutual aid. Kupat Holim was
particularly identified with the pioneering efforts of the early days
of statehood. When the mood of socialism waned, giving way to liberal capitalism, fertile ground was readied for the two laws discussed above. Kupat Holim no longer seemed fit to control the health
care scene. Tying medical services to trade union politics appeared
inappropriate. Similarly, a law guarding the rights of the individual
appeared suitable.

To sum up, changes in the economy, in the polity, and in political
culture herald a shift from an elitist patter of policy making to a
pluralist one. An oligarchic party elite, in control of the national
economy, sustained by a political culture giving priority to collective needs over individual desires, was the major actor on the welfare (health) policy scene. With the advent of change, policy making
would be expected to be more pluralistic. The major contour of pluralism, in the sense discussed here, is the inclusion of the public, in
the form of organized groups and associations, in the process of
decision making. The major argument of this chapter is that this
has not been the case. The presumed cause for leaving the people
out of the policy process is grounded in the core values on which
the Israeli polity is founded.

CORE VALUES AND THE POLICY PROCESS

Core values are change resistible (Jenkins-Smith and Sabatier
1993, 27). They are distinct from values not belonging to the core in
the four following ways. First, they are acceptable by wide portions
of the population. In every democracy divisions of opinions, orientations, and outlooks are readily identifiable, but the core is common to many sectors. Second, core values are hardly challenged.
Not only are they widely shared, but even those who do not endorse
them rarely, if at all, dare to confront them. Third, core values are
deeply rooted in the nation's history. They are part of its heritage

and are enshrined in its tradition. Being stable, they acquire new strands with the passage of time, but the hard grain of the historical experience hardly fades away. Fourth, core values differ from peripheral values in that they do not refer to an action plan propagated by specific actor or party, but are more comprehensive in nature (Inglehart 1990, 43). In each society there are several core values, which may be ordered on a hierarchical scale. This chapter deals with one core value only, not necessarily the most important one in the nation's life: the supremacy of the state.

Although changes have taken place in the economy, in the polity, and in political culture, emphasis on the state has remained intact. On account of this prominent attribute Israel has been termed a "nonliberal democracy" (Ben-Eliezer 1993). The term "state" is used here in the broadest sense. It includes state institutions, state authorities, and state personnel. To use sociological terminology, the "state" coincides with the ruling elite, including professionals and technocrats. In the jargon of policy analysis, the "state" approximates a policy community, whose members are linked by virtue of their common interests. In the case under observation, the elite comprises the Ministry of Health, the Israeli Medical Association, legislators, and officials. Studies of policy making in Israel show that the state has shifted from the state-centered model—a policy network—to a more open and society-oriented model—an issue network (Zalmanovitch 1998). The state, nevertheless, continues to be a formidable actor, situated, at least symbolically, at the center of the policy arena. State power, in the sense discussed here, is founded upon two principles: paternalism and collectivism.

Paternalism, defined as the coercive interference with the liberty of individuals to determine their own good (Dwarkin 1972; Regan 1983), is a major aspect of state supremacy (Gross 1999). It relates to a state acting on behalf of the people and not with them. Paternalism does not necessarily carry negative connotations. For example, education and health were considered issue domains where the state can and perhaps should act at the expense of individual liberty. Both are necessary conditions for human freedom and may therefore be intruded on in a one-sided fashion by the state. In Israel, paternalism was indispensable, as the state was established precisely in order to shield Jews and protect them against the horrors they suffered in their long years in the exile. Collectivism constituted the other side of the statist coin. The Zionist settlement enterprise was aimed at providing by sacrificing personal interests, putting themselves instead at the service of a movement that embodied the needs of the collectivity (Horowitz and Lissak 1989, 111). This value was not only an experience of the past. To this day, collectivism remains an overriding and overarching norm.

Expressions of paternalism and collectivism are manifold. There is an extensive and comprehensive state regulation of interest groups (Yishai 1991). Voluntary associations are required to register and submit elaborate reports on their organizational and behavioral attributes. Israeli citizens are hardly allowed to contribute to political parties or electoral campaigns. Showing distrust in the ability to refrain from corrupt politics, the state preferred to monopolize political financing. The educational system is controlled by a powerful ministry with little parent or teacher involvement. Collectivism is manifested in long military and reserve service from age eighteen through middle age (for men). Women are still called upon to create the desired "demographic balance," namely to bear many Jewish children. Land is also considered a collective enterprise, with over 93 percent held in public hands that is not, nor can it be, privately owned. People's preferences are respected, noted Goodin (1993, 235), when there is respect for the people themselves. This does not seem to be the case in Israel, where the state acts warily, treating citizens as untrustworthy subjects.

Both state paternalism and collectivism have been sustained by social paternalism, representing "concern, if not empathy, for the welfare of each individual by the community" (Gross 1999). This core value is founded on a fundamental Jewish tenet suggesting that "all Jews are responsible for one another." Judaism exemplifies a collectivist world view and social solidarity generated by historical conditions of isolation and hatred. Even though most Jews in Israel do not obey religious commandments, they have turned the spirit of communalism into a core value. Community, however, is constructed and regulated by the state. It is the state that fixes the details of the health basket regardless of the people's preferences. Likewise, committees, such as those operating under the purview of the PRA, exemplify state patronism cloaked in social responsibility. These committees, maintains Gross (1999), generate mutual concern and promote the general good; they guide individuals toward making the right decisions; they alter preferences in the direction of the collective voice, that is, in the collective assessment of what is best for the individual.

CONCLUSION

In his attempt to forestall a rise in the health tax, Histadrut's Secretary General Amir Peretz stated, "We will get every citizen out of the shell we were put into" (Broadcasting Service, 9 April

1988). The shell he referred to is the result of the patronizing state. The two health laws under consideration—the National Health Insurance Law and the Patient Rights Act—demonstrate the elitist style of welfare policy making in Israel. These laws were selected for analysis precisely because they ostensibly reflect the changes that have swept Israel in the last decade: the tendency toward privatization and toward the individualization of society. Both laws outwardly acknowledge and promote citizens' rights. Actually, however, they abide by the core value. Shuval (1992, 9) suggested that "attitudes and behavior regarding health and health care reflect deeper values of a society." The core value referred to here is the supremacy of the state. What makes the status of the state a core value is the fact that the notion is widely spread, that it has not been seriously challenged or encountered, that it is imbued with historical symbols and entrenched in historical myths, and that it does not relate to a specific or trivial policy domain. Israelis evidently did not care about the incongruency between legislative goals and reality or even noticed it. As Zalmanovitch (1997, 266) remarked, for all their new values Israelis still expect their government to ensure that they receive adequate health services as well as other goods emanating from the welfare state. They remain unconcerned about big government and do not see it as a danger; they take it for granted and even demand it.

Why were the environmental changes discussed above ineffective in introducing a shift in the policy style? Economic considerations were hardly relevant to the issues under discussion. Lip service was paid to the mounting costs of health care in the elaboration of the NHI Law, but its raison d'être was political. The political changes discussed had little relevance to the health domain, traditionally dominated by elites. Public opinion hardly mattered. In his seminal study of health policy making, Jacobs (1993) illustrates how during the post–World War II period, well-institutionalized methods developed to allow U.S. authorities to measure and monitor public opinion. Consequently, public preferences became important in the process of policy making. The leaders of Israel, one of the most computerized countries in the world, might also be expected to be attuned to the public voice. Instead, it is influenced first by rhetorical appeals to public support by politicians and second by the citizenry's experiences with preexisting governmental programs (Skocpol 1994). What did prove effective was the predominant ideology, which is the organizing principle of the third sector in Israel (Gidron 1997). A policy style based on the notion of "democracy for the people" has warded off changes in the economic, political, and even normative environment. Its tenacity is founded on the core value upholding the supremacy of the state over society.

REFERENCES

Aharoni, Y. 1998. "The Changing Political Economy of Israel." *Annals* 555, AAPSS: 127–146.

Akzin, B. 1955. "The Role of Parties in Israeli Democracy." *Journal of Politics* 17: 509–533.

Apter, D. 1965. *The Politics of Modernization*. Chicago: University of Chicago Press.

Baumgartner, R. F., and Bryan, D. J. 1993. *Agendas and Instability in American Politics*. Chicago: University of Chicago Press.

Ben-Eliezer, U. 1993. "The Meaning of Political Participation in a Nonliberal Democracy: The Israeli Experience." *Comparative Politics* 25: 397–412.

Cobb, W. R., and Elder, D. C. 1972. *Participation in American Politics: The Dynamics of Agenda-Building*. Baltimore: Johns Hopkins University Press.

Doron, A., and Kramer, R. M. 1991. *The Welfare State in Israel*. Boulder, Colo.: Westview.

Dwarkin, G. 1972. "Paternalism." *The Monist* 56: 64–84.

Easton, D. 1965. *A Systems Analysis of Political Life*. New York: John Wiley.

Gidron, B. 1997. "The Evolution of Israel's Third Sector. The Role of Predominant Ideology." *Voluntas* 8: 11–38.

Goodin, E. R. 1993. "Democracy, Preferences and Paternalism." *Policy Sciences* 26: 229–247.

Gross, M. 1999. "Autonomy and Paternalism in Communitarian Society: Patient Rights in Israel." *The Hastings Center Report* 29: 13–20.

Heclo, H. 1978. "Issue Networks and the Executive Establishment." In *The American Political System*, ed. A. King. Washington, D.C.: American Enterprise Institute.

Hofferbert, R. 1974. *The Study of Public Policy*. Indianapolis: Bobbs-Merrill.

Horowitz, D., and Lissak, M. 1989. *Trouble in Utopia: The Overburdened Polity of Israel*. Albany: State University of New York Press.

Immergut, H. 1992. *Health Politics: Interests and Institutions in Western Europe*. Cambridge: Cambridge University Press.

Inglehart, R. 1990. "Values, Ideology, and Cognitive Mobilization in New Social Movements." In *Challenging the Political Order: New Social and Political Movements in Western Democracies*, ed. R. J. Dalton and M. Kuechler. New York: Oxford University Press.

Jacobs, L. 1993. *The Health of Nations, Public Opinion and the Making of American and British Health Policy*. Ithaca, N.Y.: Cornell University Press.

Jenkins-Smith, H. C., and Sabatier, P. A. 1993. "The Study of Public Policy Processes." In *Policy Change and Learning: An Advocacy Coalition Approach*. Boulder, Colo.: Westview.

Peri, S., and Raz, R. 1997. "The Law on the Patient Rights; the Patient, the Physician and the Family." *Michtav LeChaver* (Letter to Friends) 59: 13–15.

Polsby, N. 1980. *Community Power and Political Theory*. New Haven, Conn.: Yale University Press.

Regan, D. H. 1983. "Paternalism, Freedom, Identity and Commitment." In *Paternalism*, ed. R. Sartorious. Minneapolis: University of Minnesota Press.

Sabatier, P. A. 1991. "Political Science and Public Policy." *PS: Political Science and Politics* 24: 144–156.

Shuval, J. 1992. *Social Dimensions of Health: The Israeli Experience.* Westport, Conn.: Praeger.

Skocpol, T. 1994. "From Social Security to Health Security? Opinion and Rhetoric." *PS: Political Science* 27: 21–25.

Yishai, Y. 1982. "Politics and Medicine: The Case of Israel's National Health Insurance." *Social Science and Medicine* 16: 285–291.

———. 1991. *Land of Paradoxes: Interest Politics in Israel.* Albany: State University of New York Press.

———. 1992. "From an Iron Triangle to an Iron Duet? Health Policy Making in Israel." *European Journal of Political Research* 21: 91–108.

———. 1998. "Civil Society in Transition: Interest Politics in Israel." *Annals* 555, AAPSS: 147–162.

Zalmanovitch, Y. 1997. "Some Antecedents to Healthcare Reform: Israel and the United States." *Policy and Politics* 25: 251–268.

———. 1998. "Transitions in Israeli's Policymaking Network." *Annals* 555, AAPSS: 193–208.

FURTHER READING

Eisenstadt, S. N. 1967. *Israeli Society.* New York: Basic Books.

Elazar, D. J. 1986. *Israel: Building A New Society.* Bloomington: Indiana University Press.

Elon, A. 1971. *The Israelis: Founders and Sons.* New York: Holt, Reinhart, and Winston.

Sartorious, R., ed. 1983. *Paternalism.* Minneapolis: University of Minnesota Press.

Shuval, J. 1992. *Social Dimensions of Health: The Israeli Experience.* Westport, Conn.: Praeger.

PART III

ISSUES IN THE DEVELOPMENT OF THE WELFARE STATE

10

Social Protection in the Postwar Era: The OECD Experience

Francis G. Castles

In the past few decades, there have been numerous studies in the comparative public-policy tradition seeking to determine the sources of the rise of big government and the emergence of the advanced welfare state. Such studies have tended to be partial in one of two senses: either by restricting the range of variables considered as potentially linked with the phenomena in question or by obscuring the extent to which causal linkages may, themselves, vary over time. The first source of partiality has often resulted from overenthusiastic attempts to demonstrate the role of particular factors as the key to the growth of the modern state, but has, in any case, been a natural response to the methodological problem of "too many theories and not enough cases" endemic in this kind of analysis. The second source of partiality has been a feature of more recently pooled time-series analyses, which, in seeking to bypass the small problem by assuming that the world at "time t^{-1}" is analogous to the world at "time t," have implicitly modeled change as if it were a function of an unchanging array of factors, where frequently it is a function of factors differentially relevant at different times.

In another book (Castles 1998), I have sought to plot a way through these difficulties by elaborating cross-sectional models which seek to establish which of a very wide range of theoretically derived hypotheses produce the "best fit" with data on a very wide range of postwar policy outcomes. These models are derived by utilizing statistical criteria—maximization of R^2 and t-statistics ex-

ceeding 2.00—to accept or reject alternative multivariate specifications of hypothesized relationships.[1] Clearly such models are no
less partial or misspecified than those they replace, but the degree
of misspecification is hardly greater than that which results from
reporting on only a limited range of hypotheses from the literature,
a disingenuousness by omission, which characterizes much of the
work in the field. The truth is that the small problem intrinsic to
"most similar" cross-national research designs means that all modeling exercises of this kind are inherently partial. Once that is accepted, it becomes sensible to regard findings as merely interim
conclusions to be interrogated further in light of our understanding of related phenomena. The argument of my book is that the
identification of patterned relationships across adjacent policy areas and/or across time provides the most adequate basis for such
an understanding.

Establishing the existence of such patterns requires a much
broader focus than has been common in research of this type. Focusing on variation in twenty-one OECD countries, my book seeks
to locate the antecedents of a variety of measures relevant to the
postwar expansion of the caring state, starting from overall aggre-
gates (total outlays and total receipts of government), moving on to
the major metaprograms of social spending (public consumption
expenditure and social security transfers), and concluding with
specific programs of service provision (public health and public
education). Perhaps no less relevant to questions concerning the
future of the welfare state, the book also explores a range of labor
market outcomes (male and female participation rates and unemployment rates) as well as outcomes where public policy impacts on
the realm of the personal, including cross-national differences in
home ownership, fertility, and divorce rates. Thus, the concern is
not merely with the sources of modern social policy, but also with
the ways in which the rise of the caring state has in turn shaped
economy and society. Patterns over time and trajectories of growth
are established by examining the antecedents of policy outcomes at
different points during the postwar era—1960 (usually the earliest
time for which data is available), 1974 (marking the conclusion of
the "Golden Age" of economic growth and of welfare state development), and the early 1990s (the closest the existing data allow us to
come to "where we are now")—and in respect of change over the
period as a whole.

Because this chapter is designed to provide background to a wide-
ranging discussion of the future of the welfare state, it seems appropriate that the analysis it offers should be broad gauge in
character. In what follows, we seek to identify the factors most

closely linked to postwar levels and growth in total expenditure on social protection, a category of spending not examined in my book. Total social protection is used here to designate the aggregate of social expenditures, that is, the sum of spending on benefits in the form of cash transfers or the direct provision of goods and services designed to support households and individuals under circumstances adversely affecting their welfare. Social protection includes social security insurance benefits and a wide range of welfare services, including services to the old, to families, and to employment as well as public spending on health. It does not, however, include public spending on education. The source of the definition is the OECD (1996c, 3), and the data available is for OECD countries only.

The OECD focus adopted here and in most other comparative policy outcomes research is, of course, a strategy of analysis which contributes to the small problem. However, there is no real alternative. The ILO (International Labor Organization) issued *Cost of Social Security*, the only more inclusive cross-national data set on welfare expenditure, but as their data become more and more dated, the OECD has effectively become the only source of routinely available, systematically disaggregated, and substantially comparable data on the contemporary welfare state performance of a reasonably large group of nations. The adoption of an OECD focus, however, is not just a matter of the availability of information on the dependent variable. The countries of the OECD are the only ones for which we dispose the economic, social, political, and policy data required to explore a full range of hypotheses concerning the sources of policy development over the postwar period as a whole. This means that for the growth of the state and for most other policy outcomes in the postwar period, the only story we have sufficient evidence to tell is an OECD story. Whether the account we provide here of the sources of the postwar transformation of social protection in the OECD countries has any relevance to the Israeli experience of social policy development, which is the more specific concern of our deliberations, is a matter that I discuss in the final section of this chapter.

DATA

Table 10.1 contains data for expenditure on total social protection as a percentage of gross domestic product for seventeen to twenty-one OECD countries for the years 1960, 1974, and 1993 and for change over time. Countries are grouped into "families of nations" (Castles 1993) on the basis of historical, linguistic, and cultural affinities. Four such families are identified: the English-speaking nations, the Nordic countries, continental Western Eu-

Table 10.1
Levels and Change of Total Social Protection as a Percentage of GDP in OECD Countries, 1960 to 1993

Country	1960	1974	1993	Change 1960–1993
Australia	7.4	10.5	16.4	9.0
Canada	9.1	14.1	19.8	10.6
Ireland	8.7	15.2	20.1	11.4
New Zealand	10.4	11.1	22.5	12.1
United Kingdom	10.2	14.9	23.4	13.2
United States	7.3	12.8	15.6	8.3
Denmark	---	22.7	31.0	---
Finland	8.8	15.1	35.4	26.6
Norway	7.8	18.6	29.3	21.5
Sweden	10.8	21.0	38.0	27.2
Austria	15.9	19.2	25.8	9.9
Belgium	---	22.1	27.0	---
France	13.4	17.7	28.7	15.3
Germany	18.1	23.5	28.3	10.2
Italy	13.1	19.3	25.0	11.9
The Netherlands	11.7	26.7	30.2	18.5

rope and Southern Europe. Two countries—Switzerland and Japan—are unclassified in family of nations terms. Similarities and differences between these country groupings facilitate description of the changing pattern of social protection in the OECD region during the postwar period.

Table 10.1 (*continued*)

Country	1960	1974	1993	Change 1960–1993
Greece	7.1	8.4	17.2	10.2
Portugal	---	---	16.4	---
Spain	---	---	22.5	---
Switzerland	4.9	11.5	20.6	15.7
Japan	4.1	8.1	12.4	8.4
Mean	9.9	16.5	24.1	14.1
Correlation with 1960		0.74	0.52	0.00
Coefficient of variation	37.16	32.67	28.05	

Sources: Data for 1960 and 1974 from OECD, "New Orientations for Social Policy," *Social Policy Studies* (1994); data for 1993 from OECD, *Social Expenditure Statistics of OECD Member Countries* (Provisional Version) (Paris: OECD, 1996).

Note: The figure reported in the final column is the percentage point change over the entire period; where data are missing and there are data available for a year within ±2 years of the data point, those data are given; — indicates the absence of any adjacent data point.

In terms of aggregate social spending, the story of postwar welfare state development is simply told. In the beginning and for much of the period, there were two "worlds of welfare"; but by the early 1990s, there were three. In the early period, the five biggest spenders were all continental Western European nations, while there was no obvious distinction between the English-speaking and Nordic countries. Switzerland and Japan—the two unclassified countries— had markedly the lowest spending levels in the OECD in 1960. In the mid-1970s, there were still two clear groupings, but they were not those of the earlier period. Massive Scandinavian welfare state expansion had moved the Nordic group away from an Anglo-American spending profile to a continental Western European one. This is essentially the story told by Esping-Andersen (1990) using data for 1980, although he is further able to distinguish differences between the "social democratic" Scandinavian family and the "Conservative" continental Western European one in terms of differential degrees of decommodification effected through comparable expenditure efforts. By the early 1990s, however, the threefold distinction is no less clear in expenditure than in decommodification terms. In 1993, average spending on social protection in the Nordic countries was 33.4 percent of GDP; in the countries of continental Western Europe it was 27.5 percent, and in the English-speaking world it was 19.6 percent. There was virtually no overlap between these three groupings, with the Netherlands in the continental Western European grouping the single exception in having a spending level marginally higher than Norway in the Nordic grouping (Esping-Andersen also locates the Netherlands as a sort of honorary social democratic welfare state). At the bottom of the distribution, there is much greater overlap, with no clear-cut differences in spending levels between the English-speaking nations, Southern Europe, and Switzerland. Japan remains conspicuously the lowest spender throughout.

The huge expansion of the welfare state in these years is amply testified to by a transformation in the mean level of OECD spending from 9.9 percentage points of GDP in 1960 to 24.1 percentage points in 1993, an increase of around 140 percent in thirty-three years. Somewhat counterintuitively, given the received notion of a "Golden Age" of welfare followed by a "crisis of the welfare state," the rate of change measured in percentage points of GDP was not hugely greater in the period before 1974 than afterwards. Between 1960 and 1974, the OECD mean increased by 0.47 per annum; after 1974, it increased by 0.40. Of course, there was very substantial cross-national variation in the trajectory of welfare state growth over these years. Here again, it would seem that the most appropriate account is in terms of two distinct worlds, with the Nordic counties' transformation from near laggards to outright leaders being reflected in spending growth on average around twice as high as that of either the English-speaking or continental Western European nations.

A more summary perspective of the changes taking place over the period is provided by the statistics to be found in the bottom rows of Table 10.1. The only moderate correlations between 1960 and subsequent levels of spending is indicative of the changing character of the cross-national distribution. Most of that change was, of course, a function of the growth trajectory of the Nordic countries. Indeed, excluding Finland, Norway, and Sweden from the calculation, the correlation between 1960 and 1993 values is as high as 0.85. Interestingly, in light of debates in the literature concerning welfare state convergence (see Wilensky 1975; Overbye 1994), the zero correlation between expenditure level in 1960 and expenditure change thereafter shows precisely no sign of a concerted catch-up effort in the postwar decades. The Scandinavian countries forged ahead, but the English-speaking countries apparently made little effort to bridge the gap separating their welfare performance from that of continental Western Europe.

Finally, thinking of convergence in another and more relative way, a gradually declining coefficient of variation is indicative of a modest tendency for OECD countries to become more alike with the passing of time. The significance of this trend can only be judged by comparing it with analogous trends. Calculations in Castles (1998, ch. 5) indicate coefficients of variation for social security transfers of 43.98 in 1960 and 26.20 in 1993 and for public health spending of 31.52 in 1960 and 16.16 in 1993. Thus, total social expenditure started out by being somewhat more similarly distributed across the OECD nations than income transfers, but markedly less similarly distributed than health spending. By the end of the period, total social spending was less similarly distributed than either of the categories of spending, which in most countries constitute the vast majority of that spending. This appears paradoxical only because we have provided no figures for a further category of spending on social protection that falls under neither of these headings, namely, civilian public consumption expenditure devoted to the provision of caring services. A substantial part of the story of changing cross-national profiles of welfare state development in the postwar era is told when we point out that such services scarcely existed anywhere in 1960 and today are only really strongly developed in the Nordic family of nations (Anttonen and Sipilä 1996).[2] The countries of this region have become the contemporary vanguard of the welfare state, not just because they outspend most other countries across a similar range of socially protective functions, but because they have extended the role of the state to include a whole new set of caring functions.

HYPOTHESES

Comparative public policy research has devoted more time to the search for the causes of the growth of the welfare state than to any other single topic. Over three decades, a huge range of hypotheses have been generated and tested, with socioeconomic modernization, trade exposure, demographic change, cultural preferences, ideology, and institutional arrangements only some of the more prominent categories of explanation. No area of policy research exemplifies the problem of "too many theories and not enough cases" more dramatically than the study of the determinants of welfare spending.

(Space considerations prevent us from doing much more than listing the hypotheses that we shall test in order to develop the models of social protection that are featured in the next section, with discussion limited to raising issues that emerge as particularly significant in the context of those models. For the same reason, there is only a summary consideration of issues relating to the operationalization of variables, with the presentation again highlighting only what is salient for later findings. However, all variables that are featured as components of the models presented in Tables 10.2 through 10.5 are fully defined in the notes to those tables, and all the hypotheses and related variables featured in this analysis are discussed at length in Castles [1998]. References in this section are illustrative rather than exhaustive, and a much more extensive critical analysis of the relevant literature and a fuller bibliography are also to be found in that source.)

Under the broad rubric of factors associated with economic structure and economic development, we consider propositions of three kinds. First is a broad set of hypotheses which argues that the emergence and growth of the caring state has been a function of levels of economic affluence and/or problems stemming from processes of industrialization and urbanization (essentially these are all variants of Adolf Wagner's "law of increasing state activity," first articulated in 1877—see Larkey, Stolp, and Winer 1981—and closely associated with a wide range of sociological formulations concerning the transformative role of industrial development and socioeconomic modernization—see Wilensky and Lebeaux 1957 and Flora and Heidenheimer 1981). Second are hypotheses relating to the role of international trade, with the now somewhat dated view that public spending on welfare has been largely a defensive response to trade vulnerability (Cameron 1978; Katzenstein 1985) counterposed by the more recent and wholly contradictory proposition that trade exposure reduces the capacity of domestic decision makers to flout the wishes of the markets (this is one variant of the currently fashionable globalization thesis—see Keohane and Milner 1996). Finally, we consider the possibility that an important part of the impetus to postwar welfare development was the response to the experience of World War II itself, with that response variously conceptualized in terms of public expenditure "displacement" (Peacock and Wiseman 1961), risk sharing (Goodin and Dryzek 1987), and coping with the consequences of human and material losses (the indicators we use to capture these potential effects are a war impact variable based on the severity of wartime dislocation and a war growth variable measuring the growth of real GDP per capita over the period 1937–1950).

The issue of whether welfare state development is a function of the level of economic affluence has always been of central importance in the literature, with an affirmative answer generally taken as evidence of transformative role of socioeconomic modernization and a negative answer often regarded as a prerequisite for explanations based on the role of political agency in policy determination. Although much of my previous work has been strongly associated with the latter kind of interpretation, I am far from satisfied that the intuitively obvious case that greater affluence makes it possible to devote more public resources to welfare has been rigorously enough tested. Tests of the relationship have always assumed a linear model—that more affluence means proportionately more welfare—and the twenty or so countries under investigation here have always yielded nonsignificant findings, with a number of the very richest countries—conspicuously Australia, Canada, Switzerland, and the United States—in the welfare state rearguard (Castles and McKinlay 1979). But the very fact of such a grouping of affluent welfare state laggards suggests that the linkage between affluence and welfare may have well been misspecified by friends and foes of the modernization thesis alike, with the true relationship being that high expenditure levels are characteristic of countries with middling levels of economic development and that low levels of social protection are typical of both the poorest and the richest nations.[3] In our subsequent modeling, we test for the existence of a curvilinear relationship of this nature by examining the fit between total expenditure on social protection and a simple polynomial expression of real GDP per capita.

Under the rubric of social factors, we consider two further hypotheses. The first is the argument—now widely regarded as an orthodoxy of social policy development (World Bank 1994; OECD 1996a)—that a major factor determining the size and growth of the welfare state has been the age structure of the population (Wilensky 1975; Pampel and Williamson 1989). The second is the proposition that the social policy doctrines and/or the family-oriented values of non-Protestant Christian denominations (generally Roman Catholic) have shaped welfare outcomes in countries where such doctrines and values have been culturally or politically dominant, leading to a marked preference for welfare provision via income transfers financed on a contributory basis rather than via services financed through general taxation (Castles 1995; Van Kersbergen 1995).

Accounts of political matters are as various as economic and social ones. The big divide is between explanations based on ideological preferences and those resting on an institutional logic. Within schools of thought there are additional debates and controversies concerning the significance of rival variables. Among those stressing the impact of ideology, there has been a division between a class politics analysis (Piven and Cloward 1972; Gough 1979—here we use union density as our test variable for this proposition) and one resting on partisan control, with further differences in the partisanship camp between those variously emphasizing the role of left government (Schmidt 1996a), the "power resources" of the social democratic labor movement (Esping-Andersen and Korpi 1984), and the negative salience of rightist incumbency (Castles 1982).

The belief that the institutions of government matter has an older strand which points to the role of democratization as a means of articulating popular demands (see Key 1949, but more recently Lijphart 1997) and a somewhat newer variant which stresses the way in which federalism (for a recent articulation of this argument, see Pierson 1995) and a range of other constitutional impediments to the exercise of parliamentary sovereignty (Huber, Ragin, and Stephens 1993) provide means for elites to mobilize against the growth of big government and the welfare state. Nor do all welfare-state-relevant institutions pertain to the sphere of national government. At the level of economic and societal institution-building, it has been argued that the institutional regulation of class conflict and/or its wider societal expression in corporatist structures of solidarity has been a vital element in the development of the advanced welfare state (Kemeny 1992). At a transnational level, it has been suggested that the emergence of institutional structures, such as those of the European Community, are likely to influence welfare provision in the member nations by creating pressures for uniform provision and by subordinating social protection to the imperatives of closer economic integration (Liebfried and Pierson 1995).

This brings us to a number of hypotheses roughly equivalent to the number of countries for which data were available in 1960. In respect to welfare outcomes, it is not just a matter of "too many theories and not enough cases," but of appreciably more theories than cases. We add three more, the first two relating only to growth rather than to levels of welfare expenditure and the third potentially applicable to both. The first offers us not only an account of the reasons for differential growth rates among nations, but at the same time provides a possible explanation of why welfare state expansion was not hugely greater in the Golden Age than afterward, the argument being that higher rates of economic growth permit the real expansion of welfare spending with a lesser expenditure effort measured in GDP terms (i.e., quite contrary to Wagner's law, we should expect a negative relationship between the rate of economic growth and the growth of public spending—see Wildavsky 1985). The second gives us a further reason why we might not expect too great a disparity between rates of welfare development in the immediate and late postwar periods, the argument being that high levels of inflation in the late 1970s and early 1980s were conducive to a degree of "fiscal drag" which automatically increased the revenue base available for welfare state expansion (Rose 1984). The final hypothesis we consider is the argument that a large owner-occupied housing sector is conducive to strong tax aversion amongst the electorate, leading to relatively weak popular support for public spending initiatives of all kinds (Kemeny 1981). This listing of hypotheses is still far from definitive, but even with the utilization using a technique that does not arbitrarily restrict the number of variables that can be examined, there are limits to the feasibility of extending the analysis indefinitely. In what follows, models derived on the basis of the wide range of factors listed here are presented and discussed. As we shall see, neither severally nor collectively do these models suggest an account of the postwar welfare state in which a single type of factor is featured to the exclusion of all others.

FINDINGS

Findings are presented in two stages. In Figures 10.1, 10.2, 10.3, and 10.4, we show the strength of the bivariate relationships between levels and changes in total expenditure and each of the hypothesized independent variables. In Tables 10.2, 10.3, 10.4, and 10.5, we present models, indicating which factors combine to produce the best-fitting accounts of the sources of expenditure development. As already noted, the criterion for the inclusion of terms in these models is t-values in excess of 2.00. In the case of the bivariate relationships, a correlation of around ± 0.40 is indicative of a significance level of 0.05. For those who continue to wonder at the proliferation of theories in this field, it is worth noting that each of the charts contains a substantial number of significant terms—in the case of Figure 10.2 no less than eleven. In other words, the variety of theoretical interpretations in the welfare state literature has arisen, not because researchers have ignored the facts, but because the facts have supported such a wide variety of interpretations.

Figure 10.1
1960 Total Social Protection

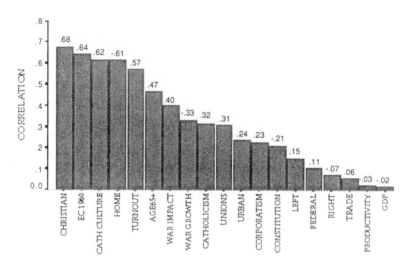

Table 10.2
Social Protection Model—1960

1960 Total Social Protection	Coefficient	Standard Error	T-value
Intercept	-8.245		
1960 Real GDP Per Capita	0.005	0.001	4.971
1960 Real GDP Per Capita Squared	-3.812E-7	8.598E-8	4.434
Catholic Cultural Impact	5.431	1.054	5.151

Adj R^2 = 0.755

Sources: 1960 Total Social Protection from Table 10.1. 1960 Real GDP Per Capita and 1960 Real GDP Per Capita Squared calculated from R. Summers and A. Heston, "The Penn World Table (Mark 5)," *Quarterly Journal of Economics* 106 (2) 327–368.

Note: Catholic Cultural Impact is a dummy variable indicating countries in which at least 75 percent of the population are baptized into a non-Protestant Christian faith or in which Christian democratic parties have held more than 40 percent of cabinet seats over the postwar era as a whole. Seventeen cases in regression.

Figure 10.2
1974 Total Social Protection

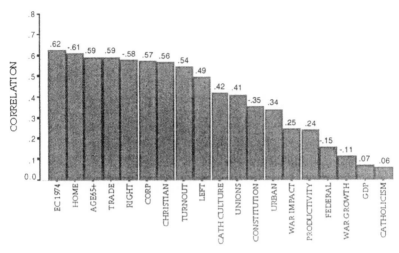

Table 10.3
Social Protection Model—1974

1974 Total Social Protection	Coefficient	Standard Error	T-value
Intercept	-20.639		
1974 Real GDP Per Capita	0.007	0.002	4.767
1974 Real GDP Per Capita Squared	-3.492E-7	7.948E-8	4.393
Catholic Cultural Impact	6.078	1.43	4.252
1950-1973 Right Cabinet Seats	-0.084	0.019	4.434

Adj R^2 = 0.767

Sources: 1974 Total Social Protection from Table 10.1. 1974 Real GDP Per Capita and 1974 Real GDP Per Capita Squared calculated from R. Summers and A. Heston, "The Penn World Table (Mark 5)," *Quarterly Journal of Economics* 106 (2) 327–368.

Note: Catholic Cultural Impact is as defined in Table 10.2; 1950–1973 Right Cabinet Seats is the average annual percentage of cabinet seats held by the major party of the right calculated from data in M. G. Schmidt, *Die parteipolitische Zusammensetzung von Regierungen in demokratischen Staaten (1945–1996)* (Heidelberg: Institut für Politische Wissenschaft, 1996b), with the definition of the major party of the right as in F. G. Castles, "The Impact of Parties on Public Expenditure," in *The Impact of Parties* (London: Sage), (Greece, Portugal, and Spain are regarded as having been ruled exclusively by rightist governments during the periods of their respective juntas). Nineteen cases in regression.

Figure 10.3
Early 1990s Total Social Protection

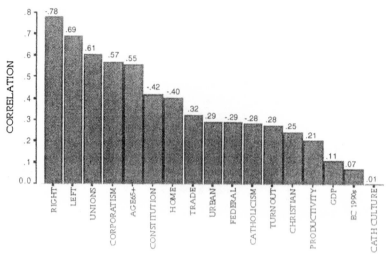

Table 10.4
Social Protection Model—1993

1993 Total Social Protection	Coefficient	Standard Error	T-value
Intercept	-11.605		
1993 Real GDP Per Capita	0.007	0.002	4.201
1974 Real GDP Per Capita Squared	-2.870E-7	6.472E-8	4.434
1993 Aged Population	0.984	0.391	2.517
1993 International Trade	-0.082	0.031	2.691
1950-1993 Right Cabinet Seats	-0.200	0.032	6.170

Adj R^2 = 0.851

Sources: 1993 Total Social Protection from Table 10.1. 1993 Real GDP Per Capita and 1993 Real GDP Per Capita Squared calculated from R. Summers and A. Heston, "The Penn World Table (Mark 5)," *Quarterly Journal of Economics* 106 (2) 327–368.

Notes: 1993 Aged Population is the percentage of the population sixty-five years and over from OECD, *Labour Force Statistics 1973–1993* (Paris: OECD, 1995). The term for the aged population is not robust and ceases to be significant if one of several cases is removed from the regression; 1993 International Trade is the sum of imports and exports expressed as a percentage of GDP from OECD, *Historical Statistics, 1960–1994* (Paris: OECD, 1996); 1950–1993 Right Cabinet Seats calculated and defined in Table 10.3. Twenty-one cases in regression.

Figure 10.4
Change in Total Social Protection

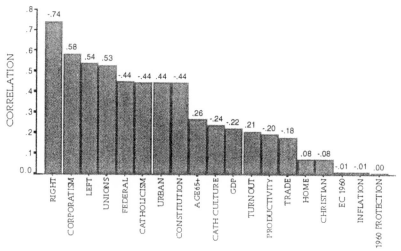

Table 10.5
Social Protection Models: Change over Time

1960-1993 Change in Total Social Protection	Coefficient	Standard Error	T-value
Intercept	23.167		
1960-1992 Growth Rate of Real GDP Per Capita	-1.541	0.430	3.585
1960-1993 Change in Aged Population	1.309	0.220	5.928
Catholicism	-0.173	0.012	14.295
1960-1993 Right Cabinet Seats	-4.790	0.658	7.284
Federalisim	-4.790	0.658	7.284
Adj R^2 = 0.962			

Sources: 1960–1993 Change in Total Social Protection from Table 10.1. 1960–1992 Growth Rate of Real GDP Per Capita calculated from R. Summers and A. Heston, "The Penn World Table (Mark 5)," *Quarterly Journal of Economics* 106 (2) 327–368.

Note: 1960–1993 Change in Aged Population is the change in the percentage of the population sixty-five years and over, with data for 1960 from OECD, *OECD Health Systems* (vol. 2) (Paris: OECD, 1993), and for 1993 from OECD, *Labour Force Statistics 1973–1993* (Paris: OECD, 1995); Catholicism is the percentage of the population baptized into the Roman Catholic or Greek Orthodox faith; 1960–1993 Right Cabinet Seats calculated and defined in Table 10.3; Federalism is a dummy variable scoring federal states as 1; others as 0; seventeen cases in regression.

Looking initially to Figure 10.1, we note that two of the strongest positive correlates of expenditure development are measures of the Catholic influence, Christian democratic incumbency and a dummy variable which we label Catholic cultural impact. A third factor, European Community (EC) membership, is clearly picking up on some of the same influences, given that the initial membership of the community consisted almost entirely of countries in which Christian democratic parties were dominant (France is the only exception). In addition, there are positive associations with a variety of other variables, including age structure of the population, electoral turnout (our proxy for democratization), and war impact. The only significant negative association is between home ownership and social expenditure. For this early period, our bivariate findings offer little support for several of the more important categories of explanations suggested in the literature. These include the role of economic development (whether measured by GDP per capita or productivity), of ideology (left or right incumbency) and of constitutional forms (federalism or the presence of other institutional impediments to parliamentary sovereignty).

The absence of a significant linear relationship between economic affluence and the development of the welfare state does not, however, mean that these variables are unrelated. As Table 10.2 shows, the best-fit model for 1960 is one which combines a curvilinear specification of real GDP per capita, with the dummy variable for Catholic cultural impact. It is worth getting an idea of the magnitude of these effects, and this is done by calculating what the coefficients reported in the model mean, in terms of estimated differences in expenditure on social protection for countries at different points in the distribution. Because Catholic cultural impact is a dummy variable, such a calculation is straightforward. Countries which were defined as Catholic in this sense spent 5.4 percentage points of GDP more on social protection in 1960 than countries which were not. In the case of real GDP, it is estimated that a country at the mean point in the OECD distribution would have spent 6.3 percentage points of GDP more than the country at the bottom of the distribution. Indicative of the strong curvilinear impact of this variable, a country with the mean level of GDP per capita would also have spent 2.1 percentage points of GDP more than the country at the top of the distribution.

A comparison of the findings reported in Figures 10.1 and 10.2 suggests elements of both stability and change. A degree of stability is testified to by the fact that, with the single exception of war impact, all the factors associated with spending in 1960 remained associated with spending in 1974. While there are signs that the link with Catholic influence was diminishing, the strength of the other relationships remained more or less constant. Change is indicated by the emergence of a range of new linkages, including international trade, corporatism, left incumbency, and union density, all of them positively associated with outcomes, as well as right incumbency, which is negatively associated with spending. Given that the hypothesis linking trade to public spending levels is premised on the defensive actions of working class organizations and parties, and that corporatism too can be interpreted as an expression of working class hegemony, the picture that emerges from Figure 10.2 is of the emergence of a new ideological dimension of welfare state development overlaying existing sources of cross-national difference.

That picture is underlined by the 1974 model which appears in Table 10.3. This model simply replicates its predecessor with the single addition of a negative term for right incumbency. In a world in which OECD spending on social protection had gone up by two-thirds between 1960 and 1974, the estimated effect of Catholic cultural impact had increased marginally to 6.1 percentage points of GDP. The estimated impact of GDP had also increased somewhat, but, once again, not fully in proportion to the increase in the level of social expenditure. In 1974, a country at the mean of the distribution of GDP per capita is estimated to have spent 7.9 percentage points of GDP more on social protection than the country at the bottom of the distribution and 3.6 percentage points more than the country at the top. Finally, a country with an average experience of right incumbency over the years of 1950 to 1973 is estimated to have spent 4.1 percentage points of GDP less than a country at the bottom of the distribution. Since the full range of the ideological distribution was from Sweden, with no experience of government by the right, to Spain and Portugal, ruled by rightist juntas throughout the postwar period, politically induced differences in spending could be very large indeed, amounting in these cases to more than an estimated 8 percentage points of GDP.

According to Figure 10.3, the cluster of political variables that had emerged in the mid-1970s had become dominant by the early 1990s. International trade, however, is no longer part of this cluster and, while still positively correlated with spending, is no longer significantly so. Apart from partisan and class-related factors, a new type of political factor had also emerged, with constitutional impediments to parliamentary sovereignty now negatively associated with expenditure levels. Of the variables originally linked to spending in 1960, only two remain of any significance: age structure of the population moderately and home ownership very modestly. The three strongest relationships of the initial period—Christian democracy, Catholic cultural impact, and EC membership—are now quite negligible.

The decline in the strength of these associations makes it a matter of little surprise that the early 1990s model in Table 10.4 no longer contains a term for Catholic influence. In other respects, however, the model is quite familiar. Once again we encounter a curvilinear real GDP effect, and right incumbency now emerges as the single most important impediment to the development of the welfare state. The early 1990s model also contains two new terms: age structure of the population and, reversing the sign of the corresponding bivariate relationship, international trade. The first of these terms is not robust and ceases to be significant if one of a number of countries is removed from the regression. The international trade finding is not dependent on sample composition and is broadly compatible with an interpretation that sees globalization of international trade as an emergent constraint on public spending.[4]

Turning now to estimated effects, we find that the magnitude of the difference between a country with an average level of real GDP and one at the bottom of the distribution is much the same as it has been in earlier years at 5.9 percentage points of GDP, but that the negative effect of increasing national wealth has become much greater, with the gap between the mean and the top of the top of the distribution now no less than 9 percentage points. Very rich countries are now, in other words, lower spenders than very poor ones. Using our standard measure of the difference in estimated expenditure between a country at the mean and at the bottom of the distribution, the estimated impacts of age structure and trade are quite moderate at 2.7 and 3.6 percentage points of GDP respectively. The right incumbency effect is much larger at 7.9 percentage points. For Sweden and Japan, at opposite ends of the postwar political spectrum, the contribution of partisan incumbency to expenditure variation in the early 1990s is a massive 18.6 percentage points of GDP.

Figure 10.4 shows that, in bivariate terms, the factors which are significantly associated with expenditure change over the postwar period as a whole are, with a single exception, political in character. On the one hand, there are the partisan and institutional correlates of ideological difference (the right, corporatism, the left, and union density) and, on the other, constitutional forms inimical to the growth of big government. The one nonpolitical factor associated with growth is a third measure of Catholic influence, the percentage of the population born into non-Protestant Christian faiths.

This variable is simply underlining the story apparent in all that has already been said of Catholic countries in the welfare vanguard in 1960 progressively dropping back until they are in the second rank by the early 1990s.

The multivariate story which emerges from the change model in Table 10.5 is, however, far from being exclusively political in character. Indeed, to someone who has, in recent years, deplored the excesses of the battle of the paradigms that has provided much of "the sound and fury" in the literature over more than two decades, there is a certain beauty in this final model, which captures the sources of welfare transformation over a third of a century. That is not so much because of the exceptionally high level of explained variation offered by the model, but rather because the array of significant terms demonstrates that virtually every major variant of theorizing in the field has some relevance to outcomes. Certainly, parties matter, but so too do economic growth, population aging, religious beliefs, and constitutional forms. Like the "Caucus Race" in Lewis Carroll's *Alice in Wonderland,* our report card on the literature is pleasing in that "all have won and all must have prizes."

Interestingly, the two factors with the strongest real effects are those most frequently and forcefully counterposed in the debate on rival causes of welfare state development: partisanship and age structure. Calculating on our normal basis, the estimated effect of right partisanship was to contain the growth of postwar welfare state expenditure in the average OECD nation by some 6.6 percentage points of GDP. An average degree of population aging increased welfare spending by 5.6 points. Other estimated real effects are somewhat smaller. Being a federal state cost a nation 4.8 percentage points of welfare growth; being characterized by an average degree of Catholic adherence weakened expenditure development by 2.7 points; and experiencing an average economic growth rate diminished it by 2.5 points. Here, as throughout this section, estimated figures should only be regarded as broadly indicative of real impacts, since calculations of average effects are strongly influenced by the shape of particular distributions.

WHY ARE RICH WELFARE STATE LAGGARDS?

An analysis of the full implications of the four models identified in the previous section is well beyond the scope of what is possible here. Although in the context of somewhat different dependent variables, interpretations of many of the most interesting issues raised by these findings are to be found in Castles (1998). There is one finding, however, that emerges in connection with our exploration of the sources of postwar expenditure on social protection, which goes somewhat farther than the results reported in my book. While these results point to the curvilinear nature of the relationships between real GDP per capita and outcomes relating to the total outlays of government in 1960 and to total receipts of government and social security transfers in both 1960 and 1974, there is no sign that these relationships persist to the present day. The findings we have reported in the previous section, however, suggest that the fact of exceptionally low aggregate expenditure levels in both rich and poor nations is a constant of postwar welfare state development and one which does not appear to be weakening with the passing of time. Because this is a new finding, and one which allows us to speculate more broadly on some of the antecedents of postwar welfare state transformation, some further analysis is warranted.

There would appear to be two available empirical strategies for identifying the factors underlying the observed curvilinear development of the welfare state. An obvious, although by definition second-best, strategy is to seek to establish the terms in the linear specification of each model that the curvilinear specification replaces. Such a strategy is second best, because we already know that the curvilinear specification accounts for a greater proportion of the variance than any linear model. Nevertheless, it seems probable that some or all of the variables which figure in the linear specifications may play some role in accounting for the tendency of rich countries to experience low levels of welfare expenditure.

On this basis, we can identify two factors that are clearly related to outcomes and that strongly point to commonalities between very rich and very poor nations. These are age structure of the population and electoral turnout, the first featuring in best-fit linear specifications throughout the period and the latter in both 1960 and 1974. We know from our change model that age structure has been a most important factor influencing postwar welfare expansion, and it obviously makes sense to see it as a factor that has contributed to the lower levels of expenditure of some of the richer nations (most notably the overseas English-speaking nations). While the disappearance of the electoral turnout term in the early 1990s models indicates that this factor could be associated with the poor welfare performance of the Southern European dictatorships prior to the mid-1970s, the continuing statistical significance of the term when these countries are excluded from the comparison suggests that this is not what is driving the relationship. Rather, whatever linkage there may be seems to be within the lower levels of participation typical of the territorial systems of electoral representation of the English-speaking countries as well as with the conditions making for low voter turnout in Switzerland both before and after the introduction of female suffrage in 1971.

A second strategy for identifying the correlates of curvilinearity is to look at the particular cases that interest us and see what they have in common. In 1960, the countries which can reasonably be described as rich welfare state laggards were the United States, Switzerland, New Zealand, Australia, and Canada, with the countries listed in order of their levels of real GDP per capita (Summers and Heston 1991). In 1974, the countries have not changed, but the ordering was the United States, Switzerland, Canada, Australia, and New Zealand. In the early 1990s, New Zealand was no longer affluent and Japan has acquired super-rich status, and the ordering is now the United States, Canada, Switzerland, Japan, and Australia. At least three commonalities can be identified: four of the five countries are federal states, all the countries except for Japan were nations which became rich and democratic in the nineteenth century, and all the countries were ones which are non-Catholic according to the criteria used in this study.

As our change model demonstrates, the federal story is one which becomes more important as the period progresses, but it is a nonstarter at the beginning, given that the remaining federal nations in the comparison—Germany and Austria—are the two leading welfare states of the early postwar era. The early development story is much more interesting in suggesting that timing and contextual issues more broadly may be implicated in shaping the long-term trajectory of social policy development. The argument is that even in countries where economic modernization had already produced adequate resources to underwrite initiatives for increasing social amelioration, and where democratic channels already existed to articulate demands for such amelioration, there are good reasons to suppose that early social policy initiatives might not take the same interventionist form as later ones.[5]

A possible reason why this should be so is the absence among mid-nineteenth century political and bureaucratic elites of a developed repertoire of welfare state responses. Self-help, friendly societies (often organized through the auspices of the labor movement), wage arbitration, and, where all else failed, means tested benefits, all of them strategies which were variously prominent in the early democratizing nations in the latter decades of the century, may well have appeared as the obvious routes to social amelioration in an age where social insurance, much less social services, had yet to be invented. As a consequence, by the time new repertoires had been established and shown to be effective elsewhere, preferred welfare strategies and conceptions of social justice in these nations were already quite highly institutionalized and resistant to change. This is a story analogous to, and indeed related to, the phenomenon of the "freezing" of Western party systems at the time of the introduction of the democratic suffrage (Lipset and Rokkan 1967). It is also a story which is connected with the earlier observation of a linkage between low turnout and weak expenditure development. Whether the connection, however, is spurious or causal is unclear. On the one hand, the link may simply reflect the fact that several of the early democratizing nations were English-speaking and that the English-speaking nations had a long historical tradition of territorial representation. On the other hand, the fact that this type of representation tends to lead to lower levels of popular participation than is typical of proportional systems may itself have been a factor contributing to the weakness of these nations' postwar welfare development.

The religious story is no less interesting and raises the question of whether there may not be quite distinct logics of social policy development in Catholic and non-Catholic countries. If we look only at Catholic countries, there is simply no story of rich welfare state laggards to be told. Taking only the countries classified as Catholic by the Catholic cultural impact variable, the bivariate correlations between real GDP per capita and total expenditure on social protection are 0.84 in 1960, 0.85 in 1974, and an astonishing 0.96 in the early 1990s. Admittedly, the number of cases is very small—seven in 1960, eight in 1974, and ten in the early 1990s—but the relationships are very clear and literally leave almost no room for alternative explanations. For the non-Catholic countries, the story is very different, with correlations of 0.15 in 1960, −0.09 in 1974, and −0.46 in the early 1990s. At the beginning of the period, affluence seems unrelated to these countries' welfare state development. At the end, although, given the small number of cases, the relationship bivariate is not statistically significant, there is a clear tendency for affluence to go along with lower levels of spending. Obviously much of the weight of accounting for the non-Catholic nations' spending levels must be carried by the other terms in the early 1990s model. Despite the fact that there are only eleven cases, the relationships are so strong that it is possible to elaborate a model for the non-Catholic countries in which age structure of the population (positively) and right incumbency and real GDP per capita (negatively) are all statistically significant predictors of outcomes and, the adjusted R2 is as high as 0.933.[6]

So our final question is whether it is possible to locate mechanisms which would make Catholicism a context favorable to a positive link between affluence and welfare and non-Catholicism a context in which there might be an emergent trend in the opposite direction. On the Catholic side of the equation, at least two mechanisms can be identified: on the one hand, a set of social policy doctrines based on the "just wage" that suggest that wages and benefits should be linked to the growth of national resources and, on the other hand, a reliance on funding through contributory social insurance which automatically increases funding as wage levels increase. On the non-Catholic side of the equation, there are two different kinds of story. There are the collectivist nations of the Nordic region in which the weakness of the right has contributed to the emergence of the advanced welfare state, with a funding mechanism based on provision from the general exchequer producing no obvious nexus between affluence and welfare effort. There are also a group of more individualistic nations in which ideological preferences focusing only on poverty alleviation provide a mechanism for a relative reduction in welfare effort as increasing affluence reduces the extent of absolute poverty. It is these latter countries which are the rich welfare state laggards.

The accounts offered in this section are not conflicting, but complementary. With the exception of Japan, all the countries in the rich welfare state laggard category are Protestant early modernizers, and each, in addition, is characterized by some combination of a youthful population, low voter turnout, strong unified parties of the right, and federalism. The United States is unique in combining all these characteristics. Most of these factors are likely to be slow to change because they affect the present through the attitudinal residues of the past or because they are the institutional forms and consequences of the democratic settlements of a previous century. The main changes in the character of postwar OECD welfare state development have arisen as a consequence of the way in which Catholic nations have responded to postwar affluence and the way in which the Nordic welfare states have been shaped by social democracy and the challenge of catering to the welfare needs of aging populations. The analysis here does not suggest that there is much risk of these countries becoming rich welfare state laggards. The only country to acquire this status over the period discussed here was Japan, and Japan did so not by changing its welfare profile, but simply because it became rich. The only country which lost its status as a rich welfare state laggard was New Zealand, and that was as a consequence of posting the OECD's poorest postwar economic growth record. The historical record says that advanced welfare states do not become rich welfare state laggards, but rather that some laggardly welfare states become rich.[7]

NOTES

1. There is nothing sacred about this or any other cutoff point for the inclusion or exclusion of terms in a model. I originally decided on a t-value of 2.00 because it corresponded more or less exactly with the conventional level of statistical significance of 0.05. I use the same criteria here to be consistent with the book, but a very large number of regression equations down the track, I am inclined to prefer a higher threshold of inclusion—somewhere between t = 2.50 and t = 3.00—which would tend to rule out instances where a term was included in a model solely because it corresponded with extreme values in a particular country.

2. Adding together early 1990s expenditures for services to the elderly, to families, and to employment (data from OECD, 1996), we find that the Nordic countries spent an average of 6.4 percent of GDP, while only three other countries (all continental Western European) spent more than 2 percent of GDP. The coefficient of variation for this category of states services was a spectacular 91.32.

3. Although, of course, it is important to emphasize that, since we measure total social protection as a percentage of GDP, the absolute quantum of welfare provided in rich countries will be hugely greater than in poor countries even where both make an identical commitment to welfare as indicated by this measuring rod.

4. This finding is stronger than the corresponding findings in my book. In that analysis, international trade featured as a negative term in models predicting early 1990 levels of total outlays, total receipts, and social security transfers, but in each case the term ceased to be significant if Ireland, one of the OECD's most internationally vulnerable economies, was excluded from the comparison.

5. Flora and Alber (1981) discuss very similar issues of timing in the context of a somewhat more restricted analysis of early welfare state development in Western Europe.

6. Obviously much of the weight of accounting for the non-Catholic nation's spending levels must be carried out by the other terms in the early 1990s model. Despite the fact that there are only eleven cases, the relationships are so strong that it is possible to elaborate a model for the non-Catholic countries in which age structure of the population (positively) and right incumbency and real GDP per capita (negatively) are all statistically significant predictors of outcomes, and the adjusted R^2 is as high as 0.933.

7. The nearest to an exception is probably New Zealand, which had some claim to being the world's most advanced welfare state in the immediate postwar period after the fifteen-year rule of New Zealand's First Labour Government (see ILO 1949). However, it seems clear—not least from the figures in Table 10.1—that national governments in the decades after 1949 managed to undermine the welfare state rather more rapidly than they undermined the economy.

REFERENCES

Anttonen, A., and Sipilä, J. "European Social Care Services: Is It Possible to Identify Models?" In *Welfare Systems and European Integration,* ed. M. Alestalo and P. Kosonen. University of Tampere, Department of Sociology and Social Psychology.

Cameron, D. 1978. "The Expansion of the Public Economy: A Comparative Analysis." *American Political Science Review* 72 (4): 1243–1261.

Castles, F. G. 1982. "The Impact of Parties on Public Expenditure." In *The Impact of Parties.* London: Sage.

———. 1993. *Families of Nations: Patterns of Public Policy in Western Democracies.* Aldershot, U.K.: Darmouth.

———. 1994. "On Religion and Public Policy: Does Catholicism Make a Difference?" *European Journal of Political Research* 25: 19–40.

———. 1995. "Welfare State Development in Southern Europe." *West European Politics* 18: 291–313.

———. 1998. *Comparative Public Policy: Patterns of Post-War Transformation.* Cheltenham, U.K.: Edward Elgar.

Castles, F. G., and McKinlay, R. 1979. "Does Politics Matter? An Analysis of the Public Welfare Commitment in Advanced Democratic States." *European Journal of Political Research* 7: 169–186.

Esping-Andersen, G. 1990. *The Three Worlds of Welfare Capitalism.* Cambridge: Polity Press.

Esping-Andersen, G., and Korpi, W. 1984. "Social Policy as Class Politics in Post-War Capitalism: Scandinavia, Austria and Germany." In *Order and Conflict in Contemporary Capitalism,* ed. J. H. Goldthorpe. Oxford: Clarendon Press.

Flora, P., and Alber, J. 1981. "Modernization, Democratization, and the Development of Welfare States in Western Europe." In *The Development of Welfare States in Europe and America,* ed. P. Flora and A. J. Heidenheimer. New Brunswick, N.J.: Transaction.

Flora, P., and Heidenheimer, A. J., eds. 1981. *The Development of Welfare States in Europe and America.* New Brunswick, N.J.: Transaction.

Goodin, R. E., and Dryzek, J. 1987. "Risk Sharing and Social Justice: The Motivational Foundations of the Post-War Welfare State." In *Not Only The Poor,* ed. R. E. Goodin and J. Le Grand. London: Allen & Unwin.

Gough, I. 1979. *The Political Economy of the Welfare State.* London: Macmillan.

Huber, E., Ragin, C., and Stephens, J. D. 1993. "Social Democracy, Christian Democracy, Constitutional Structure and the Welfare State." *American Journal of Sociology* 99 (3): 711–749.

ILO. Various Years. *The Cost of Social Security.* Geneva: ILO.

Katzenstein, P. 1985. *Small States in World Markets.* Ithaca, N.Y.: Cornell University Press.

Kemeny, J. 1981. *The Myth of Home Ownership.* London: Routledge and Kegan Paul.

———. 1992. *Housing and Social Theory.* London: Routledge and Kegan Paul.

Keohane, R. O., and Milner, H. V., eds. 1996. *Internationalization and Domestic Politics*. Cambridge: Cambridge University Press.

Kerr, C. 1960. *Industrialism and Industrial Man*. Cambridge: Harvard University Press.

Key, V. O. 1949. *Southern Politics*. New York: Alfred A. Knopf.

Larkey, P. D., Stolp, C., and Winer, M. 1981. "Theorizing About the Growth of Government: A Research Assessment." *Journal of Public Policy* 1 (2): 157–220.

Leibfried, S., and Pierson, P., eds. 1995. *European Social Policy: Between Fragmentation and Integration*. Washington, D.C.: The Brookings Institution.

Lijphart, A. 1997. "Unequal Participation: Democracy's Unresolved Dilemma." *American Political Science Review* 91: 1–14.

Lipset, S. M., and Rokkan, S. 1967. *Party Systems and Voter Alignments*. New York: The Free Press.

OECD. 1993. *OECD Health Systems*. Vol. II. Paris: OECD.

———. 1994. "New Orientations for Social Policy." *Social Policy Studies* 12. Paris: OECD.

———. 1995. *Labour Force Statistics 1973–1993*. Paris: OECD.

———. 1996a. "Ageing in OECD Countries: A Critical Policy Challenge." *Social Policy Studies* 20. Paris: OECD.

———. 1996b. *Historical Statistics 1960–1994*. Paris: OECD.

———. 1996c. *Social Expenditure Statistics of OECD Member Countries*. Provisional Version. Paris: OECD.

Overbye, E. 1994. "Convergence in Policy Outcomes: Social Security Systems in Perspective." *Journal of Public Policy* 14 (2): 147–174.

Pampel, F. C., and Williamson, J. B. 1989. *Age, Class, Politics, and the Welfare State*. Cambridge: Cambridge University Press.

Peacock, A. T., and Wiseman, J. 1961. *The Growth of Public Expenditures in the United Kingdom*. Princeton, N.J.: Princeton University Press.

Pierson, P. 1995. "Fragmented Welfare States: Federal Institutions and the Development of Social Policy." *Governance* 8 (4): 449–478.

Piven, F. F., and Cloward, R. A. 1972. *Regulating the Poor: The Functions of Public Welfare*. London: Tavistock.

Rokkan, S. 1970. *Citizens, Elections, Parties*. Oslo: Universitetsforlaget.

Rose, R. 1984. *Understanding Big Government: The Programme Approach*. London: Sage.

Schmidt, M. G. 1996a. "When Parties Matter: A Review of the Possibilities and Limits of Partisan Influence on Public Policy." *European Journal of Political Research* 30: 155–183.

———. 1996b. *Die parteipolitische Zusammensetzung von Regierungen in demokratischen Staaten (1945–1996)*. Heidelberg: Institut für Politische Wissenschaft.

Schmidt, S. 1989. "Convergence Theory, Labor Movements, and Corporatism." *Scandinavian Housing and Planning Research* 6 (2): 83–101.

Summers, R., and Heston, A. 1991. "The Penn World Table (Mark 5)." *Quarterly Journal of Economics* 106 (2): 327–368.

Van Kersbergen, K. 1995. *Social Capitalism: A Study of Christian Democracy and the Welfare State*. London: Routledge.
Wildavsky, A. 1985. "The Logic of Public Sector Growth." In *State and Market: The Politics of the Public and the Private*, ed. J-E. Lane. London: Sage.
Wilensky, H. L. 1975. *The Welfare State and Equality*. Berkeley and Los Angeles: University of California Press.
Wilensky, H. L., and Lebeaux, C. N. 1957. *Industrial Society and Social Welfare*. New York: Russell Sage Foundation.
World Bank. 1994. *Averting the Old Age Crisis*. New York: Oxford University Press.

FURTHER READING

Castles, F. G. 1998. *Comparative Public Policy: Patterns of Post-War Transformation*. Cheltenham, U.K.: Edward Elgar.
Esping-Anderson, G. 1990. *The Three Worlds of Welfare Capitalism*. Cambridge, U.K.: Polity Press.
Huber, E.R.C., Ragin, C., and Stephens, J. D. 1993. "Social Democracy, Christian Democracy, Constitutional Structure and the Welfare State." *American Journal of Sociology* 99 (3): 711–749.
Schmidt, M. G. 1996. "When Parties Matter: A Review of the Possibilities and Limits of Partisan Influence on Public Policy." *European Journal of Political Research* 30: 155–183.

11

Privatization and Commercialization in a Global Context

Ernie S. Lightman

Like some aging but still unproved wonder drug, privatization continues to be promoted as the cure-all for everything that ails the welfare state. And, like that same wonder drug, backed by the immense political power of a multinational drug company, privatization remains high on the global remedy list, notwithstanding its dubious efficacy after years of rigorous clinical testing.

In the early years, privatization was advocated on the basis of its alleged greater efficiency compared to the public sector; the ideological arguments were often subsumed within nominally positivist debate over least cost provision of quality service. More recently, however, the promotion of private sector remedies to the welfare state ills has shifted ground; ideology has come to the fore, the nominal pursuit of equality formally abandoned, and the case for privatization is now overtly normative, based on the fundamental unacceptability of state structures and service provision within a market economy.

This chapter examines this transition over time. It begins with a matter of definition and then proceeds to review the arguments surrounding privatization, focusing on the more interesting ideological issues; it looks at the forms of privatization, noting that the process can occur on both the demand and the supply sides, with the former perhaps less recognized in the literature. We consider a number of case examples of "good" and "bad" privatization and conclude by raising two critical questions: Is it *desirable* to oppose all trends toward privatization; and is it *possible* to resist, within a context of increasing globalization?

A KEY DISTINCTION

Privatization has often been viewed as a process or an approach in which "market criteria such as profit or ability to pay are used to ration or distribute benefits and services" (Walker 1984, 20). However, the concept can be broader than this, and may encompass all forms of nongovernmental decision making. "Private" in this sense simply refers to "outside government." Thus we may distinguish two discrete concepts:

- Commercialization, which connotes the introduction of for profit service provision.
- Privatization, which is more comprehensive, involving the reduction of state activity in favor of all forms of private (or nonstate) decision making. This would include for profit provision (commercialization), as well as that of NGOs, QUANGOs, agencies, communities, and even families.

Viewed in this way, government offloading of responsibility to individuals and families reflects privatization every bit as much as the sale of a public asset such as council housing or El Al.

THE REASONS TO PRIVATIZE

Though there are many arguments in favor of privatization, they can be usefully grouped under general headings. LeGrand and Robinson (1984) use four categories: efficiency, equality, liberty, and community. Johnson (1987) uses three: efficiency, choice and freedom, and equality. Today many advocates of privatization would reject equality as a relevant variable on normative grounds. (We note, of course, that any categorization is inevitably subjective to some extent.) For present purposes, we use two categories: the case for efficiency ("We can do it better outside government") and the case for ideology ("It is better done outside government").

THE CASE FOR EFFICIENCY

The efficiency argument, in principle at least, is subject to assessment and measurement: Governmental and nongovernmental modes of service delivery can be compared and the relative costs compared for a given set of outcomes. The alternative that offers the highest quality for a given cost, or the lowest cost for a given quality, is the most efficient mode of service delivery, and is therefore preferred, be it in the public or private domain.

Some of the best empirical data of this type deals with deinstitutionalization (Knapp 1992; Netten and Beecham 1993; Wright 1994) and institutional closure. However, the empirical case for privatization remains ultimately unproved. The methodological difficulties in cost–benefit (or cost-effectiveness) analysis are well documented and focus largely on the problems of output (or outcome) measurement in the human services (Smith 1996). If the generalized argument for privatized service delivery is to stand or fall on the basis of an alleged greater empirical efficiency, the issue is as yet open.

Cost reduction and minimizing public spending (without particular regard to ultimate outcome) are common goals of privatization. Selling off public assets is often described as disposing of the family jewels to pay the rent and may lead to huge profits for a fortunate few (Doron 1990; Doron and Karger 1993; Lightman and Epstein 1997). On the operating level, cost reduction through privatization usually stresses the lowering of labor costs; clearly this was a primary consideration in the Thatcher policies (Wilson 1993) and is also important in Israel today. An allied goal is that of breaking the power of large, public sector unions—a central theme in many settings including Israel. On 1 July 1996, for example, some 400,000 workers went on a one-hour warning strike "as part of (the Histadrut's) fight against the government's plans for privatization that will probably lead to mass dismissals" (Yudelman 1996; Alexander 1996; Morav, cited in Doron 1995a, 17; Rosenberg 1997). Permanent, unionized, well-paid jobs in the public sector are replaced by casual, often part-time work, typically without effective union protection (Chamberlain 1998). Abraham Doron (1994b; 1995b) has shown in some detail how a primary motivation around the new National Health Bill was based on opposition by the Likud to the power of the Histadrut. According to Kim (1994, cited in Doron 1995b), then leader of the opposition Netanyahu admitted that his party supported the new health care bill because it separated the Histadrut from the Kupat Holim Clalit, a price worth paying. While asset disposal, often at fire-sale prices, typically leads to short-term revenue enhancement, the reduction of labor costs tends to focus on decreasing public expenditure. Either of these paths—increasing revenue or decreasing costs—leads to a short-term decrease in government spending (disregarding severance payments and transitional costs). Though the cost reduction route is more ideologically compatible with the operative ideology, the sale of assets often avoids direct labor conflict and may be easier to achieve in practice.

THE CASE FOR IDEOLOGY

The more interesting argument for privatization refers to the ideological basis, a broad heading that, for present purposes, encompasses in effect everything not quantifiable. There is theoretical support for this position in both economics (supply side) (Gilder 1981) and social welfare (public burden model) (Walker 1984; Titmuss 1968). The argument is made that state spending represents a drag on private entrepreneurial activity and that it is necessary to vacate and make room for the private market. The supply side theories, and the associated Laffer curve, were popular among economists of the right during the Reagan years in America, but they ultimately proved void of any identifiable empirical basis. "Public burden" is an older concept, deeply rooted in traditional American antipathy to active government, but it is only a descriptive label without analytic content. Notwithstanding these theories, there was and is no evidence to suggest the public sector is inherently more or less productive or efficient than the private market. Reducing the former to make room for the latter does not automatically eliminate a drag in favor of a dynamo.

Central to the ideological case for privatization is the argument for freedom, choice, and individual liberty. There is little to be added to this debate, except to reiterate the obvious distinction between active and passive freedom, freedom from interference (which is the concern of the proponents) as distinct from the freedom to exercise choice (which requires resources). We are clearly all free to stay at the King David Hotel, but some of us are freer to do so than others. And for those without resources, we can, in consolation, recall Janis Joplin's famous observation that "Freedom is just another word, For nothing left to lose."

In exploring the drive to privatization in Israel, Abraham Doron (1990; Doron and Karger 1993) places much emphasis on the economic interests of the service providers and the potential benefits for "the new conservative Israeli middle class elites" (Doron 1994b, 199) "Freedom" means the opportunity to get rich off the spoils of privatization (see Lightman and Epstein 1997) while "choice" leads to the maintenance and enhancement of existing patterns of class division (Doron 1990) and the creation of "private welfare states . . . for selected, stronger and better off groups of the working population" (Doron 1990, 16; see also De la Roca 1997). The result, in Doron's words, has been the "marginalisation" of the welfare state (Doron 1994c). And in this process, it is important for outsiders to appreciate that there has been no significant difference between Labour and the Likud (Alexander 1996).

The final major consideration is that of accountability, the presumption that the private market will place a greater onus on service suppliers to ensure consumer satisfaction, compared to state provision. The ability of the consumer to go elsewhere ostensibly guarantees effort and activity by the provider so as to retain purchaser loyalty.

MARKET FAILURE

What is important to note is that *all* these alleged benefits of privatization are implicitly based on the emergence of a competitive market: that is, a market is *assumed*, rather than *assured*. On the supply side, it is assumed there will be a variety of suppliers, and an absence of monopoly or monopsony; hence, there will be competition (to replace a public monopoly with a private monopoly may still be rationalized in terms of promised cost reduction or the breaking of a public sector union, but on its own, it clearly does not enhance choice or create a competitive market). On the demand side, it is assumed that sovereign consumers will have information–mobility–access and usually adequate resources. These premises of a competitive market are often overlooked in this debate, because, frankly, they are rarely upheld (Johnson 1987; Esping-Andersen 1996).

There are two traditional responses to market failure. The first of these is to go outside the market to utilize an alternative method to meet needs and allocate resources. This was, in effect, the reasoning that led to state provision of benefits in the first place—a recognition that the market could not or did not lead to socially equitable outcomes. The second response to market failure is to try and make the market work better—to ensure, for example, that there are competing suppliers in the marketplace so as to attain greater efficiency, accountability, and the normative goals of choice; or, on the demand side, to assist consumers in making informed choices and to ensure they have the resources to act on their preferences. Doron and Karger (1993) note the traditional culture in Israel which, as a matter of course, denies the public access to all forms of government information without reason or justification. They suggest that this culture, which would lead to a weak regulatory environment, creates the central dangers in implementing privatization in Israel (for an interesting Canadian example in this area, see Lightman and Aviram 1998).

Privatization implies a rejection of the first avenue which would entail a return (or embrace) of nonmarket systems of allocation. The challenge facing the privatizers, then, is to provide resources and supports sufficient to approximate a functioning market. In market terms, it would not, for example, be acceptable to privatize child care or accommodation for seniors without ensuring that the consumers (particularly those with greater needs) have information, access, and resources to make appropriate decisions in the marketplace. One must also ensure that the market responds appropriately by making available the necessary services.

THE FORMS OF PRIVATIZATION

Most of the literature focuses on privatization as a supply side phenomenon, taking three forms: reductions in state provision; reductions in state subsidy; and reductions in state regulation (LeGrand and Robinson 1984). The first two involve rationing (Doron 1983) and herald a direct decline in services delivered by the state, while the third leads to an increase in nonstate provision through a lowering of the barriers to entry.

The alternative perspective on privatization, viewing it as a demand side process, involves offloading of government decision making to a variety of possible recipients: to individual consumers; to the voluntary sector–agencies–charities; to local communities; to families or friends; or to private commercial interests such as corporations and/or unions. Any of these groups can be given the responsibility (either on their own behalf or on behalf of consumers) to make decisions which were previously reached on collective basis through the agency of the state. Ultimate accountability (the regulatory authority) can either remain with the state, can simply be ignored, or can be formally lodged with one of the privatized interests.

ON THE SUPPLY SIDE

Undoubtedly the most insidious form of privatization—and that showing the greatest growth potential in Canada today, and perhaps Israel tomorrow—is supply-side commercialization, American-style (Lightman, Freiler, and Gandy 1990).

The Thatcher approach, using internal markets and quasi-markets has not been followed in Canada; traces can be found, however, in the new Israeli health bill (see the next section in this chapter). The appeal of privatization to government is both ideological (in that it reduces that size of the public sector) and operational (assuming that provider profit can be generated from future cost savings).

Esping-Andersen notes the privatization of social security—specifically pensions—involves the replacement of public state-assured income in old age with private, often employer-run pension entitlements. A public monopoly is, in effect, replaced with a private monopoly, as vesting requirements inhibit labor mobility, and no competitive market is created. Furthermore, the use of private pensions, such as American IRAs, determine postretirement income on the basis of prior productivity and earnings; the element of social solidarity and the public commitment to adequacy which are hallmarks of many public pensions are absent. The market focuses on the individual rather than the group and makes no apologies for this. But the alleged benefits of consumer sovereignty—choice, autonomy, alternatives—may be entirely absent (in the case of company-provided pensions or other benefits tied to a specific job) or partially absent (in the case of IRAs, being denied to those without the available discretionary income). In other cases, the results of privatization may be more benign: responsibility for pensions can be devolved to a bilateral union–management committee, which may permit a better meeting of local needs—assuming there is rough parity of bargaining power between the parties; that there is no problem of excluded groups; and that there is no broader public interest involved.

In Ontario, an American multinational firm with a dubious history was recently hired, without public tender, to open a youth boot camp. Unfortunately, the official opening had to be canceled when the kids hot-wired a car and drove away before the minister's arrival. Andersen Consulting, a worldwide behemoth, has been contracted to clean up the provincial welfare system with a contract that has not been made public. For the first time ever, the Ontario government is putting out to commercial tender (including to foreign multinationals) the authority to write a series of new high school textbooks, rather than doing this work in-house as in the past. What is occurring in all these cases is that core central functions of the welfare state are being assigned to commercial interests whose responsibilities include a fiduciary obligation to shareholders and possibly a service link to some bureaucracy—but nothing to the ultimate consumers. The accountability of the political process is replaced by the accountability of the stock exchange. Changes of the sort described, with the import of traditional American commercialized values into what is left of the Canadian welfare state, will have a profound and fundamental impact on the society. Once the responsibilities have been devolved, it will be difficult, if not impossible in practice, to ever recover them to the public sector.

IN ISRAEL

Several years ago, Doron and Karger (1993) discussed the inevitability of American-style privatization being imported into Israel. It is not surprising that we now witness its acceleration, given the simple-minded appeal of the approach and the American affinities of the prime minister and his key advisors. Before his election, Netanyahu promised to privatize fifty out of some 160 government-owned companies over four years (Harris and Makovsky 1996). A listing of the new Likud government's guidelines in June 1996 stated, "To increase revenue, the government will significantly expand privatisation" (Government of Israel Press Office 1996).

Most activity to date has been outside the social services and has involved the sale of state assets such as El Al and the banks, or the end of monopolies such as Egged in certain areas. In fact, the entire 1997 budget deficit of NIS 8.1 billion was covered by the proceeds from privatization, which amounted to NIS 8.5 billion; of this total, the sale of banks alone generated NIS 7.5 billion (*Ha'aretz*, 8 January 1997). To illustrate how little has been done in the area of deregulation, Netanyahu has pointed out there is as yet no Hebrew term to describe the concept (Harris and Makovsky 1996). As well, the private sector has become involved in the development of infrastructure such as railways and the Trans-Israel Highway, typically on a BOT (Build–Operate–Transfer) basis (Harris 1997). Under BOT, a private company or consortium secures the financing to construct a public infrastructure project. The developer then owns, maintains, and manages the facility for a concessionary period and recoups the investment through charges or tolls. At the end of this period, ownership and operation are transferred to the government or state authority. Last year there was concern that the stock of public housing might be sold to friends of the Likud in the for profit sector, resulting in the dehousing of some 200,000 low-income individuals (Lightman and Epstein 1997). Cutbacks in subsidies to state schools to fund the *yeshivot* have made a joke of "free" public education, as parents by 1993 were directly paying 24 percent of the total national expenditure on education: "[This] creeping privatisation of . . . education . . . more than in any other social service system . . . marks the ideological contest over the nature of Israeli society in future" (Doron 1994c, 13).

In the health area, the state comptroller in 1985 explicitly stated that the financial interests of private owners of long-term care facilities were "clearly incompatible with the interests of elderly and sick clients" (cited in Doron and Karger 1993, 93; see also De la Roca 1997). The new health care law—a long time coming (Doron

1980)—was actively promoted as increasing the role of private medicine (Doron 1994b; 1995a; 1995b). Specific measures included user fees, private supplementary insurance, a move toward preferred access in hospitals for "clubs of rich supporters" (Doron 1995a), more reliance on private practice, and contracting out—all advocated by the economists in the Bank of Israel and the Treasury (Doron 1994b; 1995a; 1995b) and endorsed by politicians in both major parties. A major point of debate for the 1998 state budget was the failure to adequately fund the new Kupat Holim, which led to creaming of the less costly cases and insufficient coverage for people with cancer, HIV–AIDS, and other high cost illnesses. Currently, many persons with anorexia—often young women—are denied access to eating-disorder clinics (where the cost is high) and shifted instead to the mental hospitals (where there is no cost to the Kupat Holim) (Gross 1998).

Consider Abraham Doron's angry words of betrayal at this American-style privatization in Israel (Doron and Karger 1993):

In contrast [to the United States] the privatization of Israel's social services symbolises a radical departure from its collectivist roots of government action and responsibility. . . . In effect it is a repudiation of almost 50 years of a collectivist ideology of government responsibility and a rewriting of the social contract that has bound Israeli society together since before the period of Independence.

There is a consequence of these privatization activities in Israel that directly affects the broader political arena as well: When the state does not provide necessary services such as child care, school lunches, health care, or even basic education, it falls to other nongovernmental bodies to take up the slack. Undoubtedly much of the electoral strength of the ultraorthodox party Shas flows directly from its role as a provider of these very social services (Goodman 1997). Gesher and Shas compete, in part, for the same constituency of poor Sephardim, relatively few of whom are deeply religiously observant. The greater success of Shas, in a context where there might be a more natural affinity between secular voters and Gesher, can be attributable in part to Shas's extensive network of social services, nurseries, and educational institutions. And given the considerable political capital which Shas derives from the provision of these services, it is not surprising that Gesher calls for the extension of state programs (as a way to undercut Shas), while Shas tacitly opposes such moves, in order to protect its political base.

Within the Arab community, a similar process occurs: the Moslem Brotherhood within the Green Line and Hamas in the West

Bank and Gaza also exert a tremendous pull on the population because they provide an array of social and health services not otherwise available to the poor in the community (Abu 1997).

The failure of the state, both Israeli and the Palestinian Authority, to provide universally accessible, affordable, and quality services leaves a gap, which the middle class can fill by private purchase from the commercial sector. But for the poor, the unmet needs are filled by ethnically and community-based organizations that exact a price as part of much wider political struggles and debates with unpredictable longer-term consequences.

ON THE DEMAND SIDE

On the demand side, the key to privatization is that government vacates, abdicates, or delegates decision-making authority to some "other" nongovernmental body which is authorized to make decisions on behalf of the consumer. The problem is that this other decision maker may not be willing, capable, or suitable to serve as a proxy. Consider, for example, the deinstitutionalization of psychiatric patients: Typically, we shut beds, or entire buildings, and return the individuals to the community, giving them inadequate financial support, and modest or no human support. With a firm handshake, we wish them well as definitionally competent consumers in a market economy. If we care at all about what happens subsequently, we assume that in place of government responsibility, someone else (such as family) will somehow appear to save the day. Yet, the family may not exist or cannot be found; the family may not be willing to assume the responsibilities; the family may not be able (financially or socially) to assume the responsibilities; or the consumer may not want the family to be involved.

This privatization to the family (and within the family as well) has been much discussed within the feminist literature. Eichler (1997) addresses the obvious gender implications of what she describes as the "individual responsibility model" of the family, which results in the privatization of parenting. Freiler and Cerny (1998) note that gender equality will never be achieved as long as caring for dependent family members continues to be seen as a strictly private matter.

Over thirty years ago, Richard Titmuss (1968) presented his famous list of reasons why a market should not prevail in health care, and most of these had to do with uncertainty and unpredictability for the future along with limited competence for the consumer. His solution, of course, was to keep health care outside market parameters and to provide services on the basis of need.

Such reliance on "experts" has been criticized as excessive (Reisman 1977); yet, today, we find ourselves in the same situation. The internal markets for health care found in the Thatcher reforms and copied to some extent in the new Israeli health law replace decision making by the state (or its agent) with the private authority of the managed caregiver. The autonomy of consumers and attempts to enhance their competence in decision making seem to be lost. Privatization does not appear to involve a transfer of authority from the state to the individual (as market principles would dictate), but instead a shift from one proxy to another, as we substitute private (profit or not for profit) authority for that of the state. Individual well being, of course, will depend on the benevolence, as well as the competence, of the new privatized decision makers, but in the aggregate the net welfare gain is hard to observe.

There are cases where privatized decision making seems to work. Perhaps the best example involves individualized funding for persons with disabilities, sometimes referred to as "independent living." In these cases, which are most commonly used for people with physical disabilities, decision-making authority is transferred from the state, or from a case manager, to the individuals themselves. A budget based on estimated needs is drawn up with the active involvement of the consumer, and then the lump sum, either in cash or in voucher form, is given to the individual who is free to determine his or her own wishes and priorities. In place of a worker from an agency, consumers hire their own staff; rather than state–client dependence, there exists a formalized employer–employee relationship, which may even include withholding of income tax and payment of benefits.

This approach is highly praised by virtually all those who come in contact with it; it represents an exciting positive development in the area of privatization. Decision-making authority is transferred from one proxy (the state), not to another proxy (a case manager), but rather devolved all the way to the consumer. Given adequate supports, there is no reason in principle why this model could not be extended to other vulnerable groups, including seniors and persons with psychiatric or developmental disabilities (Lightman and Aviram 1998).

The only obstacle is on the supply side where the market may not respond. While the consumer may have the financial capacity to buy services, there is no guarantee the private sector will necessarily offer them for sale. In practice, some state provision of service (or other assurance of service availability) may be needed, but this should not hinder the transference of decision-making authority from the state (case manager) to the consumers themselves. The preference for independent living compared to managed care, as alternate forms of privatized service delivery, could not be more clear.

SOME THOUGHTS FOR THE FUTURE

Should Privatization Be Reversed?

The basic premise with which most welfare advocates have traditionally approached the issue of privatization is that it is generally a bad thing: It introduces the form of the market, though not usually the substance; and it deals inadequately with externalities and replaces the collective meeting of needs with the individual satisfaction of wants (for those with sufficient resources).

Yet this chapter has suggested that privatization is in reality a more complex concept. Donnison (1984) talked of the "progressive potential" of privatization. To Esping-Andersen (1996, 26), it is a response "to the more differentiated and individualistic demands of post-industrial society." In some cases, privatization on the demand side may replace an insensitive state bureaucracy with a caring or responsive not for profit agency or community. Independent living, as we have seen, has adherents and few detractors.

But privatized demand does not create its own supply: The sale of public housing and its replacement with cash allowances does not ensure adequate—or even inadequate—housing in a tight market, where cash infusions may simply translate into higher rental costs with no assurance of affordability. Child care payments to parents do nothing to ensure the availability of adequate numbers of quality places in regulated centres. Even in the independent living models, the authority to decide one's own needs does not mean the desired services will necessarily be available.

We have also seen, however, that commercialization typically has little to commend it: Most commonly, it reflects an abdication of collective responsibility in favor of profits for large corporations without effective accountability. We receive the form of the market without the content.

CAN PRIVATIZATION BE REVERSED?

The final issue is whether it is possible to delay or reverse current trends toward privatization. At a microlevel, it is, of course, easy to destroy and hard to build. The disposal of state assets (physical capital) is hard to reverse, as the tax revenues necessary to build new welfare state structures are not readily forthcoming. The political limits of taxation are a reality. Human capital is perhaps more easy to replace, and is probably less demanding of tax revenues, but the time lags involved for planning, training, and delivery can be substantial.

It is at a macrolevel within a global context, however, that the picture is even more gloomy (Yergin and Stanislaw 1998). Though international treaties and free trade agreements are generally viewed with favor in Israel and within the left in Europe, there is a different perspective in Canada. The Free Trade Agreement between Canada and the United States, for example, subsequently expanded to NAFTA, the North American Free Trade Agreement, and will blossom next into the Free Trade Area of the Americas (FTAA) (Diebel 1998). It assigns primacy to the rights of private capital and private property and severely limits the ability of a so-called sovereign state to act on behalf of its residents. There are clauses in NAFTA that would prevent Canada from introducing a national Medicare plan if it did not already have one. Such an initiative would be seen as expropriating the business rights of private American health providers and massive compensation (for future profits foregone) would have to be paid. Were attempts made to introduce a national dental care, home care, or pharmacare (drug) plan, the American multinationals might well have a legal claim against the Canadian government.

Going a step further, consider the Multinational Agreement on Investment (MAI), an initiative of the twenty-nine-member OECD (Rowan 1998). The ideas embedded in this treaty are much the same as in NAFTA, giving corporations the right to sue governments for restricting their private, for profit investment opportunities. This agreement has now been delayed and shifted to the World Trade Organization (WTO), hopefully never to reappear.

Regardless of the MAI, the clear and powerful worldwide trend, promoted by the World Bank, the IMF, and their allies on Wall Street, is toward a hegemony of the private market. After meeting with Netanyahu in December 1997, U.S. Under-Secretary of State for Economic Affairs Stuart Eizenstat complimented the prime minister on his privatization plan, saying it was the most far-reaching in Israeli history (*Ha'Aretz*, 18 December 1997). These trends may involve American-based multinational corporations as direct providers of welfare state services, or it may result from global treaties and agreements which limit the rights of sovereign governments. In either case, what we are witnessing is an abdication of control by the state in favor of multinational corporations and the rights of private property. And as McQuaig (1998) has argued, we are not even allowed to question: "It's not just that we're powerless to stop being pushed over the edge of the cliff in the new global world order. But to even try to prevent ourselves from being pushed over the cliff is a sign of regressive thinking." Within such a context, it would certainly be difficult to reverse the seemingly inexorable trend toward private, for profit delivery of services on any significant scale. But commercialization clearly is only one of the undesirable outcomes of this process. Far more serious in the long run, I fear, is the widespread loss of democratic control in the face of market globalization.

REFERENCES

Abu, T. K. 1997. "From Cradle to Grave." *Jerusalem Report*, 4 September.

Alexander, E. 1996. "Dumping the Welfare State." *Challenge—A Jerusalem Magazine on the Israeli–Palestinian Conflict* (September–October).

Chamberlain, A. 1998. "Home Care Nurses Strike for Contract with Private Firm." *Toronto Star*, 21 January.

De la Roca, J. 1997. "Retiring in Style at Affordable Prices: Special Advertising Supplement." *Jerusalem Post*, 21 April.

Diebel, L. 1998. "Mammoth Trade Zone Proposed." *Toronto Star*, 20 April.

Donnison, D. 1984. "The Progressive Potential of Privatization." In *Privatization and the Welfare State*, ed. J. Le Grand and R. Robinson. London: Allen and Unwin.

Doron, A. 1980. "The Ailing Health Services." *The Jerusalem Quarterly* 14 (Winter).

———. 1983. "The Welfare State: Issues of Rationing and Allocation of Resources." In *Evaluating the Welfare State: Social and Political Perspectives*. New York: Academic Press.

———. 1990. *Alternative Futures for Social Security*. Jerusalem: Hebrew University. Unpublished.

———. 1994a. "The Effectiveness of the Beveridge Model at Different Stages of Socio-Economic Development: The Israeli Experience." in *Beveridge and Social Security: An International Retrospective*, ed. J. Hills, J. Ditch, and H. Glennerster. Oxford: Oxford University Press.

———. 1994b. "The Health Services in Israel: The Prospect of the 1990s." *Social Security* (Israel; special English edition) 3 (August): 9–24.

———. 1994c. *Marginalization of the Welfare State: The Case of Israel.* Jerusalem: Hebrew University. Unpublished.

———. 1995a. "Health Care in Israel: The Uncertain Future." Paper presented at the International Conference on Social Work and Health, Jerusalem.

———. 1995b. "Health Care Systems in Transition: The Israeli Experience." Paper prepared for the Conference on Comparative Research on Welfare State Reform, University of Pavia, Italy, 14–17 September.

Doron, A., and Karger, J. H. 1993. "The Privatization of Social Services in Israel and its Effects on Israeli Society." *Scandinavian Journal of Social Welfare* 2: 88–95.

Eichler, M. 1997. *Family Shifts: Families, Policies and Gender Equality.* Toronto: Oxford University Press.

Esping-Andersen, G. 1996. *Welfare States in Transition: National Adaptations in Global Economics.* London: Sage.

Freiler, C., and Cerny, J. 1998. *Benefiting Canada's Children: Perspectives on Gender and Social Responsibility.* Ottawa: Status of Women Canada.

Gilder, G. 1981. *Wealth and Poverty.* New York: Basic Books.

Goodman, H. 1997. "Masters at Their Game." *Jerusalem Report,* 13 November.

Government of Israel, Government Press Office. 1996. *The New Government's Guidelines.* Jerusalem: Government Press.

Gross, N. 1998. "Anorexia Patients Suffer as Health Funds Try to Cut Costs." *Jerusalem Report,* 30 April.

Harris, D. 1997. "Jerusalem Rail Tender to Be Issued in 1998." *Jerusalem Post,* 5 December.

Harris, D., and Makovsky, D. 1996. "Cabinet Approves NIS 4.9 Billion Budget Cut." *Jerusalem Post,* 3 July.

Johnson, N. 1987. *The Welfare State in Transition.* Brighton: Wheatsheaf.

Knapp, M. 1992. *Care in the Community: Challenge and Demonstration.* Canterbury: University of Kent, PSSRU.

LeGrand, J., and Robinson, R. 1984. *Privatisation and the Welfare* State. London: Allen and Unwin.

Lightman, E., and Aviram, U. 1998. "Too Much; Too Late: The Advocacy Act in Ontario." Unpublished paper.

Lightman, E., Freiler, C., and Gandy, J. 1990. "A Transatlantic View: Privatisation, Canadian-Style." In *Privatisation,* ed. R. Parry. London: Jessica Kingsley.

Lightman, E., and Epstein, B. 1997. "See the Poor Get Poorer." *Jerusalem Post,* 1 June.

McQuaig, L. 1998. *The Cult of Impotence: Selling the Myth of Powerlessness in the Global Economy.* Toronto: Penguin Canada.

Netten, A., and Beecahm, J. 1993. *Costing Community Care.* Canterbury: University of Kent: PSSRU.

Reisman, D. 1977. *Richard Titmuss: Welfare and Society.* London: Heinemann.

Rosenberg, D. 1997. "Labor under an Illusion." *Jerusalem Report,* 30 October.

Rowan, D. 1998. "Meet the New World Government." *The Guardian,* 13 February.

Smith, P., ed. 1996. *Measuring Outcome in the Public Sector.* London: Taylor and Francis.

Titmuss, R. 1968. *Commitment to Welfare* (Ch. 12). London: Allen and Unwin.

Walker, A. 1984. "The Political Economy of Privatisation." In *Privatisation and the Welfare State,* ed. J. LeGrand and R. Robinson. London: Allen and Unwin.

Wilson, J. 1993. "Privatisation." In *Public Services and the 1990's,* ed. J. Wilson and P. Head. Sevenoaks, Kent: Hodder and Stoughton.

Wright, K. 1994. *Evaluating Community Care*. Buckingham: Open University Press.

Yergin, D., and Stanislaw, J. 1998. *The Commanding Heights: The Battle between Government and the Marketplace That Is Remaking the Modern World*. New York: Simon and Schuster.

Yudelman, M. 1996. "400,000 to Strike in Protest of Government's Economic Proposals." *Jerusalem Post*, 1 July.

FURTHER READING

Broad, D., and Wayne, A., eds. 1999. *Citizens or Consumers? Social Policy in a Market Economy*. Halifax, Canada: Fernwood.

Eichler, M. 1997. *Family Shifts: Families, Policies and Gender Equality*. Toronto: Oxford University Press.

Esping-Anderson, G. 1996. *Welfare States in Transition: National Adaptations in Global Economics*. London: Sage.

McQuaig, L. 1998. *The Cult of Impotence: Selling the Myth of Powerlessness in the Global Economy*. Toronto: Penguin Canada.

Mullaly, B. 1997. *Structural Social Work*. Toronto: Oxford University Press.

Yergin, D., and Stanislaw, J. 1998. *The Commanding Heights: The Battle between Government and the Marketplace That Is Remaking the Modern World*. New York: Simon and Schuster.

12

Dominance, Contest, and Reframing

Martin Rein

One subject that has fascinated scholars of comparative social policy is how to classify and compare welfare state policies of different countries.[1] Most efforts to derive a typology of types, regimes, or schemes are based on cross-sectional comparisons at a point in time. The patterns that emerge from such an analysis are, by their nature, static and presume that there is stability over time. Not surprisingly, there has been a rather large body of literature that has criticized these various efforts at developing a typology of social policy across countries. This criticism has tended to identify an important elision, that is, a significant dimension that has not been taken into account, such as gender. Critics have in turn responded by developing a new classification that is based on the omitted variable. A good example is the scheme to take account of recent feminist debate, classifying countries by the extent to which they follow a strong, moderate, or weak male breadwinner model.

But this is not sufficient to address what I believe is the fundamental weakness of the regime approach to comparative social policy. The weakness is that these efforts are based on a static, cross-sectional snapshot of prevailing policies. Such an approach requires the acceptance of an implicit assumption about the underlying nature of policy making, namely that policies are stable over time and that countries can unambiguously be assigned to one type. I know that these assumptions are false. The approach I want to pursue is based on different premises: The essential characteristic of social policy is that it changes over time, that actual social policies are both path dependent and the result of current competing ideological, social, and political forces, and not really "intellectually and pragmatically unified packages of programs and policies, values and institutions" (Goodin, Headey, Muffels, and Driven 1999, 6).

As a first step in the development of a framework focused on complexity, evolution, and the process of change, I propose to look at a group that is a focus of current public policy controversy, that of lone mothers, and to try to identify the way in which the public response to this group has been framed and reframed over time. I focus on recent challenge and reframing of policies and consider how organized groups or social movements challenge the taken-for-granted consensus on which the frame rests. Examples of current policy change in the United States illustrate the process. Finally, I propose a general interpretation of how internal and external change provide windows of opportunity to challenge dominant frames. The discussion of the early French experience in dealing with lone parents draws primarily on the excellent work of Nadine Lefaucheur (for the most recent English version of her work see Lefaucheur 1998; Lefaucheur and Rein 1999).

DOMINANCE, CONTEST, AND REFRAMING

While welfare and economic dependency is on center stage in the American political debate today, other frames with respect to single mothers and illegitimacy have not vanished altogether; they have only become subordinate. In the American context it seems clear that the liberal emphasis on antipoverty and antiinequality frames and political disenfranchisement as a measure of proper citizenship have been substantially weakened and that public policy legislation has gravitated toward frames which focus on demarriage, antidependency, and antiabsent father. What has been reframed is the priorities of how to socially construct the issues of lone mothering. What has remained relatively stable is the repertoire of choice within the paradigm and frames, a repertoire which highlights continuities and discontinuities with the past.

For example, many countries have historically struggled with how to deal with infanticide. The French solution followed a pattern adopted in many Catholic countries of permitting the mother to more or less secretly surrender the unwanted child to the hospital (and the church in the early middle ages), sometimes through a device known as *Le Tour* (or "the wheel"). This practice fell into disrepute at the end of the nineteenth century, when the size of institutional population became a major concern, since many of these children died because of the difficulty of finding wet nurses to feed them. But in 1993, a modern version of the policy of permitting mothers to anonymously surrender children was reinforced in France (where it had been introduced in the Family Law of 1938 to 1941), when the parliament passed a civil code legislature permitting the mothers who are about to give birth not to tell their name or to ask their identity being kept secret (this practice is known as *l'accouchement sous X*). This legislation made it impossible for a grown child to identify the mother later in life, but it preserved the anonymity of the mother. There is now a major debate about how to resolve this dilemma. There are surprisingly many sponsors of this frame, such as feminist groups who stress women's rights to anonymity; adoption agencies and adoptive family associations also have an obvious stake in protecting their interests. The result is a political struggle of the process of reframing both within a frame and shifting across frames. And it is this interesting puzzle I want to explore in this chapter.

As a first step in elaborating these ideas, I need first to clarify what I mean by hegemonic dominance, frame contest, and reframing, including the difference between changes within a frame (frame alignment) and changes across frames (frame shifting). These definitions set the stage for the development of my views about the nature of the claiming process, which is essential to understanding the dynamics of policy change.

FRAME DOMINANCE

I start with the distinction between dominance and hegemony. A paradigm can be dominant in that it is normatively secure as the accepted course of action to be pursued. Hegemony implies that the dominant position of the paradigm is maintained, without being engaged in a contest for dominance with other competing paradigms. Christian morality, from the twelfth to the early part of the eighteenth century, was the dominant and hegemonic approach for dealing with illegitimacy in most Catholic countries. There was virtually no important and successful challenge to the Christian paradigm. The Church was the important social institution with the power to implement its interpretation of Christian morality and to impose its rules and norms on the state and the local communities. By contrast, a paradigm can retain a position of dominance even though its hegemonic position is constantly being challenged. The model of medical health care policy in the United States and other countries offers a good example. The medical profession, like the clergy, enjoyed both a dominant and hegemonic position for long periods of time, but in recent years, once cost entered the equation, its hegemonic position as the only profession providing relevant professional values was contested. With health expenditures in the United States accounting for more than 14 percent of the GDP, financial managers are seeking to undermine the hegemonic position of the doctor. The outcome of the contest is still evolving. It is important therefore to distinguish between dominance and hegemony.

By elaborating the meaning of *dominance*, we find that during certain historic periods, the policy environment can be relatively quiet and settled, with little overt evidence of turbulence, challenge, and controversy. This is an era of policy dominance. The essential characteristic of a period of dominance is described by Habermas, when, in a somewhat different context , he introduced the idea of a "normatively secure" discourse. This idea involves forms of action which "are coordinated on the basis of a conventional, pre-reflective, taken-for-granted consensus about values and ends, . . . rooted in the pre-critical internalization of socialization and cultural tradition" (quoted in Frazer 1997, 131). When a paradigm has the standing of being normatively secure, its assumptions are simply assumed to be the natural, correct, self-evident, and taken-for-granted ways to deal with a social problem. In the case of illegitimacy, the repertoire of available choice has been narrowed to a particular collective choice which is accepted as the morally correct response, not open for negotiation. There is no critical discourse on alternatives. Of course, this does not negate the existence of the repertoire of other choices, only that in some historic settings the full repertoire is not open for discussion.

To understand the evolution of the institutions on which historically dominant frames or paradigms are found, MacIntyre (1984, 266) points out that one needs to locate these frames in a specific historic setting or context. A setting has a history, a history within which the histories of the specific institutions, professional practice, and roles of individual agents have to be situated. Without introducing the idea of a broader setting and its change, the history of the policy frames and its changes cannot be understood. Accepting this line of reasoning, we can agree that dominance and hegemony depend on the relative stability of the setting in which the policy institutions exist. Of course, it is not always easy to separate the setting from the institutional response or to understand what aspects of the setting are important.

Consider for example the era of Christian Angelism. The term was developed by Nadine Lefaucheur (1998) in her historic analysis of the evolution of policy paradigm in Catholic countries during the seventeenth century and later "when the Church in partnership with the State greatly extended its control over sexuality and reproduction in Catholic Europe and when the Church in partnership with the State established a thorough network of social control, designed to enforce its surveillance over pregnant, unwed women and the illegitimate children they bore." The practice of social control continued during the eighteenth and nineteenth centuries, and Kertzer's (1983, 16–22, 37) research tried to describe and explain why and how this practice was stable and why it changed. He notes that on the one hand, "a sizeable minority of all women gave birth to an illegitimate child. [But] there were tremendous differences in the prevalence of illegitimacy within countries, as is evident in France." The size of the caseload of bastard children in the institution known as *Le Tour* and the cost of the care to the community for maintaining this program can be interpreted both as the response to the setting but also as a cause for the shift in the setting. Disentangling the direction of causality is not self-evident. The point I want to make here, however, is much simpler—policy choices are both context dependent and historically contingent. If we accept this assumption, then we would anticipate that dramatic shifts in the economic, political, cultural, and religious context would be accompanied by equally dramatic changes in the direction of policy, after some reasonable time lag. It also follows that when we observe continuity in the political choices accepted by society, we can reasonably assume a fair measure of stability both in the setting and the dominance of the prevailing policy frame.

FRAME CONTEST

A contest can intuitively be contrasted with dominance, because it implies that, instead of finding a normatively secure, taken-for-granted set of paradigms, one encounters a contested terrain. But the concept of a contest needs to be further unraveled into three closely linked, but separate components: controversy, challenge, and contest.

A *controversy* can erupt when there is a sense that something is wrong and needs to be fixed, but when there is no clear name for the phenomenon and an even less clear idea about how to rectify the troubling situation. Betty Friedan graphically described the process in the *Feminine Mystique*, when she explained that she knew something was wrong about the treatment of women in society, but she struggled for a long time before she could name the trouble on which modern feminism is based. So, "naming" is central for an understanding of what is at issue at that stage in a controversy when the issues have not yet crystalized.

A *challenge* involves a process of mobilizing resources into a strategy of action, which in turn implies a reasonably coherent approach in framing what the controversy is about and how best to react and what is the worst evil that needs to be avoided. To mount a challenge against a dominant frame requires that there also be challengers who can mobilize resources. Of course, the entry of challengers does not insure that the contest will be successful. An empirical example of a lost contest about demarriage is discussed to illustrate the idea of a challenge.

Who are the challengers that sponsor competing frames? In the modern evolution of social policy about lone mothers, social scientists and professionals have all played important roles as sponsors of competing frames. For a historic example, consider Lefaucheur's analysis of the role that political economists have played in the transition from the concern about Christian morality to the concern about pauperism, and the role that clinicians, policy intellectuals, and policy entrepreneurs played in the emergence of the "healthy and proper citizens" frames. These experts make a claim for scientific knowledge, but the nature of the policy paradigms pose moral questions about how to care for the children in the absence of both parents. To signal the underlying moral debate, I have followed the work of Nadine Lefaucheur (1998) who interpreted the historic paradigms she studied in strong normative terms, using the terminology of worse and lesser evils. In an earlier work on controversy, reflection, and reframing (Schon and Rein 1994), we emphasized that reframing could usefully be conceptualized as a dialectic process, but I want now to argue that the dialectic actually rests on a much earlier tradition, which is cast in terms of good and evil. Hanna Arendt makes this point very eloquently, when, in a discussion of power and violence, she observes,

Hegel's and Marx's greater trust in the dialectical "power of negation," by virtue of which opposites do not destroy but smoothly develop into each other because contradictions promote and do not paralyze development, rests on a much older philosophical prejudice: that evil is no more than a privative *modus* of the good, than good can come out of evil; that, in short, evil is but a temporary manifestation of a still hidden good. (1986, 71)

Of course, much of the modern discourse about the justification of competing frames is cast more neutrally, in terms of scientific knowledge. But a discussion of the sponsors of frames posed as a central issue in scientific policy analysis tends to obscure to the competing and complementary roles of both knowledge and morality in debates about the reframing of policy toward single mothers.

REFRAMING

Viewed substantively, a contest arises when there is a controversy about how to reframe the balance of choices in the limited repertoire of feasible responses to the condition of single mothers. Sponsors of competing frames are the active agents in the process of reframing. To launch a successful challenge, challengers must try to promote coalitions among the active agents, who represent such varied groups as social movements, bureaucrats, politicians, the general public, social scientists, intellectuals, and professionals. The media plays an important, perhaps critical role as intermediary between the gallery of the public acting as observers of the contest and the key players who sponsor competing frames. In practice, the contest is worked out in specific forum, such as the legal, the legislative, the academic, and the professional. Each forum has its own rules about what is appropriate in terms of discourse and decision.

Further differentiating the concept of reframing is needed. Of course, challengers do not necessarily want to resolve a controversy. In the case of symbolic contests, challengers may want to keep the contest alive without resolution, since when deeply held norms are at stake, they are doubtful that a successful coalition supporting reframing is possible. It can also be the case that challengers may not have the intention of threatening the dominance of the paradigm at all. What they hope to accomplish is an internal change within the paradigm.

I propose a vocabulary to distinguish two types of reframing: frame shifting and frame alignment. The former involves shifting the definition of what is taken to be the supremely worse evil that the paradigm is trying to eliminate. Frame shifting involves a fundamental readjustment of what is essential to the paradigm, by trying pragmatically to "hitch on" to important changes that have occurred in the context. By contrast, frame alignment seeks to modify the definition of what is the lesser evil, in order to assure that the redefinition of the worse evil can realistically be reduced or eliminated.

Recent experience in the United States helps to illustrate this point. The shift in welfare has dramatically increased support for low income workers and withdrawn support for unrestricted, cash grants to lone mothers in need. The shift from need-based programs to work-conditioned benefits represents an important example of the reframing of welfare policy. Earlier welfare reform efforts such as the introduction of social services, training, or financial incentives are examples of frame alignment since the innovations did not challenge the fundamental premise on which the policy was based.

A close examination of administrative practice should reveal important changes in practice, leading to a process of accommodation or "frame alignment," defined as a change in practice, not in response to changes in the context or setting, but to internal changes which surface from dilemmas, contradictions, and flaws in the policy design of the paradigm. Frame alignment does not threaten the paradigm itself because it keeps the definition of what is taken to be the worse evil intact, and only modifies the meaning of acceptable lesser evils. Another way to say this is that the goals and mission are stable, but the constraints in the choice of means change. If this interpretation is correct, even within a dominant and hegemonic paradigm, both controversy and reframing within the frame or paradigm can occur and are expressed via a process of "frame realignment."

To consider the direction of change in reconstructing the repertoire of policy option, an account needs to be taken of both processes of reframing: shifting across frames and realignment within a frame. The empirical task of unraveling which process of reframing has occurred may be difficult, especially since a frame contest may be fought out at the symbolic level, which might be different than the way the actual practice unfolds. To illustrate the three ideas which provide a framework for understanding policy change, I draw on an account of the evolution of recent American welfare policy.

DOMINANCE, CONTEST, AND REFRAMING IN THE UNITED STATES

I interpret the story of the evolution of American welfare policy for lone mothers as a series of contests involving controversy, challenge, and reframing against a dominant policy paradigm. This analysis makes use of the concepts introduced in the preceding section. The schema is presented in the eight cells of Table 12.1, which presents a stylized account of the main narrative of frame shifting and frame realignment in the American welfare reform story. The example also shows how the effort of making the lesser evil in one period is transformed into the worse evil in another period.

The following are the stylized facts used to construct Table 12.1. The first period was characterized by the movement to create mothers' pensions and the Social Security Act, based on the assumption that the worse evil was that poverty alone should be a cause of separating a widowed mother from her child and the lesser evil was long-term dependency. In the second period, widows became a minority among single parents, replaced first by mothers who were divorced and then by mothers who were never married. At the same

Table 12.1
Dominance, Contest, and Reframing in the United States: 1935–1996

	Antipoverty	Antidependency	Antidemarriage
Time period	1920-1935	1960-1996	1992-1996
Worse evil	forced separation of mother and child	Long-term dependency	demarriage and illegitimacy
Lesser evil	long-term dependency	Time limits and demarriage	forced separation inst. placement

time the work patterns of mothers changed; the married-mothers labor force grew larger than that of single mothers, and the fraction of single mothers on AFDC (Aid for Families with Dependent Children) grew sharply. In this new context, the worse evil was seen as long-term dependency, and the lesser evil was imposing time limits on how long a mother could receive welfare before having to work. In the third period, one sees a willingness to dramatically increase the financial outlays to reduce poverty for the working poor and to accept as a lesser evil and weakened support for single mothers who cannot work. The last frame challenges the dominant reframing of welfare policy based on work test rather than need test and assumes that the worse evil is demarriage, that is, raising children outside of the traditional marriage of a husband and a wife. The lesser evil is to place children in institutions, a foster home, or to sever parental rights and place the child up for adoption. This challenge for frame dominance has not been accepted in congressional legislation, although some important concessions to this frame can be identified in the new welfare reform.

ANTIPOVERTY FRAME DOMINANCE

The underlying logic of the antipoverty frame was that a woman should not be separated from her child simply because she was poor. This was a strong moral position about the sanctity of motherhood. Based on this normative position, the state had a social obligation to pay for the care of the child as it developed into adulthood. The social benefit was conceived of as an entitlement, meaning that anyone who met the qualification standards had a legal entitlement to the benefit. Transfers were distributed on the principle of consumer sovereignty, that is, the mother received an unrestricted cash grant, which meant that she alone made the consumption choice of how the transfers would be spent, unconstrained by collective choice as to what was an appropriate allocation of consumption.

The worse evil in this antipoverty program was forced, parental separation of a mother from her child because of the lack of money to care for the child. No attempt is made here to trace the history of the contest between this frame, the pauper frame, and the institution of the workhouse which preceded it except to note that, preceding and including the 1920s, the mothers' pension movement at the state level set the historic background for this national initiative. Forced separation was morally offensive because it violated the natural, maternal bond of a mother and her child. There was also an implicit instrumental argument which reinforced the moral argument, that the child would develop better into a healthy and proper citizen if it was raised under the care of the mother. The primary argument at this time was moral and not scientific.

The lesser evil was the acceptance of economic dependence on means tested cash transfers. The lesser evil was mitigated by a number of assumptions and facts. The program initially was very small, the relative cost trivial, and it was assumed that the program would decline over time, since the widows receiving benefits would eventually be integrated into the maturing and expanding social insurance program.

ANTIDEPENDENCY FRAME

In 1996, a Republican-dominated Congress and a Democratic president passed a law which not only reversed virtually all of the principles embodied in the antipoverty frame but ushered in a new, dominant, antidependency frame. Some background facts to the new antidependency frame will clarify how radically it departed from the antipoverty frame. Consider first some of the major changes in direction that this reframing implied: from a national entitlement to a temporary state program based on time limits, from a national social obligation to personal responsibility, from unrestricted cash grants to controlling and supervising the behavior of the mother (the "new paternalism"), from needs come first to work comes first (Mead 1997).

Clearly the 1996 welfare legislation did not see the program as an antipoverty program designed so that income would not be a justification for separating a mother from her child. It was a means tested program, but that did not make it a program focused on dependency (i.e., long-term receipt of welfare as an undesirable aim). In 1935, the Social Security Act framed lone motherhood as an antipoverty paradigm.

The consensus on the nature of the worse evil in the antidependency frame has to be understood as a change in context. First, there was a clear shift in norms. By 1990, more than two-thirds of wives who were mothers with young children were in the paid labor force, a practice which rejected the norm that children needed the mother to be at home; hence economic dependency on the state was much less politically acceptable. Second, in 1995, among female-headed families, two-fifths of black mothers, one-third of Hispanics, and one-fifth of white mothers had never been married. In the same year, 23 percent of all children resided in a lone parent household including half of all black children. For those who disapproved of unmarried parenthood, there was growing reluctance to "reward" unmarried mothers with unconditional support for their children. One feature making the American experience distinctive is the role that minority and black mothers play in the politics of welfare, since the public perception of the program was that it largely serves unmarried, black mothers (Cherlin 1998, 40).

The logic of the shift from antipoverty to antidependency needs to be briefly elaborated because it represents a rather dramatic departure in principle from the preceding antipoverty frame. The new focus is based on three major premises: personal obligation; solving social problems, and not merely meeting need; and redefinition of welfare as a work-tested rather than need-tested program. Each is briefly elaborated here.

The center of welfare reform debate turned on the ancient moral question of the correct balance to be placed on personal responsibility and social obligation. In the conservative view, the underlying dynamic of welfare dependency was created when welfare benefits were simply given away, without an expectation of reciprocal obligation. It was an entitlement, a right unaccompanied by an expectation of a behavioral change on the part of the welfare client. Here the focus was not on deviant behavior or illegitimacy but on the lack of any personal obligations. What was the implication of this diagnosis? Most important was the belief developed by Mead that work engenders self-discipline and provides a routine which organizes and structures time; it also engenders cooperation and demands consistent behavior responses from a set of demands imposed by the authority of the supervisor. Taken together, these beneficial effects of work have an important impact on an individual's personal character. This conservative analysis is strikingly similar to the argument developed by William Julius Wilson

(1998, 334) on the liberal side about the deleterious effect of jobless ghettos. They differ, however, in the prescription they recommend for action: job creation as a social obligation rather than supervision of the poor to create personal responsibility.

The emphasis on the failure to require that something be given by the recipient in return for the benefits received from welfare was interpreted by policy intellectuals and entrepreneurs like Mead as the need for a new paternalism. It was a call for authoritarian programs to force people to work, that is, to make work mandatory, to set time limits, and to have a tight definition of work that excludes by and large the idea that people should first be trained for a job. The new initiative stresses that work comes first for the reasons described, and training could follow, but not precede, work. In the new legislation there are sanctions on the states if they fail to meet standards stipulating the percentage of the population to be at work, and sanctions on the individual if they failed to get a job in a defined time limit. This is intended to be a serious set of work requirements, although states can exempt about 20 percent of caseloads. At the moment, the labor market in the United States is tight. In this situation national AFDC caseloads declined by 11.4 percent between 1993 and 1996, but the decline was over 25 percent in states like Massachusetts, Indiana, Oregon, and Wisconsin (Friedman and Rein 1998). Between 1993 and 1998, the decline was approaching 50 percent. While many welfare recipients found work, one cannot predict the direction that policy will take, especially when the inevitable economic recession occurs.

The next assumption is more subtle. It assumes that public spending should be directed toward solving social problems and not merely ameliorating personal hardship and meeting needs. This issue is fundamental, because it raises the central question of what is the purpose, the ultimate goals, against which the effectiveness of the program can ultimately be judged. What complicates the answer to this question is that sponsors of an antipoverty approach oversold what the programs could achieve. Poverty involves a host of symptoms—economic deprivation, family breakdown, joblessness, crime—and the identification of a "root" cause or causes offers the hope of potentially solving a range of different problems with a single cure (Rein and Winship 1999). For example, the political left in the United States has long taken the position that the elimination of economic deprivation would substantially eliminate the other symptoms of poverty. This position was most strongly stated by President Lyndon Johnson in the 1964 *Economic Report of the President*, noting that poverty's "ugly by-products include ignorance, disease, delinquency, crime, irresponsibility, immorality, and indifference.

None of these social evils and hazards will, of course, wholly disappear with the elimination of poverty. But their severity will be markedly reduced."

Now the conservative right is using this rhetoric to insist that more social spending should have beneficial effects on the list of social problems that Johnson itemized. If there is no effect, there is no justification to continue the programs. In the new paternalism, there is a willingness to impose personal responsibility, to supervise the poor so that they are held to a standard which insists on behavior change in school attendance, absence of drugs, and work behavior. In this approach of supervising the poor, there is no pretense this could be done without more public spending, which is not a call to reduce public spending in general, although the conservatives were opposed to guaranteeing public jobs.

The heart of the American welfare system traditionally has been an income-conditioned benefit. It has been restricted categorically in various ways, such as covering mainly single mothers with children. For those who are categorically eligible, however, the benefit formula has been tied to income and has been intended to reduce the poverty of the household. American policy has tried a long string of supplemental policies to encourage work within the context of the income-conditioned benefit. There have been social services, improved work incentives in the benefit formula, work requirements (or at least job search requirements), and training programs. While some of these supplemental efforts may have encouraged work, the effects have generally been modest or stronger, and still have failed to alleviate public concern that welfare recipients should be working (Friedman and Rein 1998).

Now the new antidependency initiative implies a dramatic change in design from a needs-based program to a work-based program of entitlement. The core of the American welfare system for nonaged poor has long focused on alleviating poverty (at least partially) through an income-conditioned benefit. This benefit would then be supplemented by various policies intended to promote work. The recent welfare reform has the potential to turn this around. The intention of the reformed system is to make the core of the system be work, to be supplemented by policies to alleviate poverty conditional on work. It is too early to know how the new policies will work or to understand their full consequences.

The new frame clearly shifts the focus to expecting something from the poor, namely that they work, and sets a time limit to make sure that they work within two years. After that the legislation mandates that mothers take a public job, where earnings are used as a substitute for the welfare grant. All this seems reasonably clear. What is ambiguous is the logic of the five-year limit. This rule means that welfare is only temporary, during a person's lifetime. But I do not know why 20 percent of mothers that start a welfare spell stay on welfare for over ten years, twice the new maximum limit. Maybe the proportion will shrink as those who can work are forced to early in their spell and will continue to do so thereafter. This could be the group whose motives and capability deteriorate the longer they stay on welfare. The problem is that the group of long-term recipients is likely to be heterogeneous. What about the rest of the population who cannot benefit from work? Some are mentally defective, some mentally ill, some on drugs, some have AIDS. In other words, the residual group may lack the capability of work. Moral capability and responsibility are linked. I cannot expect someone lacking in capability to be responsible for work, unless I find a way of improving her capability. But that is hard to do if I do not even know the cause of her lack of capability. The five-year limit could represent a potential hole in the safety net, leading to an increase in poverty and homelessness. Maybe the five-year time limit will lead to the substitution of new institutions with a different function to play than the role of caring for those lacking capabilities that the welfare system played. Recent reports suggest that half of those presently in prisons are mentally ill. Alternatively, the unresolved mystery of the long-term dependent may set the stage for the next step in the evolution of welfare policy, namely a change in the logic of the five-year term limits.

There was a consensus regarding what was the worse evil and a debate about what constituted the lesser evils. Liberals wanted training before jobs, the guarantee of a job before time limits, child care and health benefits to protect children, and child support from the father which permitted the mother to augment her income rather than have her benefits reduced. On most of these lesser evils the liberals lost or compromised. Buoyed by a strong economy and a tight labor market, the antidependency frame became dominant.

THE REEMERGENCE OF THE ANTIPOVERTY FRAME

A dramatic reframing of current welfare policy is now underway, leading to a surprisingly large increase in financial support of low-income families who work. The new consensus is based on a widely accepted assumption that if you work, you should not be poor. What is more surprising is that the antipoverty frame could in principle support those formerly on welfare rolls. The national welfare caseloads has declined by 45 percent since 1994. Of course not all of these mothers are working. But the Bureau of Labor Statistics reports that since 1996 there has been an annual net increase in employment of mothers who are heads of families.

The mothers who are most likely to enter employment are low income mothers. Between 1993 and 1998 the percentage of never married mothers who were employed increased from 44 percent to 62 percent. And many of these mothers can benefit in the expanded transfer system that is available to the working poor. Consider the following trend. In the late 1980s, low income working families were eligible for about $5 billion in aid. By 1996 the total expenditure was approaching $50 billion, and about half of this growth was due to the expansion of the Earned Income Tax Credit, which is "a refundable tax credit of up to 40% of earning for low income families. In 1996 the maximum benefit was $3,600 for a family with two children. All low income families with children can apply."

The lesser evil is to accept the economic dependency of people who were unable to work. After all there is evidence that there is a substantial group of mothers who are actually worse off as a result of welfare reform. And as Haskins argues, conservatives should agree that "every effort should be made to figure out ways to help these families."

Another lesser evil is the potential problem of discouraging marriage and the incentive of low income wives to work. These problems arise because programs that supported low income working families favored families with one low wage worker.

ANTIDEMARRIAGE AND ILLEGITIMACY

The fourth frame contest, about demarriage (presented in column four of Table 12.1), has a different policy outcome than the other frames. This was a conflict largely among conservative sponsors. A coalition of religious organizations in concert with conservative think tanks argued that the single largest threat to society was the problem of illegitimacy and the weakening of the institution of marriage as the appropriate setting for sex and child rearing. The thinking was that this problem should be addressed by a "family cap," which cut mothers off welfare if they had a second illegitimate child. The problem of long-term dependency and the failure of welfare recipients to work was only a lesser evil. They launched an aggressive campaign which failed to be added to the national agenda in the end. This story of a contest that did not lead to dominance is interesting and worth briefly recounting here.

Illegitimacy was a particularly divisive issue within the Republican Party. For some conservatives, illegitimacy was the most serious threat to society, because it was interpreted as the root cause of welfare dependency, crime, and violence. Hence "illegitimacy, not mandatory work, needed to head the Republican on welfare reform." This was the worse evil that needed to be addressed. The sponsors of this competing frame included organizations like the Christian Coalition, The Family Research Council, The Heritage Foundation, and many others. Of course, the private philanthropic foundations sponsored research designed to show that AFDC contributed to and was associated with illegitimacy. Liberal researchers responded by showing that an association between two variables cannot be interpreted as empirical evidence of a causal link (Rein and Winship 1999). But the argument does not depend on resolving the scientific and technical debate about causality, since the underlying issue was without doubt a moral question. It is wrong to have sex outside of marriage and to give birth to children that the parents could not afford to support. The preservation of Christian morality about sexuality and marriage was the central issue, even if this position ran against changing the norms and behavior of young people.

But the more difficult question was what specific action to remedy the situation should be proposed. What was the lesser evil that needed to be accepted to resolve the supreme evil of illegitimacy? Charles Murrray, who wanted to make illegitimacy the central issue in the welfare debate, advocated the most radical solution to combat this supreme evil. He wanted to "cut children off all welfare benefits for the duration of their childhood." This proposal for welfare reform came to be known as the "family cap." This solution was rejected, perhaps largely because it seemed too harsh a penalty to impose on children, who were victims of the environment in which they were born. While compassion may have receded in the new balance between personal responsibility and social obligation, the family cap debate shows that it was not totally out of fashion. If the family cap was not accepted, there were other stringent policies "that were capable of increasing sexual abstinence as the way to reducing pregnancy, or promoting marriage."

Nevertheless, the new legislation does contain a host of provisions that make it clear that the issue of demarriage has, by no means, died on the political agenda. Consider only a partial list of the numerous programs in the new legislation designed to provide performance bonus to states for reducing illegitimacy: abstinence education which rejects the safe sex message and, perhaps most important, continued experimentation at the state level. Twenty states have already introduced experimental "family caps," which were rejected by the national legislation. There is little doubt that Christian morality with its definition of demarriage as the worst evil is still alive and thriving, even if it did not rise to displace the dominant frame introduced by the new legislation, which renamed AFDC as Transitional Assistance for Needy Families (TANF) and was based on the view that "work comes first" in the American welfare reform.

Why did antiillegitimacy fail to win national support? A partial answer is that the moral position would have created a serious split between law and public opinion; and the scientific argument to support the moral position created a serious split among the community of scholars.

The only morally correct position is abstinence for the sponsors of this frame. The problem, of course, is that this position conflicts with the prevailing social norms, which may be ambivalent about the moral question, but clear that, from the perspective of behavior, premarital sex, contraception, and abortion are acceptable. The changing social norms undermined a serious moral debate in the public sector.

The intellectual justification was provided by policy intellectuals and entrepreneurs based on conservative think tanks. There are three main elements in the argument they advanced. First, illegitimacy is the root cause of dependency, and other problems such as drugs, crime, and delinquency. Whatever the scientific evidence may be, the argument appealed to the general public, who could readily accept the intuition that guaranteed and generously provided welfare benefits contributed to illegitimacy. Second, white illegitimacy is now approaching the rate that black illegitimacy held twenty-five years earlier. Hence there is a social threat that a white underclass is emerging. Charles Murray developed this argument in a very influential op-ed article that appeared in *The Wall Street Journal* (Murray 1995). The argument was exported to Britain, where it also had a significant impact on a receptive conservative audience sympathetic to the position. Third, single parenting has a negative effect on the cognitive development of young children compared to children growing up in a traditional, two-parent family unit.

Let me briefly summarize why the antiillegitimacy frame could not challenge the antidependency or the antipoverty frames for a dominant position. This frame failed to lead to a shift of frames, but it did lead to a frame alignment. In a significant way it became an important component of the lesser evil in the antidependency frame, although it has not influenced the antipoverty of the working poor frame. Many provisions in the final welfare law were designed to combat rising illegitimacy.

There are three main reasons why the contest did not lead to reframing of the antidependency definition of the worse evil. First, there was a conflict between morality and compassion. The family cap may have contributed to a reduction in illegitimacy, but it would have challenged an equally important value of compassion for the children who would have lost economic resources. There is an obvious conflict of aims in trying to alter the behavior of the mother but also protect the interest of the child. Second, the intellectual justification was shaped by an academic debate which favored the liberal position. While there is scientific evidence of a statistical association between dependency and illegitimacy, there is no evidence of a strong causal relationship. As Haskins points out, "Conservatives did not allow the lack of consensus in the social science literature to dull their claims about illegitimacy." The conservatives rested their justification for the emphasis on illegitimacy largely on public judgment and on weak evidence of a negative impact of illegitimacy on the mother's ability to raise her children. So both the value and intellectual arguments were ambivalent and weak, and this contributed to the failure to achieve a dominant reframing from dependency to illegitimacy.

DYNAMICS OF POLICY CHANGE

In the final section of this chapter, I revisit the discussion of dominance, contest, and reframing and offer a complementary approach for examining the dynamics of policy change. I consider change from three different dimensions. It is my intention to extend and deepen the early discussion. At this stage it is another cut at the same set of issues, which in future work should be integrated into a single framework. These include the *internal*, by which I mean the dilemmas which arise from any specific course of action which has been elected to follow; the *external*, which deals with changes in the context within which action takes place; and the opportunity for the *challenge* to launch oppositional movements to the normatively established and taken-for-granted norms of action, while recognizing that the same forces can give rise to the counter-movements that these challenges spawned. The discussion draws on examples of situated, policy changes that describe the historical situation in France and other Catholic countries and the United States.

THE INTERNAL DIMENSION: THE DILEMMAS OF ACTION

Historical paradigms provide good examples of how dilemmas can arise from the courses of action suggested by a prevailing paradigm. Kertzer's excellent study of policies to deal with infant abandonment in the eighteenth and nineteenth centuries in Italy offers a good example. The paradigm of Christian morality tried to discourage the unmarried mother from raising her own child or alternatively to commit infanticide as a way of avoiding undertaking this responsibility. Either course of action was unacceptable in the Christian doctrine of the time. The socially accepted solution of the time was to create a foundling institution, making use of *Le Tour*, or the "wheel," a device facilitating the abandonment (in the institutional practice, a foundling hospital), where the mother could anonymously leave her child in the care of the church, the state, or later, a nonprofit, secular institution. But such a policy had three unintended byproducts. First, the very anonymity of the process also made it possible for married couples who were not able financially to care for their children to make use of this institutional arrangement. Thus, a policy directed at one specific group spilled over to other groups, enabling another group equally to be able to take advantage of the policy. Second, the very policy of anonymity also provided an incentive to promote the condition whose consequences the policy was trying to avoid. In other words, the very existence of foundling hospitals in the view of later critiques was that the policy inadvertently "encouraged" women to have children out of wedlock because there was an easily available way of disposing of children in a socially acceptable way. The third dilemma in this system was that it relieved the mother of the obligation to pay for the care of the child that she conceived, thereby increasing the cost of the care for the state. In the historic period where children were fed by wet nurses, the shortage of women who could perform this service led to the mass death of infants left in the care of the church. This in turn led the church to find a pragmatic solution by enlisting the mother as a wet nurse for the care of children other than just her own, or a policy of charging the mother a fee for the care of the child. Both policies undermined the principle of anonymity and hence the larger goal upon which the program rested (Kertzer 1993, 16–37).

There is a modern parallel to this set of dilemmas which I call the inclusion–exclusion dilemma. The very essence of any means tested, social program is that it should be directed toward those for whom it was intended, and not be made available to those for whom the program was not intended. But the very effort to achieve either of these goals undermines the possibility of achieving the other. Specifically, in order to exclude those who are not eligible for a program, policies are developed to make access more difficult and more stigmatizing to ensure that the value of the benefit received is only very modest. This very process of discouraging noneligible persons from using services also leads to a very low utilization of the program by eligible people for whom it was designed. Yet, if the program is made attractive, accessible, and destigmatized so that higher proportions of eligible persons make use of the program, there will always be the danger of increasing the proportion of noneligible users due to administrative error or intentional abuse on the part of the recipient. This inclusion–exclusion dilemma tends to surface periodically when the size of the population receiving means tested benefits rises precipitously, which raises the specter that there is a loss of control over the administration of the program and that collective intervention "crowds out" the prevailing system of social ties that provide informal support via the family, the church, nonprofit institutions, and the local community of friends and neighbors. There appears to be a difficult-to-define threshold between collective and informal social ties which, when crossed, leads to a shift from policies to promote generosity (a concern with takeup and adequate benefit levels) to policies characterized by stringency (a concern for fraud, abuse, and moral hazard).

EXTERNAL CHANGE

Probably the most important external change is the decreasing importance of the institution of marriage as the appropriate institution for raising children and having sexual relations, a trend that Lefaucheur has described as "demarriage." Two important consequences follow from this trend: Most women will spend some time in their life living alone with their children, and its corollary, that most men will also spend time apart from their children (Ford and Miller 1998).

As a result of these changes in the norms and values, the metonym for *mother* has dramatically changed, reflecting this important cultural shift in the meaning of motherhood (Lakoff 1987). A metonym is a part of a category that is taken to represent the whole category. It serves as an exemplar or a prototype for the category as a whole. In the past, the metonym for *mother* was a stay-at-home mother fulfilling the wiving role for the husband and the mothering role for the child. The extent of the change in practice is suggested by a survey in the United States in 1995 which showed that only about 20 percent of all children reside in a household in which there is an employed father and a stay-at-home mother, as compared to 57 percent in 1960 (Cherlin 1998, 40).

Another trend that appears to be visible in the United States is the pattern of children living apart from both natural parents. In 1995, 4.3 percent of all children under age eighteen lived without a mother or a father. Desegregating by race, there were 3 percent of all white children living apart from both parents and 10.8 percent of black children. These children lived in foster homes, institutional settings, and with grandparents (Swingle 1998). Part of the growth of welfare caseloads during the 1990s can be traced to a rise in cases where the benefit goes only to the child and not to the mother. It seems clear then that there has been a significant rise in all industrial countries in births out of wedlock, divorce, and in the rise of women who were never married or not currently cohabiting with a man.

Most accounts of the story of demarriage has been focused on the living arrangements of children or the phenomenon of lone mothers. Ackerloff (1998) tried to recount the story from the perspective of the man, arguing that there has been a decline in the proportion of young men who marry. He observed that between 1968 and 1993, the fraction of men twenty-five to thirty-four who were householders living with children declined from 66 percent to 40 percent. His essay tried to examine the causes and the consequences of this decline in the marriage rates of men. The argument can be briefly stated as follows. One of his central points was technology change, where women have access to birth control and abortion and therefore are in a position to control conception. This change has caused men to respond in two important ways. First, there was a sharp decline in "shotgun" marriages since men no longer felt fully and solely responsible for the outcome of an unwanted pregnancy. Accompanying the decline in coerced marriage, there has been a general decrease in overall marriage rates. This could have a beneficial effect if the men, instead of marrying, spent more time at school and pursuing a career. But by and large this has not happened, as marriage itself symbolizes the adoption of a new identity by both the bride and the groom, a rite of passage from one stage of life to another. Hence, marriage itself presages a change in behavior in terms of attachment to work, signaled by the fact that married men earn more, that their earnings increase more rapidly compared to single men, and that they accumulate more financial assets since they are likely to invest in buying a home in preparation for raising a family. The fact that men do not marry, in Ackerloff's interpretation, is a causal factor in the increase in crime and drugs and other forms of deviant behavior. His solution is not to encourage men to marry or to reintroduce "shotgun" marriages, however, but instead to do more to improve the economic condition of those who are single mothers. In his view, the causes for the dissatisfaction in welfare is the disparity in the economic position between working and nonworking families, and his solution is to do more to increase the income of low income families who are at work.

CHALLENGES

The policy environment is set to receive challengers and counter-challengers once sponsors of paradigms come to recognize the dilemmas provoked by direct personal experience in the use of the action frame that they are pursuing, and once there is recognition that the least–worse solution is redefined as the supremely worse solution (e.g., in Kertzer's study of illegitimacy, the worse problem was redefined as not that children were not being baptized, but that they were being slaughtered). Once the problem was so redefined, there was a sense that the external or exogenous environment had opened a window of opportunity to permit a fundamental reframing to occur, such as in the Christain Angelism frame, leading eventually to the view that the best place to care for the children was with the mother, within the community, supported by state funding. In this new setting, there is a sense that the direction of the paradigm is threatened and that a new direction is needed. At the early stage of this process, there is a deep sense of malaise, but the nature of the problem has not yet been named, and hence the new direction to be pursued is not yet defined. What is known is that the past no longer serves as a guide for an unfolding future. There is a breakdown in that the process of coping has been disrupted, leading to a sense of not knowing where we want to be, what we want to preserve from the past, or what we want to take with us in the future (Piore 1994, 423). In this process, it is not only the direction of change that is unfolding—the analytic categories are also becoming unglued as well as distinctions that serve as the vocabulary for conventional deliberation about the issue. One example is the insistence by feminists that women be seen as active agents making claims for resources and direction and not merely as clients who are the objects of policy established by a legislative process, from which they are excluded in the claiming process. Frazer argues forcefully that the source of the difficulty arises because of the culturally accepted dichotomy between the private-life sphere of the family and the official open space of political participation in the public life world. She believes that the split is themed by gender where women are presumed to function naturally in the private-life world of the family and that this assignment of women's role to the private sphere denies them an active role in the public sphere as citizens of society. Women should then learn to play an active role as an agent in the political process, interpreting the nature and causes of lone parenting and in communicating what course of action should be followed in response to the phenomenon of lone parenting (Frazer 1997, 131).

Gamson (1999, 25) provides evidence to show that, at least in the United States, this passive role of women is changing because the media "in legitimating experiential knowledge and personal narratives," plays a central role in opening discursive opportunities for women to present themselves as "agents." Whether this optimism is warranted is not clear, given the direction in which public policy appears to be moving. What is clear is the importance of recognizing political participation as an important positive element in the raising of proper citizens.

An example is provided to illustrate the general process in which challengers arise and establish new claims on the "normatively secure" forms of action. What I have been arguing is that when these normatively secure foundations on which the existing policy paradigm rests weaken because of, on the one hand, external changes, which signal important value changes in society and, on the other, by the internal dilemmas that surface in the pursuit of any single paradigm. When these situations combine, they can lead toward oppositional movements which challenge the established paradigm. These challenges are expressed in many ways. In the case of the rise of social movements they can actively take the form of militant protest. But they can also follow a more discursive form which leads toward a rational, critical discourse where a new course of action is "communicatively achieved." Habermas defines this as a process "coordinated on the basis of explicit, relatively achieved consensus, consensus reached by unconstrained discussions under normal conditions of freedom, equality and fairness" (in Frazer 1995, 28). Of course, the process of change can combine both an initial, oppositional phase followed by a more deliberative process. I do not believe that it is possible to integrate the modern frames reviewed in Table 12.1 into a coherent, integrated set of policies toward lone parenting. The answer is an obvious no, by construction, since frames differ by what they consider as the worst evils and cannot be reconciled as far as "worse evils" are concerned. There will always be many different groups seeking to define the nature of the needed changes and projecting desired outcomes in contradictory, inconsistent, and incompatible directions (Ford and Miller 1998, 2). As analysts, the best that we can hope to achieve is to identify the rationale or logic which justifies a worst scenario (i.e., the "dystopia") and comment critically on its plausibility, or to call attention to an important frame that has been repressed in the current discourse. The move in the opposite direction of trying to establish a utopian vision which integrates the conflicting paradigms into a new whole, however, is perhaps likely to lead nowhere.

NOTE

1. This chapter is an extensive elaboration and expansion of an earlier essay by Nadine Lefaucheur and Martin Rein, "Framing and Reframing Social Policy Paradigms: The Case of Lone Parents," in *Fighting Poverty: Caring for Children, Parents, the Elderly and Health*, ed. R. Stein and R. de Jong (Aldershot, U.K.: Ashgate Publishing Ltd., 1999).

REFERENCES

Ackerloff, G. A. 1998. "Men without Children." *Economic Journal* 108 (445): 287–309.

Arendt, H. 1986. "Communicative Power." In *Power*, ed. S. Lukes. New York: University Press.

Blau, F. 1998. "Trends in the Well Being of Women, 1970–1995." *Journal of Economic Literature* 36 (1): 112–165.

Bradshaw, J. 1998. "International Comparisons of Support for Lone Parents." In *Private Lives and Public Responses*, ed. R. Ford and J. Millar. London: Policy Studies Institute.

Cherlin, A. J. 1998. "By the Numbers." *The New York Times Magazine*, 5 April.

Crowther, M. A. 1981. *The Workhouse System 1834–1929*. London: Methuen Press.

Ford, R., and Miller, J. 1998. "Lone Parenthood in the UK: Policy Dilemmas and Solutions." In *Private Lives and Public Responses*. London: Policy Studies Institute.

Frazer, N. 1989. *Unruly Practices: Power, Discourse and Gender in Contemporary Social Theory*. Minneapolis: University of Minnesota Press.

———. 1995. "What Is Critical about Critical Theory." In *Feminists Read Habermas*, ed. J. Meehan. New York : Rutledge Press.

———. 1997. "Geneology of 'Dependency.'" In *Justice Interruptus: Critical Reflections on the "Post-Socialist" Condition*, ed. N. Frazer. New York: Rutledge Press.

Friedman, B., and Rein, M. 1998. "Working and Poor: Challenges in Implementing America's 'Work First' Strategy." Paper presented at a U.N.–European followup meeting to the World Summit for Social Development on Innovative Employment Initiatives, European Center, Vienna, Austria, 20 December.

Gamson, W. A. 1999. "Policy Discourse and the Language of the Life—World." Forthcoming in *Self Dynamics of Social Processes: Festschrift in Honor of Friedhelm Neidhardt*. Isdeutscher, Germany: Verlag Opladen.

Goodin, R., Headey, B., Muffels, R., and Driven, H. J. 1999. *The Real Worlds of Welfare Capitalism*. Cambridge: Cambridge University Press.

Habermas, J. 1993. "On the Pragmatic, the Ethical, and the Moral Employment of Practical Reason." In *Justification and Application*, ed. J. Habermas. Cambridge, Mass. MIT Press.

Jencks, C., and Mayer, S. 1996. "Do Official Poverty Rates Provide Useful Information about Trends in Children's Economic Welfare?" Mimeograph, 30 May.

Kertzer, D. 1993. *Sacrificed for Honor: Italian Infant Abandonment and the Politics of Reproductive Control*. Boston: Beacon Press.

Lakoff, G. 1987. *Women Fire and Other Dangerous Things*. Chicago: University of Chicago Press.

Land, H., and Lewis, J. 1998. "The Problem of Lone Motherhood in the British Context." in *Private Lives and Public Responses*, ed. R. Ford and J. Miller. London: Policy Studies Institute.

Lefaucheur, N. 1998. "Fatherless Children, Lone Parents: A Paradigmatic Approach." Paper presented at the Workshop of Current European Research on Lone Mothers, Gutenberg University, Mainz, 24–25 April.

Lefaucheur, N., and Rein, M. "Framing and Refaming Social Policy Paradigms: The Case of Lone Parents." In *Fighting Poverty: Caring for Children, Parents, the Elderly and Health*, ed. S. Ringen and P. R. de Jong. Aldershot, U.K.: Ashgate Publishing Ltd.

Le Grand, J. 1997. "Knights, Knaves or Pawns? Human Behavior and Social Policy." *Journal of Social Policy* 26: 6.

Lerman, R. I. 1998. "Separating Income Support from Income Supplementation." Washington, D.C.: Urban Institute Report.

Levy, F. 1999. *The New Dollars and Dreams: American Incomes in the Late 1990's*. New York: Russell Sage Foundation.

Lewis, J. 1995. "The Problem of Lone Mother Families in Twentieth Century Britain." Discussion paper WSP/114, Welfare State Program, London School of Economics, August.

MacIntyre, A. 1984. *After Virtue: A Study in Moral Theory*. Notre Dame, Ind.: University of Notre Dame Press.

Mead, L., ed. 1997. *The New Paternalism: Supervisory Approaches to Poverty*. Washington, D.C.: The Brookings Institution.

Murray, C. 1995. "Welfare Hysteria." Op-ed, *The New York Times*, 14 November.

Piore, M. J., Lester, R. K., Kufman, F. M., and Malek, K. M. 1994. "The Organization of Product Development." *Industrial and Corporate Change* 3 (2): 405–434.

Rein, M., and Winship, C. 1999. "The Dangers of 'Strong' Causal Reasoning in Social Policy." *Society* 36 (5): 38–46.

Schon, D., and Rein, M. 1994. *Frame Reflection: Toward the Resolution of Intractable Policy Controversies*. New York: Basic Books.

Sen, A. 1998. "Mortality as an Indicator of Economic Success and Failure." *Economic Journal* 108 (446): 1–25.

Solow, R. 1998. *Work and Welfare*. Princeton, N.J.: Princeton University Press, Tanner Lectures.

Swingle, J. 1998. "Children in Flux: The Frequency and Risk Factor of Children Living Apart from Both Parents." Mimeograph.

Wilson, J. Q. 1997. "Paternalism, Democracy and Bureaucracy." In *The New Paternalism: Supervisory Approaches to Poverty*, ed. L. Mead. Washington, D.C.: The Brookings Institution.

Wolfe, A. 1998. *Whose Keepers? Social Science and Moral Obligation.* Berkeley and Los Angeles: University of California Press.

FURTHER READING

Ellwood, D. T. 1996. "Welfare Reform As I Knew It: When Bad Things Happen to Good Policies." *The American Prospect* 26 (May–June).

Haskins, R. 1992. "Is Anything More Important Than Day-Care Quality?" In *Child Care in the 1990's*, ed. A. Booth. Hillsdale, N.J.: Lawrence Erlbaum Associates.

Rein, M., and Goodin, R. "Regimes and Pillars." Forthcoming.

Troublesome Targeting: On the Multilevel Causes of Nontake-Up

Wim van Oorschot

Talking about the targeting of social security benefits may easily lead to misunderstandings. In the Scandinavian social policy debate, for instance, targeting tends to be equated with means testing as a way of distinguishing between those people who are entitled to a benefit and those who are not (Palme and Wennemo 1998). A similar view is at the base of Andries's account of recent Belgian social security developments (Andries 1996). In the British debate, however, means testing is called selectivity (Spicker 1998), a term that by other authors is used just to indicate that benefits do not cover all citizens (like universal benefits do), but only certain categories among them (Ferge 1997). Given this conceptual confusion I feel a need to start by saying that here I follow the idea that targeting in social policy most generally means that policies are directed at someone or something (Spicker 1998). In this sense all social security benefits are targeted, be it at categories of citizens (e.g., unemployed workers, pensioners, or families with children), at needy groups (sick or disabled people), or at people whose means fall below subsistence level (the "poor"). Furthermore, I regard policies that are targeted at more narrowly defined target populations as being more selective, and those aimed at more broadly defined groups of people as more universal in character. From the viewpoint of the efficiency and effectiveness of the implementation of targeted policies, the differences between more universal and more selective policies may not be that large in the case where the targeting variables are confined to neutral and objective sociodemographic and socioeconomic categories. When they include degrees of neediness and/or income level, however, a qualitative difference emerges, which negatively affects both the implementation's efficiency and effectiveness. With regard to efficiency this effect stems from the difficulties in assessing and controlling for levels of neediness and income, which makes for higher administrative costs for policies targeted at need and/or income per unit assessed (see Deacon and Bradshaw 1983 for the United Kingdom, and Aarts and De Jong 1998 for Dutch figures). With regard to effectiveness the negative effect stems from under consumption or nontake-up of benefits and services which is inherent to income testing or means testing (Deacon and Bradshaw 1983; Van Oorschot 1995), but which may occur in case of disability testing too (Blunn and Small 1984; Cohen 1983; Corden 1987).

Seen from the goal of social policy, which is to deliver a benefit or a service to a target population, the problem of ineffectiveness is more serious than that of inefficiency. And the same is true seen from the viewpoint of the target population itself. Both are good reasons to direct this contribution on the targeting of social security benefits to the problem of ineffectiveness, and more specifically, to the underconsumption of rights related to means testing.

First, I will discuss the problem of ineffective targeting in a broader context, claiming that nontake-up of benefits still is underemphasized, though it has become a more pressing problem in the recent past and will remain one in future, due to the increasing role of means testing in social policy. Second, I will elaborate on the causes of nontake-up, arguing that one should not blame nonrecipients for their underconsumption, since the causes are to be found, not only at the client level, but at the level of administration and scheme structure too. Finally, I will present an empirical analysis showing the causal links between a number of factors from these three levels, which together influence the take-up of a number of Dutch benefits.

TARGETING AND TAKE-UP

In an ideal world a scheme targeted at a certain population is implemented effectively: All those entitled receive the benefit, and all recipients are entitled. All who are entitled belong to the specific population policy makers had in mind when establishing the scheme. In other words, there is a perfect correspondence between target population, eligible population, and recipients population (van Oorschot 1995). In practice, however, mistargeting may occur, which may be of different kinds, depending on the population at issue. This is shown in Table 13.1, where subgroups e + g represent mistargeting due to nontake-up, when eligible people do not receive the benefit at issue. Another form of mistargeting at the level of the eligible population is shown by b + d, the ineligible recipients. Mistargeting at the level of the target population is shown by b + f (members of the target population who are not eligible), and by c + g (eligible people who do not belong to the target population).

Table 13.1 relates to what Vincent, Ashworth, and Walker (1991) call the *tactical* level of targeting, which is distinguished from the *strategic* level. At the strategic level, targeting consists of allocating resources between different categories of need or of needy groups of people. Strategic targeting is about the ideological and political question of who should get what and why. Tactical targeting is of a more pragmatic character and has two meanings. The first concerns the degree to which practical definitions of need accurately match those prescribed by those recognized socially and interpreted through the political process. In terms of Table 13.1, this meaning concerns the correspondence between the target population and eligible population. The second meaning of tactical targeting relates to the extent to which people with qualifying levels of need receive benefit. In terms of Table 13.1, this concerns the correspondence between the populations of eligible people and recipients.

From the perspective of the targeting of existing (i.e., already defined) benefits, the effectiveness of the implementation within the population of eligible people is at stake. At this level ineffectiveness can on principle take the two forms of overconsumption of rights (abuse) and underconsumption (nontake-up). In practice both might be present at the same time.

From the viewpoint of the poor at least, the latter form of ineffectiveness is more serious than the first. And, as we shall see, there

Table 13.1
The Three Populations of a Benefit Scheme: Targeting and Mistargeting

		Target population			
		yes		no	
		Eligible population			
		yes	no	yes	no
Recipients	yes	a	b	c	d
population	no	e	f	g	h

are good reasons for policy makers and administrators to be concerned about underconsumption of rights too. However, looking over the literature on the functioning of welfare states in general or the literature on how people cope with poverty or react to the supply of welfare state benefits, it quickly becomes clear that overconsumption usually receives much more attention than nontake-up (Golding and Middleton 1982; van Oorschot and Kolkhuis 1989). Somehow it seems that the importance of nontake-up, which is the phenomenon whereby people or households do not receive the amount of benefit to which they are legally entitled, is not self-evident. This is despite the fact that as early as the 1970s, studies in different countries had already showed the existence of it (see Lister 1974 for the United Kingdom, Catrice-Lorey 1976 for France, Bijsterveldt 1975 for The Netherlands, Geissler 1976 for Germany, and Doron and Ruter 1978 for Israel).

There may be several reasons for this bias, but one of the most important factors is the widespread idea that the modern citizen is a rational, calculating individual seeking personal profit from any relationship with the state, not bothered by cultural and personal barriers such as, for instance, feelings of shame and insufficient "bureaucratic skills." Indeed, from this perspective the proper functioning of social policy is seen as being endangered more by overconsumption than by underconsumption of social rights. And as a consequence the existence of underconsumption may easily be underrated. Another widespread idea is that, in the few cases of nontake-up that may exist, it is believed that people do not want the benefit, either as a result of calculation (they do not think the benefit is worth the effort), or on principle (they do not want to depend on what they believe is "charity"). In both situations, according to the common view, the nonclaimants do not really need the benefit to which they are entitled. This leads to the judgment that there is not generally a serious problem of nontake-up, at least not for the nonclaimants themselves, and, usually therefore, neither for the administration nor for policy makers.

Although there will be cases of nontake-up which are aligned with this common view, results from studies on the topic show that such cases are rare. They also show that in the case of means tested benefits (and sometimes also for nonmeans tested benefits) it is a normal situation for large proportions of eligible populations not to receive the benefits in question. There even seems to be a sort of "natural ceiling," of about 80 percent to 85 percent, above which take-up rates of means tested benefits can not reach (van Oorschot 1995). Studies show also that many people who are eligible for social security benefits do not behave as well-informed, rational, calculating individuals, and that only in a minority of cases do nonclaimants explicitly not want the benefit to which they are entitled.

All this implies that nontake-up is to be regarded as a serious problem in targeted social policy. Some authors take a strong standpoint by evaluating the existence of nontake-up as evidence of the failure of the means test as an instrument for social security (Hartmann 1985), or even as indicating the failure of the very principle of selectivity (Lynes 1972, 505). Lister (1974, 21) concludes from her review of early British take-up studies that "the selectivist solution to poverty has been tried, and it has failed." Others take a more moderate standpoint by stating that nontake-up generally should be regarded as an important problem in social policy but not, or to a lesser extent, if only small amounts are forgone (Bendick 1985); if people genuinely do not want to claim (Beltram 1984); if nontake-up is only fractional (Adler 1977); or if people are entitled or nonclaiming only for a short period of time (Supplementary Benefits Administration [SBC] 1978; Richardson and Naidoo 1978). Atkinson (1984) would assert that in all such cases nontake-up nevertheless indicates the existence of nontrivial costs associated with claiming. These costs, which claimants will also experience, may justify attention to the problem apart from the amount of unclaimed money or the nonclaimants' motivations.

Such attention is also justified because nontake-up can be a cause of poverty and other problems related to low incomes. Furthermore, because it implies a fundamental injustice due to the inequality that exists between claiming and nonclaiming citizens in realizing their rights. Especially in the field of social security, injustice in a scheme's implementation should be a matter of concern. Not only because social security is the institution par excellence that can promote a just distribution of resources in modern society, but also because many people who are entitled to a benefit are in a situation of real need. And attention is finally justified because of the fact that strategic targeting has become significantly more selective in the welfare systems of many countries since the economic crisis of the 1980s (Gough 1994). At the general social policy level, this process has been referred to as "individualisation of the social" (Ferge 1997) and at the level of systems of social security as "a shift from insurance to assistance" (van Oorschot and Schell 1991). The increased selectivity of strategic targeting has resulted at the tactical level in an expansion of means testing and thus in a growing importance of the nontake-up phenomenon. Given this actual trend the question of what are the exact causes of nontake-up becomes pressing.

CAUSES OF NONTAKE-UP:
CLIENTS, ADMINISTRATION, AND SCHEME STRUCTURE

Reviews of nontake-up research all show that traditionally the causes of nontake-up of social security benefits are studied at the client level only (Corden 1981; Falkingham 1985; van Oorschot and Kolkhuis 1989; Craig 1991). That is, in trying to explain why people do not receive the benefits to which they are entitled, the focus has been on eligible people's knowledge, perceptions, attitudes, motivations, experiences, and circumstances. Influencing factors possibly operating at the levels of scheme structure and administration have largely been ignored thus far in empirical research (see also Whyley and Huby 1993; Corden 1995). Nevertheless, the literature on nontake-up contains much evidence on the importance of influential factors at these two levels, be it that there is little direct proof.

It is commonly acknowledged that the administration of services and benefits can have a great influence generally on what citizens actually receive compared to what is originally intended, strategically or tactically, by policy makers (see Blau 1955; Handler and Hollingsworth 1971; Catrice-Lorey 1976; Leibfried 1976; Ringeling 1981; Lipsky 1980; Mashaw 1983; Walker 1985). About administrative influences on the nontake-up of means tested social security benefits in particular, however, little is known exactly. This is especially so in the case of direct influences, which occur when administrators decide wrongly to reject a claim or when they award a smaller amount than a claimant is actually due. Examples of such wrong decisions can be found in Berthoud (1983, 1984) and Vos (1991). Other studies have shown that administrators of means tested social security schemes tend to make decisions on the basis of biased and/or insufficient information (Howe 1985; Vos 1991; Beltram 1984; Knegt 1986), leading most probably to false rejections in at least some cases. In comparison with the direct influences, there is more documentation about indirect influences of the administration on a scheme's nontake-up. Such indirect influences arise from practical administrative arrangements and administrators' behavior, which can set constraints on clients or lay stumbling blocks in their paths. Clear examples can be found in Briggs and Rees (1980), Corden (1983, 1987), Graham (1984), Richardson and Naidoo (1978), and Davies and Ritchie (1988). From these studies the main factors at the level of administration that enhance the probability of nontake-up can be summarized as follows:

- A way of handling claims and claimants that is experienced by claimants as humiliating or degrading.

- Combining a "service" and a "fraud control" function.
- Poor quality of communication with clients, giving insufficient information and advice.
- Using complex application forms.
- Poor quality of decision making (e.g., making decisions on the basis of insufficient information or on the basis of client stereotyping).
- Poor quality of technical administrative procedures.
- Wrong interpretation of scheme rules by administrators.

Recently, Corden elaborated this list of main factors on the basis of British findings and improved it by offering and applying an alternative, sequential classification of administrative aspects that are influential: aspects of information supply, of service provision, and of application procedure and outcome. Corden presents a wide variety of evidence on the influence of these administrative aspects on nontake-up and concludes that "every aspect of administration can potentially affect take-up" (1995, 58).

Factors at the level of benefit structure will lead indirectly to nontake-up because they constitute to a large extent the context in which the behavior of administrators and clients takes place, thereby offering opportunities for and constraints on the behavior of both sets of actors. From the rather scattered information available, I concluded elsewhere (van Oorschot and Kolkhuis 1989) that the probability of the occurrence of nontake-up is larger in schemes that

- Contain a means test.
- Have a "density" (i.e., a large number) of rules and guidelines.
- Contain complicated rules.
- Contain vague (i.e., imprecise), indistinct, and/or discretionary entitlement criteria.
- Supplement other sources of income.
- Are aimed at groups in society which are the subject of negative valuation.
- Provide only small amounts of benefit.
- Leave the initiative to start the claiming process fully to the applicant.
- Provide for a variety of expenses (i.e., comprehensive schemes).
- Provide for incidental instead of regular expenses.
- Offer an unstable entitlement.

Corden (1995) also applied this list to the British social security system and claimed to have found considerable supporting evidence as to its validity, while at the same time offering a few additional features that certainly are of relevance. She suggests that not only may a test of means have a deterrent effect on take-up, but also because of feelings of shame involved, that is, a test of disability (proof of which can be found in Bradshaw and Lawton 1982; Blunn and Small 1984; and Corden 1987). Furthermore, she suggests that effects exist from overlap and interaction between different benefits in respect of the criteria for entitlement, and from structural aspects of benefits which challenge cultural norms, and she rightly points to the fact that structural aspects of time influence nontake-up. Of course, of the structural aspects, the presence of a means test is most widely recognized as a factor inherently associated with nontake-up (Bendick 1980; Hartmann 1985; Deacon and Bradshaw 1983).

The three different levels—scheme structure, administration, and client—can be distinguished analytically quite easily, but the research literature and reviews of it show that in practice the factors influencing nontake-up form a complex whole. We propose to see nontake-up as the result of a mix of interrelated factors from different interacting levels, as pictured in Figure 13.1.

The different factors may be directly or indirectly influential and the actual mix of factors may and usually will differ between particular situations (i.e., between different schemes, administrative arrangements, client groups, times, and places). Looking at the causes of nontake-up in this way for one thing helps us understand how different studies focusing on the reasons for nontake-up at the client level have come to quite different, indeed sometimes opposite, conclusions about the relative influence of separate factors (e.g., "knowledge," "stigma," "perception of eligibility," and "need"; see Craig 1991 for examples). Namely, these studies were about different schemes and different client groups (pensioners, lone parents, working poor, or social assistance beneficiaries); and they were carried out at different times, in different places, and in the context of different administrative arrangements. The view on the causes of nontake-up as a mix of multilevel factors furthermore leads to recognizing that it is not only citizens who are responsible for the problem of nontake-up. Policy makers and administrators also play their role and can be held responsible. Denying this would be a clear case of "blaming the victim" (Townsend 1979). As for the question of primary responsibility, one must realize that often the answer is just a matter of which viewpoint is taken. For instance, who is responsible for the nontake-up resulting from lack of sufficient knowledge by eligible people? Is it the clients, as is commonly assumed? Or is it the administration, for not being active enough in distributing information and giving advice? Or are the policy makers to blame, for designing a large number of complex, vague, and therefore incomprehensible rules and guidelines? Note, how-

Figure 13.1
The Multilevel Influences on Nontake-Up: An Interactive Model

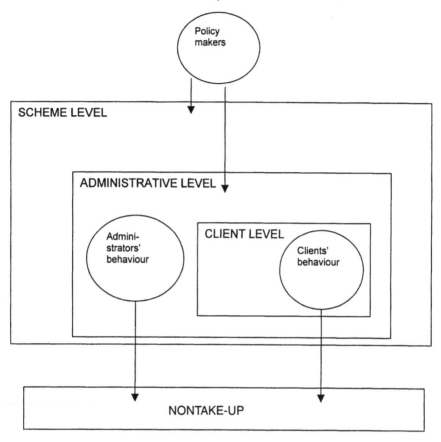

ever, that in the most direct sense nontake-up is the result of the specific behavior of two groups of actors (see Figure 13.1): administrators, who may make false decisions regarding applications of clients, and clients, who for whatever reason may omit putting in a claim or withdraw a claim. Policy makers are of importance because of their role in setting the scheme's rules in deciding on the budget and personnel available and outlining the main factors of the scheme's administration. In doing so they define the legal and organizational context in which administrators and clients act. Clients also act within a specific administrative context, that is, their relevant knowledge, perceptions, attitudes, experiences, and behavior are all influenced by characteristics of the administrative level (e.g., the amount and quality of information and advice given, the barriers raised in the practical procedures, the location of offices, and the treatment by administrators).

AN EMPIRICAL APPLICATION: DUTCH HOUSING BENEFIT

When studying the causes of nontake-up and viewing them as a mix of interacting factors from different levels, comparative research is needed, in which different scheme structures, different administrative practices, and different client groups can be observed and compared. In the beginning of the 1990s, such research was carried out in The Netherlands, in which the nontake-up of five different schemes among groups of elderly people (N = 1370) and social assistance beneficiaries (N = 520) in two major cities, Rotterdam and Nijmegen, was studied. In the course of 1991, random samples were taken from the municipal registry office's records and from the records of the municipal social service of the major Dutch cities of Rotterdam and Nijmegen to obtain respectively samples from the population of elderly people (sixty-five years of age and over) and social assistance clients. Among the sampled households, oral, structured interviews were carried out for assessing entitlement to and take-up of a number of benefits, as well as for assessing knowledge, perceptions, attitudes, and behavioral factors that might be relevant for understanding the causal factors playing a role at the client level. On the basis of the interview data, eligible claimants and eligible nonclaimants of the various schemes involved were distinguished, and per scheme weighted least squares regression analyses were carried out for analyzing differences between the two groups regarding their behavior, perceptions, attitudes, and awareness of the scheme involved. For studying factors playing a role at the level of administration, administrative practices were observed and people working in the administration were interviewed. The structures of schemes were compared to obtain information on causal factors possible operating at the level of scheme structure.

Table 13.2 shows that considerable nontake-up of the schemes included in our study existed. In itself this is not surprising because all these schemes are means tested, and all supplement existing sources of finance for those entitled. What does attract attention, however, is not only that there is such a wide variation in the percentages found, from 8 percent to as much as 72 percent, but that two patterns are visible. The first one is that, within each separate group, housing benefit has (by far) the lowest rate of nontake-up. The second is that, with the exception of special assistance, the nontake-up of all other benefits is lowest among the Nijmegen social assistance beneficiaries. The question put forward here is how these patterns can be explained.

Table 13.2
Nontake-Up Rates in Percentages

	Rotterdam		Nijmegen	
	Social assistance clients	**Elderly people**	**Social assistance clients**	**Elderly people**
Housing benefit	26	22	8	20
Special assistance	63	50	53	72
Exemption property tax	40	38	16	50
Exemption garbage tax	70	69	25	54
Declaration fund			54	72

Note: Eligible nonrecipients as percentage of sum of recipients and eligible nonrecipients.

Housing Benefit

Why housing benefit in every group has the lowest rate of nontake-up cannot be understood fully from client level factors alone (i.e., from possible differences in the composition of the eligible populations). This is because there is a large overlap of about 80 percent to 90 percent between the target population for housing benefit and the target populations of the other schemes. This means that to a large degree the people involved in the high take-up of housing benefit are the very same people involved in the low take-up of the other schemes. Therefore, the answer mainly has to come from comparisons of characteristics of scheme structures and of administrative practices.

At the *structural* level we compared the position of housing benefit based on the factors summarized earlier as enhancing the probability of nontake-up, with the position of the other schemes. Housing benefit is no different from the other schemes in respect of it being means tested and supplemental to other sources of income. The scheme does not contain much clearer entitlement conditions, and as the other schemes, it leaves to the applicant the initiative to start the claiming process. Nevertheless, housing benefit does have some distinctive structural features which create a strongly claim promoting context. These features are related to the types of household and the types of cost at which housing benefit is directed, as well as to features of the benefit itself. The following mix of favorable characteristics is typical for Dutch housing benefit: It offers a relatively large amount of benefit which is awarded for a whole year; the scheme is directed at a single type of expense which recurs regularly (monthly rent); it offers a stable entitlement over a period of some years (entitlement criteria do not change much, and most people do not move frequently); it has a fixed application date (making possible well-targeted campaigns); it counts as means last year's taxable income (which for clients is a rather easy definition of the means test); and finally, it is not directed only at the poorest households (i.e., it is less selective, in that families with incomes up to about 150 percent of the minimum wage may be entitled).

We also compared the housing benefit's position at the *administrative* level with that of the other schemes. Relevant features that appeared from our study were that the atmosphere surrounding the housing benefit application process is less dominated by the administration's function of fraud control. And most importantly, that each year during June, the month preceding the application date of 1 July, housing corporations undertake intensive and well-targeted information campaigns directed at stimulating housing benefit take-up. Both these claim-promoting administrative features are directly linked to certain structural features of the scheme. The first is linked to the fact that housing benefit counts as means last year's taxable income (which is easy to check in most cases), and the second to the fixed application date (campaigns of the quality and intensity of those organized by the housing corporations in June could not be sustained throughout the year).

To complete the analysis of multilevel influences we compared at the *client* level the people eligible for housing benefit with those eligible for the other benefits on two sets of factors (see van Oorschot 1995 for the theoretical and empirical validation of the importance of these factors):

1. Benefit-specific informational factors, including awareness of a benefit; the type of source of the first information about the benefit; the degree of knowledge of the entitlement criteria; and whether people have searched intensively for information about the benefit.

2. Image factors, including the expected amount of a specific benefit; the perceived character of the benefit (i.e., whether one sees it mainly as a right or as a matter of charity); the perceived degree of disapproval from acquaintances with regard to claiming the benefit; and the perceived difficulty of applying for that benefit.

The analyses showed that the high take-up of housing benefit can be understood at the client level from the facts that it is a much better known scheme, as well as a more acceptable one. That is, among its population of eligible people the level of awareness is much higher compared to other schemes (nearly 100% against on average 75%). And, in contrast to the other schemes, it is thought to offer large amounts of benefit, to be easy to apply for, and to carry less of a stigma (i.e., more seen as a matter of right and less perceived disapproval of acquaintances). The structural and administrative features of housing benefit mentioned form the context in which the claiming behavior of the eligible people takes place, and some of these features are directly linked to factors found to play a role at the client level. That is, the higher level of basic knowledge is directly linked to the intensive claim-promoting activities undertaken at the administrative level, which are specific for housing benefit. The image factors are linked to administrative as well as to structural features: the justified expectation of substantial amounts of benefit, being easier to get (linked to simpler means test, more information and help), and being less stigmatized (linked to less fraud control and less selectivity).

The Nijmegen Social Assistance Clients

In order to understand the factors causing the pattern that the nontake-up rates of all schemes (with the exception of social assistance) are lower among the Nijmegen social assistance clients than among the other subgroups, we shall again look for explanations at different levels. The structural level is irrelevant here, however, because we are dealing with a phenomenon that is a group characteristic and which goes beyond the structure of separate benefits. Furthermore, the structures of the separate schemes involved do not differ among the subgroups.

Starting at the *client* level, we compared the Nijmegen social assistance clients with the other subgroups on

1. Personal characteristics (e.g., sex, age, marital status, household composition and nationality) (compared only with the Rotterdam social assistance clients).
2. Common concepts in nontake-up research, including basic knowledge of schemes, perceptions of need and utility of schemes, and general attitudes.
3. General informational aspects, including difficulties generally experienced in understanding information, perception of availability of information, main source of information generally used, and having received advice to claim.

The analyses revealed that the Nijmegen social assistance clients as a group do not differ from the Rotterdam clients on the personal characteristics. So, here there is no explanation of the favorable take-up position of the Nijmegen subgroup. Furthermore, the Nijmegen clients do not differ on any of the common concepts: They have comparable levels of need (indicated by disposable income and perception of making ends meet); they attach the same degree of utility to certain amounts of benefit; and they have the same attitudes toward administrators and their behavior (completing) application forms, giving personal information when applying for benefits, (dis)approving reactions of acquaintances, and benefits and subsidies in general. There were clear differences, however, regarding the third type of variables, the informational aspects. The Nijmegen social assistance clients had clearly higher levels of basic knowledge of all schemes, and less difficulty in understanding information. They perceived more information as being readily available, and as a group they experienced greater encouragement to claim.

That from these factors their favorable take-up position can be understood became clearer when factors were analyzed at the *administrative* level. The most significant finding from comparing the administrative context of the subgroups was, very briefly, the fact that the Nijmegen social service was especially active in informing its clients about other benefits and subsidies *in addition to* the social assistance benefit for which it is formally responsible only. This happened not only by means of well-targeted, up-to-date written information, but also during personal contacts with their clients. Elderly Dutch people lack structural contacts with any bureaucracy that could inform them regularly and systematically on benefits and rights. The Rotterdam social assistance clients did not profit from their structural contacts with the Rotterdam social service, because this service proved to be very passive in offering information to its clients, compared to the social service of Nijmegen.

The multilevel mix of influencing factors explaining the high take-up of schemes among the Nijmegen social assistance clients thus can be summarized as follows: The active Nijmegen social service created a claim promoting environment for its clients, resulting in a favorable informational position, and thus higher take-up. (That the nontake-up of social assistance is at a relatively high level among the Nijmegen social assistance clients too, could be explained by the fact that in the year of the study welfare workers had been told to be cautious with this benefit for reason of an expected budget deficit).

CONCLUSION

Nontake-up of social security benefits manifests ineffective targeting. Contrary to common belief, such ineffectiveness does not occur only marginally, but can be regarded as a phenomenon inherent to selective targeting, especially to means testing. Nontake-up results from an interaction of factors at the levels of scheme structure, administration, and clients. To demonstrate such interaction, comparative research was necessary, that is, research in which the nontake-up of a number of benefits among different populations and/or time periods was studied.

After a theoretical discussion of the significance and causes of nontake-up this chapter presented the results of an empirical, comparative study undertaken in The Netherlands. The central question of the empirical section was how differences in nontake-up rates between types of benefit and groups of eligible people could be explained.

By analyzing the results, I want to state as a first general conclusion that differences in levels of knowledge about available benefits between groups of eligible people depend strongly on the extent to which the context surrounding claiming decisions and claiming behavior tends to promote such knowledge. That is, people eligible for housing benefit and the Nijmegen social assistance clients as a whole have exceptionally high levels of awareness, not because they are special people, but because at the administrative level they are exposed to an exceptionally high level of information. The knowledge people have of schemes thus is an important overall factor. A recurrent comment in the research literature is that lack of such knowledge is too easy and superficial an explanation of nontake-up, and that the deeper causes are situated in fundamental negative attitudes and fear of stigmatization (Craig 1991). If this were true in my research, I would have found combinations of high levels of basic knowledge together with high levels of nontake-up. Such combinations were not found. What was found were low levels of awareness along with lower take-up and higher awareness levels with higher take-up rates.

A second conclusion is that the administrative level seems to play a most important role in the multilevel mix of influencing factors. If administrations are actively targeting and distributing information, they can enhance levels of awareness and therefore the level of take-up. In practice, however, it is here that the main problem seems to lie. It was my experience that administrations usually care little about the problem of nonclaiming: Their ambitions and feelings of responsibility often do not seem to go beyond processing claims, let alone being concerned with the take-up of benefits that are formally administered by other agencies. "Take it or leave it" is the administrative attitude toward claiming that was encountered most.

A third conclusion is that the argument promoting structural elements as a factor in nontake-up can be divided into two types: those which facilitate matters at the administrative level by providing the conditions in which well-targeted information and advice activities can be designed and implemented (such as a fixed application date, being directed at a single type of expense, or being directed at a regular expense); and those that facilitate matters at the client level by promoting a positive image of a scheme (e.g., not being targeted only at the poorest, by offering a certain type of benefit, such as a larger amount or a more stable entitlement).

In general, realizing a right to benefits is not a matter of isolated individual beneficiaries deciding at a particular time to go out and claim or not. Instead it is a long process which starts from the moment the structure of a scheme is defined (i.e., when the concrete eligibility criteria are determined by policy makers). These criteria establish to a considerable extent the degree to which administrators and clients will experience serious obstacles later in the process. Analytically, on the microlevel, the process ends when the benefit is actually received by those people who are entitled to it. In practice and on the macrolevel, however, the process does not end, because at any one time there will always be eligible nonrecipients left, usually marginal numbers in the case of nonmeans tested benefits, but much higher proportions in the case of means tested benefits. Between the establishment of a scheme's structure and benefit receipt, administrative bodies and administrators play an important role. They have to implement the scheme, with a primary aim to ensure that the benefit reaches its eligible population. Whether they fulfill this task completely depends not only on contextual constraints over which they usually have no control (e.g., elements of scheme structure, budget, time and/or prescribed procedures), but also on their own efforts and activities within such constraints. Delivery of entitlements within each scheme can meet higher or lower standards, in a technical administrative or procedural sense, along with variable degrees of conviction and commitment to clients' needs. The clients of the administration—the people who are or might be entitled to the benefit—are not discharged from any responsibility within the administrative process. On the contrary, they are justifiably expected to try as hard as possible to find solutions to problems experienced, such as by seeking further information about possible benefits and by claiming those available. This is different, however, from expecting them to be fully self-confident, rational, active, and bureaucratically competent. Only if all clients were like this would it be justifiable to allot the main responsibility for the ineffectiveness of targeted social policies to them.

REFERENCES

Aarts, L., and De Jong, P. 1998. "Privatization of Social Insurance and Welfare State Efficiency." Paper presented to the Second Research Conference of the International Social Security Association, Jerusalem, 25–27 January.

Adler, M. 1977. *Research Priorities for Improving the Take-Up of Benefits*. Edinburgh: Social Security Research Policy Committee.

Andries, M. 1996. "The Politics of Targeting: The Belgian Case." *Journal of European Social Policy* 6 (3): 209–233.

Atkinson, A. B. 1984. "Take-Up of Social Security Benefits." Discussion Paper 65, International Centre for Economics and Related Disciplines, London.

Beltram, G. 1984. *Testing the Safety Net: An Enquiry into the Reformed Supplementary Benefit Scheme*. London: Bedford Square Press.

Bendick, M. 1980. "Failure to Enroll in Public Assistance Programs." *Social Work* 25 (4): 268–274.

———. 1985. *Improved Program Administration Can Benefit Both Public Assistance Recipients and Oregon Taxpayers*. Washington, D.C.: The Urban Institute.

Berthoud, R. 1983. *Study of the Reformed Supplementary Benefit Scheme, Working Paper D: Welfare Rights Advice Experiment*. London: Policy Studies Institute.

———. 1984. *The Reform of Supplementary Benefit, Working Paper E: Analysis of DHSS Records of Single Payment Decisions*. London: Policy Studies Institute.

Bijsterveldt, Q. M. 1975. *Een sociale voorziening en haar cliënten: een onderzoek naar de bijstandsverlening aan vrouwelijke gezinshoofden*. Tilburg: Proefschrift, Katholieke Hogeschool Tilburg.

Blau, P. M. 1955. *The Dynamics of Bureaucracy*. Chicago: University of Chicago Press.

Blunn, C., and Small, M. 1984. "The Anomalies of Attendance Allowance." *Community Care* 16: 18–20.

Bradshaw, J., and Lawton, D. 1982. "Utilisation of the Family Fund." *Child Care, Health and Development* 8: 227–237.

Briggs, E., and Rees, A. M. 1980. *Supplementary Benefits and the Consumer*. London: Bedford Square Press.

Catrice-Lorey, A. 1976. *Inégalités d'accès aux systèmes de protection sociale et pauvreté culturelle*. Revue Française des Affaires Sociales: Ministère du Travail.

Cohen, R. 1983. *Able to Claim? A Report of Work with Occupational Thera-pists and Physiotherapists to Improve Take-Up of Disability Benefits.* London: Islington Peoples Rights.

Corden, A. 1981. *The Process of Claiming FIS, Background Paper II: Re-view of Previous Studies on the Take-Up of Means-Tested Benefits and Their Relevance to a Study of Fis-Take-Up.* York: SPRU, University of York.

———. 1983. *Taking Up a Means-Tested Benefit: The Process of Claiming Family Income Supplement.* London: Department of Health and Social Security, HMSO.

———. 1987. *Disappointed Applicants: A Study of Unsuccessful Claims for Family Income Supplement.* Aldershot, U.K.: Avebury.

———. 1995. *New Perspectives on Take-Up: A Literature Review.* London: HMSO.

Craig, P. 1991. "Costs and Benefits: A Review of Research on Take-Up of Income-Related Benefits." *Journal of Social Policy* 20 (4): 537–565.

Davies, C., and Ritchie, J. 1988. *Tipping the Balance: A Study of Non-Take-Up of Benefits in an Inner City Area.* DHSS Research Report No. 16. London: HMSO.

Deacon, A., and Bradshaw, J. 1995. *Reserved for the Poor: The Means-Test in British Social Policy.* Oxford: Blackwell.

Doron, A., and Ruter, R. 1978. *Low Wage Earners and Low Wage Subsi-dies.* Jerusalem: National Insurance Institute.

Falkingham, F. 1985. *Take-Up of Benefits: A Literature Review.* Benefits Research Unit Review Paper 1:85, Department of Social Administration, University of Nottingham, Nottingham.

Ferge, S. 1997. "A Central European Perspective on the Social Quality of Europe." In *The Social Quality of Europe*, ed. E. Beck, L. van der Maesen, and A. Walker. The Hague: Kluwer Law International.

Geissler, H. 1976. *Die neue soziale Frage.* Freiburg im Breisgau: Herder Verlag.

Golding, P., and Middleton, S. 1982. *Images of Welfare: Press and Public Attitudes to Poverty.* Oxford: Robertson.

Gough, I. 1994. *Means-Tested Benefits in a Comparative Perspective.* Presentation at the Richard Titmuss Memorial Lecture, Hebrew University of Jerusalem, 31 May.

Graham, J. 1984. *Take-Up of FIS: Knowledge, Attitudes and Experience, Claimants and Non-Claimants.* Stormont: Social Research Division, PPRU, Department of Finance and Personnel.

Handler, J., and Hollingsworth, E. J. 1971. *The Deserving Poor: A Study of Welfare Administration.* Chicago: Markham.

Hartmann, H. 1985. "Armut trotz Sozialhilfe: Zur nichtinanspruchnahme von Sozialhilfe in der Bundesrepublik." In *Politik der Armut und die Spaltung des Sozialstaats*, ed. S. Leibfried and F. Tennstedt. Frankfurt am Main: Suhrkamp.

Howe, L.E.A. 1985. "The 'Deserving' and the 'Undeserving': Practice in an Urban Local Security Office." *Journal of Social Policy* 14 (1): 49–72.

Knegt, R. 1986. *Regels en redelijkheid in de bijstandsverlening: Participerende observatie bij een Sociale Dienst.* Amsterdam: Proefschrift, Universiteit van Amsterdam.

Kramer, G. L. 1975. "Bureaucratic Competence and Success in Dealing with Public Bureaucracies." *Social Problems* 23: 197–208.

Leibfried, S. 1976. "Armutspotential und Sozialhilfe in der Bundesrepublik: Zum Prozess des Filterns von Anspruchen auf Sozialhilfe." *Kritische Justiz* 9: 376–393.

Lipsky, M. 1980. *Street Level Bureaucracy: Dilemmas of the Individual in Public Services.* New York: Russell Sage Foundation.

Lister, R. 1974. *Take-Up of Means-Tested Benefits.* Poverty Research Series 18, Child Poverty Action Group, London.

Lynes, T. 1972. "Welfare Men." *New Society* 21 (September): 505–506.

Mashaw, J. L. 1983. *Bureaucratic Justice: Managing Social Security Disability Claims.* New Haven, Conn.: Yale University Press.

Palme, J., and Wennemo, I. 1998. *Swedish Social Security in the 1990s: Reform and Retrenchment.* Stockholm: SOFI, Stockholm University.

Richardson, A., and Naidoo, J. 1978. *The Take-Up of Supplementary Benefits: A Report on a Survey of Claimants.* London: Chelsea College, University of London.

Ringeling, A. 1981. "The Passivity of the Administration." *Policy and Politics* 9 (3): 295–309.

Spicker, P. 1998. *Targeting and Strategic Intervention.* Paper presented at the Second Research Conference of the International Social Security Association, Jerusalem, 25–27 January.

Supplementary Benefits Administration (SBC). *Take-Up of Supplementary Benefits.* Supplementary Benefits Administration Paper No. 7. London: HMSO.

Townsend, P. 1979. *Poverty in the United Kingdom: A Survey of Household Resources and Standards of Living.* Middlesex: Penguin Books.

van Oorschot, W. 1995. *Realizing Rights: A Multilevel Approach to Non-Take-Up of Means-Tested Benefits.* London: Avebury.

van Oorschot, W., and Kolkhuis, P. T. 1989. *Niet-gebruik van sociale zekerheid; feiten, theorieën, onderzoeksmethoden,* COSZ-series, 16, The Hague.

van Oorschot, W., and Schell, J. 1991. "Means-Testing in Europe: A Growing Concern." In *The Sociology of Social Security,* ed. M. Adler, C. Bell, J. Clasen, and A. Sinfield. Edinburgh: Edinburgh University Press.

Vincent, J., Ashworth, K., and Walker, R. 1991. *Taking Account of Time in the Targeting and Administration of Benefits.* Center for Research on Social Policy: Loughborough University.

Vos, J. G. 1991. *Recht hebben en recht krijgen: Een studie over beleidsvrijheid, niet-gebruik van rechten en verantwoord ambtelijk handelen.* Lelystad, The Netherlands: Vermande.

Walker, R., with A. Hedges. 1985. *Housing Benefit: The Experience of Implementation.* London: Housing Centre Trust.

Whyley, C., and Huby, M. 1993. *Take-Up and the Social Fund: Applying the Concept of Take-Up to a Discretionary Benefit*. York: SPRU, University of York.

FURTHER READING

Corden, A. 1995. *New Perspectives on Take-Up: A Literature Review*. London: HMSO.

Deacon, A., and Bradshaw, J. 1995. *Reserved for the Poor: The Means-Test in British Social Policy*. Oxford: Blackwell.

Handler, J., and Hollingsworth, E. J. 1971. *The Deserving Poor: A Study of Welfare Administration*. Chicago: Markham.

Lipsky, M. 1980. *Street Level Bureaucracy: Dilemmas of the Individual in Public Services*. New York: Russel Sage Foundation.

van Oorshot, W. *Realizing Rights: A Multilevel Approach to Non-Take-Up of Means-Tested Benefits*. London: Avebury.

14

The Future of Social Policy Making

Hugh Heclo

There is a certain symmetry in what can be said about the future of social policy making and the future of any particular individual. For both, the details of the near future are often much harder to discern than are the large features in the farther distance. Each of us, for example, may have trouble saying exactly what we will be doing a year or two from now, but all of us can be fairly certain that the twenty-first century as a whole contains the date when virtually every person reading this sentence will die. For both collectivities and individuals, horizons are sometimes much clearer than foregrounds.

This chapter tries to look beyond the hazy foreground to the yonder landscape of social policy. Though in the distance, it is also a territory toward which Western societies seem to be moving with great rapidity. In this essay I will try to describe the future of social policy making in light of equally large features that mark the path by which we have arrived at our current point of departure. The following sections trace three big "moves" of the past one hundred or so years and the fourth movement that—if it is not presumptuous to say so—clearly lies ahead. It is not historically accurate to treat these as distinct stages in a continuous line of development, much less as mechanical outputs whereby one stage is the product of the former. It is more realistic to think of melding or overlapping movements where one phase is the transformation of the other. Such conversions in policy-making regimes, expressed in different forms and varying durations in different countries, represent rough archetypes of development rather than direct cause and effect sequences in modern social policy. Or as Hannah Arendt put it in another context, "The event illuminates its own past, but it can never be deduced from it."

FROM CHARITABLE EXPERIMENTATION TO WELFARE STATE CONSOLIDATION

Throughout the Western world a long period of turmoil ensued as premodern, agrarian societies puzzled and struggled over their transformations into market-based, industrial societies. Trying to grasp the upheavals of the last four or five centuries, economic historians have painted a rich picture of the development of trade and financial markets, the commercialization of agriculture, and the growth of the factory system and industrial production. Social historians have described the immense dislocations as European populations moved from small-scale rural communities to mass urban agglomerations. Theorists of modernization have taught us to conceptualize the changing ways of life from status to contract, from ascription to achievement, from personalistic loyalties to bureaucratic organization, from inner-directed to other-directed norms of social character. All together it has been an astounding few centuries of world history. And for much of this time, public intellectuals in the West have been struggling to grasp what modern society has been doing to itself—a collective self-consciousness that is itself a mark of modernity.

Experimentation

Practical political efforts to cope with this social situation launched a host of experiments, first at local and then at national levels. In first one way and then another, reformers throughout the nineteenth century sought to modernize their premodern poor laws. Traditional religious provisions for alms and local charity strained against the new movements of population and new forms of destitution that developed. Innovations proliferated, not only in early industrializing countries like Britain but among other European nations whose circles of reformers often learned from each other. Outdoor relief, local wage subsidies, workhouses, vagrancy laws, benevolent societies, classification of the poor, public hospitals and reformatories, "scientific charity"—these were only a few of the innovations. By the beginning of the twentieth century, the "social question"—a mass society of wage earners dependent on impersonal, uncontrollable market forces—bedeviled Western nations. Currents of class self-interest blended with traditional Christian morality and new social sciences to "reform" the touchstone of advanced thought spanning liberal and conservative perspectives. To be serious minded was to be reform minded.

Behind all of this social policy experimentation lay a basic idea. That idea was to reconcile the growth of a commodified, market economy, whose rules seemed to have a dynamic life of their own, with religious-based aspirations for a moral society. In effect, from the late eighteenth century through the early twentieth century, the disparate movements of social reformers were forever puzzling over practical action at the intersection of Adam Smith's two books: *The Wealth of Nations* (1776) and *The Theory of Moral Sentiments* (1759).

Gradually, as the twentieth century proceeded, a complex sifting process yielded the emerging features of what, by the end of World War II, was coming to be called the "welfare state." For purposes of this chapter, it can be said that all of this complicated experimentation with public policy gradually produced two broad categories of results.

First, regulation of business and social insurance for workers emerged as enduring features of national policy regimes. In the late 1930s, with both fascism and communism seemingly in ascendence, it became popular in the beleagured democracies to speak of "the third way" (a term revived in the 1990s). But the fact is that for well over one-hundred years, third ways were really what the hodgepodge of policy experimentation was gradually yielding. This was the de facto agenda and accomplishment—neither laissez faire nor collectivist ownership, something between top-down regimentation and bottom-up social leveling. Business regulation and worker protection laws gradually came to dominate over grander schemes of public ownership. Income maintenance programs focussed on methods of social insurance for wage earners. Publicly underwritten access to and/or provision of health care was instituted for more citizens and began gradually to be taken for granted as a social entitlement in many Western nations.

The second general result of all this experimentation is often less obvious to us today. It was the tendency for social policy initiatives with overtly moral claims to eventually fail or become greatly scaled back in their ambitions. Examples are the various temperence movements that swelled in the nineteenth century and then lost force as the twentieth century proceeded. Demands for a government-mandated "just" living wage were rebuffed except where the brute power of the strongest labor unions could prevail. Free citizenship (i.e., noncontributory) pensions proved to be a policy dead end. High-minded experiments to model utopian communities for the rest of society soon languished, as did more mundane attempts to enforce moral strictures on the poor, or what nineteenth century elites had unabashedly described as the "lower orders." Looking back from today, observers often dismiss this crusading, moralistic face of past social experimentation as quaint and naïve. But that observation is itself a comment on the "demoralized" presuppositions of our own late twentieth century perspective that is now taken for granted. In effect, social policy experimentation in the Western democracies turned out to be a kind of evolutionary process that selected against programs premised on deference to traditional moral authorities and in favor of programs pointing toward helping people maintain or even improve their consumption standards in volatile, impersonal, and increasingly nationalized economic markets.

Expansion

Standing by itself, the term "expansion" is a rather empty concept. What it means here is that policy initiatives—forays into new uses of government that were often contingent and experimental before World War II—took root and grew rapidly in the unexpected prosperity of the post–World War II decades.

To be sure, socialist and social democratic parties still battled for control over the egalitarian agenda. Conservative parties both resisted and pushed their own reforms to defend the increasingly affluent capitalist order. And with the 1960s came youth-led upheavals against "the system," protests reminiscent of romantic revolts and religious awakenings of earlier centuries. All of this sent a shudder throughout Western societies. But the overarching fact is that, despite a flood of radical critiques launched by the New Left and others against postwar liberal society, the basic structures of regulatory and social policy not only held together, they expanded. New regimes of government social regulation came into existence on behalf of women's and minorities' rights. By the same token, issues of environmental and consumer protection had been a modest and erratic concern earlier in the century. After the 1960s such policies grew into a major part of the public agenda and a source of government's continually growing presence in peoples' lives.

Throughout the postwar decades, the heartland of modern social policy remained an expanding body of social insurance and health care programs, generally providing ever-improved benefits and covering a growing portion of the population. Hence it is not surprising that in the last half of the twentieth century these programs assumed a growing portion of national government budgets throughout the Western world. Such vigorous expansion of government income maintenance policies was well attuned to—in fact in vital partnership with—the expanding mass consumer markets and affluent culture of the developed nations.

Of course many in the World War II generation carried forward feelings of solidarity elicited by the Great Depression and wartime austerity of the 1930s and 1940s. But as the years and that generation passed, these became a fading recollection to add to the attic trunk containing the more distant memories of nineteenth century moral crusades. In effect, modern social policy—sophisticated as it became in techniques of social insurance, professionalized services, and bureaucratic administration—institutionalized the secularization of moral obligation. Provision for the aged is perhaps the most prominent example. Toward the end of the nineteenth century, reformers' concerns for the destitute elderly had begun by trying to destigmatize poor law charity and protect the "deserving" poor. Eventually such attention to the income needs of aging workers unlocked new approaches to old age insurance for wage earners and their dependents. As the twentieth century unfolded after the Depression and war years, Western societies literally invented a new life stage of leisure and consumption called "retirement."

Consolidation

The decades of unexpectedly rapid economic growth after World War II allowed social policy commitments to expand without a great deal of attention to their coordination or long-term consequences. Doing more for more people was a relatively painless political exercise amid the bountiful tax revenues that flowed from modern tax structures in a context of sustained economic expansion. If anything, economic growth and technological advances now struck the Western nations with greater enduring force than had been the case in the nineteenth century. Deep boom and bust cycles of the earlier era were now being smoothed out through new government commitments to fiscal and monetary economic management. Earlier scientific advances in electricity, transportation, communication, and medicine now worked their way into applied technologies which produced a cornucopia of consumer goods and services that more people had the growing incomes to buy in increasingly integrated national and international markets. The results were sustained increases in living standards for the masses of national populations, realizations of affluence that would have been unthinkable at the beginning of the twentieth century.

By the middle of the 1970s, however, the economic growth that had sustained relatively painless expansions in social policy was coming undone. Immense hikes in energy and raw material prices produced unexpected slowdowns and dislocations in the developed economies. An unexpected combination of economic stagnation, higher unemployment, and accelerating inflation bewildered economic managers in all countries. To be sure, Western societies continued to maintain levels of material well-being that were the envy of the rest of the world; however, many Westerners' expectations were now pegged to the good times of recent postwar experience. While relative, the sense of deprivation and scarcity that set in during the 1970s and 1980s was nonetheless real.

The economic troubles constituted only one of two major forces, however, that interacted so as to precipitate a new move in the contours of social policy making. This second factor was the accumulating weight of past social policy decisions themselves. Roughly from the mid-1970s onward, the cumulative impact of social policy growth began to suggest limits to endless expansion. Quietly at first, and then more boldly, social critics argued that entitlements to social welfare programs were accumulating into an unsustainable load of precommitments on future tax resources. Taxpayer resistance became more widespread in the middle bulge of the income distribution, even as public expectations on national governments to solve problems remained high. Mounting budget deficits and recurring fiscal crises became a nagging problem throughout the developed world.

What might be called an era of social policy consolidation now ensued. "Consolidation" identifies a period when the focus in social policy making changed from expanding to managing commitments. New attention was given to harmonizing overlapping programs, to tightening delivery of benefits and services, and to weighing and sometimes cutting back the accumulation of government obligations. Expansion still could and did occur in social programs, but now it was surrounded by much more controversy and painful trade-offs than had been the case in the earlier postwar period.

The political manifestations of this third phase brought a new round of ostensibly ideological debate over the future of the welfare state. To critics on the socialist left, the troubles represented a "crisis of legitimacy" for the capitalist order. But this was the minor key of those times. As the 1970s and 1980s proceeded, the major key was sounded by conservative forces that now rose to intellectual and electoral prominence in many countries. The various moves and countermoves of the ensuing struggle need not detain us here. Suffice it to say that leaders such as Reagan, Thatcher, and many others on the newly energized right vowed to overturn dependence on Big Government and high taxes. The result was a kind of de facto, rolling referendum on the welfare state carried out in innumerable election venues and policy clashes across the developed world. The politics was a messy, ambiguous process, far from an elevated debate on theories of government and public policy. However, as the twentieth century waned, enough dust had settled to leave the results of this era of consolidation fairly clear. Social policy making in the twenty-first century will be reacting within and against this recent context. These are the "givens" for what comes next. Three interrelated features constitute this point of departure:

As it turned out, there was no enduring crisis of legitimacy in the capitalist order and no dismantling of the welfare state anywhere. By the last decade of the twentieth century, neither left nor right political persuasions were claiming with any plausibility that they could solve the major problems of modernity by dramatically reconstructing political society. In strictly political terms, the victorious forces of consolidation were those of the pragmatic center. They were leaders and parties who emerged as moderate supporters of market mechanisms, individual opportunity, and well-furbished safety nets for an essentially pro-middle-class welfare state.

In rejecting ideological agendas of right or left, democratic peoples reaffirmed tendencies that had been sporadically taking shape throughout the dramatic upheavals of the twentieth century. What the overwhelming mass of people increasingly demanded from government was not simply security in the basic necessities of life—an aspiration that more or less exhausted social policy reformers' experimental vision of one-hundred years earlier. Far beyond that, democratic peoples by the end of the twentieth century had learned to expect even more affluent security, an assurance of being able to satisfy growing consumption desires throughout their lives. In their technology-driven, mass market systems—with social programs of the welfare state as a central component of that social order—wants were needs. The age-old idea of necessity had now become effectively redefined as the need for more—more of whatever could be wanted.

By withstanding its consolidationist critics, activist government became more deeply entrenched in its preexisting tendencies. Essentially this meant reenforcing an "economistic" view of the relationship between government and citizens. The citizen is hereby conceived as one who balances an assembly of roles, with paid employment more than ever the key axis of identity. Government is to facilitate this balancing act through its programs in education, health care, social insurance, childcare, and so on down through the vast menu of contemporary social programs. The social bonds expressed in such a sociopolitical order are essentially instrumental and contractlike, mirroring the market culture itself.

What does all of this history, sketchy though it is, mean for the future of social policy making? The answer lies in more than a vague generality about history shaping possibilities for the future. The relevance is more concrete and ultimately disruptive. Modern social policy has evolved into a very specific, institutionalized world view, a framework for ascribing meaning not only to government but to society as a life system that engages individuals in some ways and not in others. This self-understanding that has been so laboriously acquired over the past century, consolidated amid attacks on the "welfare state" and institutionalized in modern social policy, will be deeply challenged by the fourth move that lies ahead. Developments in this fourth phase promise to tear off the veil of secular neutrality to reveal and require collective social choices of an essentially cultural–religious nature. The current appearances of "third way" complacency about the welfare state are deceiving. With conservatives accepting (reluctantly) Big Government and socialists accepting (reluctantly) competitive markets, and everyone (gleefully) accepting the collective pursuit of mass prosperity, it might seem that this thing called the modern mixed-economy welfare state will live happily ever after. But no, the future of social policy making promises something quite different.

SOCIAL POLICY AS CULTURAL POLICY

The argument of this chapter is that the fourth movement will be a growing realization that making social policy choices means making cultural choices—not a small matter, since at the center of all culture stands religion. Culture refers to the deep-seated understandings people use to construct the shared identities and strategies of action carried out in everyday life. Cultural understandings help people give meaning to who they are, how they should act to others, and who these others are. This is the direction I am pointing toward in referring to the "cultural dimensions" of social policy.

As a general rule, most people spend little time philosophizing about the basic questions of cultural identity: Who am I? How should I act? What do I owe to and am owed by other people? Who are these relevant other people? But everyone does spend a great deal of time, in fact all of their time, living *some* answer to these questions. If culture is the broad term used for the lived answers to these basic questions, social policy is the means for self-consciously making collective choices that are enforceable answers to these difficult questions under the coercive power of the state. We can expect that debate about social policy and the role of government will grow ever more troubled precisely because it will occur amid a growing and inescapable tangle of certain kinds of demands.

These are not the traditional contestations over economic inequality that energized so much of the welfare state drama over the past one hundred or so years. Compared with the past, the modern welfare state and market culture displays widespread moral indifference to growing inequality. That may be regrettable, but it is not the point now. The policy demands now coming into view are of a kind that will press Western society to make, and to keep making, very public choices about its moral identity and the deep rules that should govern its ways of life. My claim is not that people want to take up such issues, but that the affluent people of the world are living in the kinds of societies where they will be forced constantly to readdress the cultural dimensions of social policy. More than that, they will have to do so in economistic welfare states that over time have developed an acquired incapacity to carry on such moral deliberations. There are four interrelated features that deserve attention. These have to do with essential properties of modernity: its technology, cultural ambivalence, self-consciousness, and godlessness.

The Imperatives of Technology

Modern social policy will have no choice but to make cultural choices forced on it by developments in scientific knowledge and technology. Even a cursory review of the news during the past few years makes it clear that scientific advances and technological change are presenting ever-greater challenges for democratic peoples to think about who they are and what should be the rules of the game in their culture. Of course scientific knowledge has been accumulating over many centuries of discovery. But it is particularly within the past few decades that this earlier investment in basic scientific research has cumulated in technological applications of that knowledge so as to affect everyday human life on a massive scale.

For example, after more than fifty centuries of recorded history, the existence of the human egg was discovered in 1827, the DNA structure of life became known only in the middle of our own century, the first test tube (in vitro fertilized) human baby born in 1978, and the cloning of mammals begun in the 1990s. What at the beginning of this century was a crude, self-contained eugenics movement has become by the end of the century a technically sophisticated, highly organized, and commercially viable presence in Western societies. The implications for social policy are immense, uncharted, and only now beginning to be consumed in public debate (Pernick 1996; Maranto 1996).

Advances in biological and medical sciences will increasingly require portentous new questions to be faced about controlling the genetic characteristics of human life; about the cultivation, use, and commerce in human body parts; about access to organ regeneration for pursuing immortality; about the meaning and prolongation of death; about reconfiguring the brain and meaning of what it is to be human, to mention only a few. In these areas, cultural understandings are going to come under constant challenge if only because the inescapable question will now be omnipresent: If it is technologically possible to do certain things, why shouldn't we do them? And if they can be done for some people, why not others?

Or we might consider the cultural-forcing mechanism of science and technology at the other end of the spectrum. It is only since the middle of this century that there has been a well-developed environmental movement, the effect of which has been to create an awareness that (quite apart from questions of nuclear war) human institutions are in control of choices affecting the sustainability of life on Earth itself. This point is not that issues such as ozone depletion, species extinction, and global warming are settled facts but that they are the kinds of things people never before had to think about or imagine making collective decisions about. For many people this too raises deepening questions about a culture's way of life.

All these particular changes are well known, but their cumulative impact is difficult for any citizen to grasp and make sense of. Modern technological civilization is the first to span outward, bringing all societies within a common global destiny, and it is also the first that has penetrated inward to put the very structures of life into the control of human hands. The point is not a simple question of information overload. Rather, uncertainties about cultural commitments are the natural companion of ever more fateful and inescapable choices citizens must face, thanks to our growing scientific knowledge and technological capabilities.

Being profound, the choices are unsettling at a very deep cultural level. The natural scientist may blithely say, "Wind back life's tape to the dawn of time and let it play again—and you will never get humans a second time. We cannot read the meaning of life passively in the facts of nature. We must construct these answers ourselves—from our own wisdom and ethical sense. There is no other way." The social scientist may boast, "If you can change everything else about life, if you can even tamper with genes, why not culture? There is nothing sacred about it; it is our creation." But it is the poet who sees our coming social problems clearest when he says, "There is, in truth a terror in the world. . . . It is the silence of apprehension. We do not trust our time, and the reason we do not trust our time is because it is we who have made the time, and we do not trust ourselves. We have played the hero's part, mastered the monsters, accomplished the labors, become gods—and we do not trust ourselves as gods. We know what we are" (Gould 1991, 33; Gillis 1997; McLeish 1967).

An Inclusiveness That Divides

And yet, do we know who we are as distinctive societies? Immigration laws notwithstanding, it seems clear that in the years ahead, economically advanced societies will have to digest a growing diet of differences among ever more mobile populations. Dramatic illustrations of this geographic loosening of people is the international movement of labor forces, not to mention the worldwide spread of contagious diseases such as AIDS. Whatever economically developed country one lives in, there is a growing likelihood that those who come and go will be people who are "unlike us." In the long run more people can be expected to have moved out of ethnic neighborhoods and married outside their "home" groups. Any given "minority situation" is likely itself to become a more kaleidoscopic array of minorities within minorities. In the United States, for example, blacks, who in the 1960s were over 90 percent of America's minority population, were only about one-half in 1990 and within fifty years can be expected to be less than one-third of the nonwhite "minority" population (Passel and Edmonston 1992).

"Virtual" movements of people are likely to become even more fluid. Unprecedented innovations in electronic technology are making it increasingly possible for more and more people to construct and live in personalized communication subcultures, currently ranging from twenty-four-hour multimedia religious programming to all-porn fantasy worlds. In a disorienting larger culture, this new opportunity may enhance a form of psychological security in the short run, but it bodes ill for common cultural understandings on which people in any given society can depend in the long run.

The cultural challenges go deeper, however, than physical migration or self-made, virtual realities. In the contemporary social order that elevates the supreme importance and legitimizing power of individual choice, the very idea of assimilation has become problematic in a way that it was not the case earlier in this century. In those earlier times, life, while not fairer, certainly was clearer regarding cultural expectations. A relatively fixed structure of who is in and who is out of the cultural mainstream was enforced by self-confident elites convinced that movement from the outside depended on becoming like those on the inside. Particularly since the cultural upheaval known generically as "the Sixties," ideals of equal human dignity and inclusiveness have acquired much greater legal and social reality in many countries. Long-standing sexist, racist, and nativist prejudices have been increasingly delegitimized by court decisions, legislation, and social norms. By the end of the twentieth century, "post-Christian" developed nations have developed tolerances for vast religious differences, secularized public education, freedom of expression, and personal "lifestyles." Likewise, rules of exclusion have fallen away for some of the historically most marginalized persons—as in the treatment of unmarried mothers, the mentally ill, physically disabled, homeless, homosexuals, and others. These changes have typically been based less on the traditional idea of rights-as-individual-freedoms and more on a newer view of rights as claims for personal fulfillment and group liberation (Wiebe 1995).

Such progress in pushing for greater inclusiveness will continue to set in motion a chain reaction of cultural ambivalence. This seems inescapable. As barriers against exclusion fall, new uncertainties are raised about what it actually means to belong. And the greater the range of differences included in the mainstream, the greater the turmoil of having to get along in the same social space where the meaning of belonging is itself disputable. Thus the paradox of an "inclusiveness that divides" that will be played out on a number of policy fronts (e.g., claims for so-called identity politics, demands for subnational autonomy, the civil rights claims of alien workers, challenges to traditional concepts of marriage and family).[1] Even if the imperatives of technology were not going to present us with so many portentous collective choices to make, the result of growing social inclusiveness will be deepening arguments about cultural identity. Politically active traditionalists will demand a return to the uniformities of a single national culture. Active multiculturalists will seek what is really an inverse uniformity by demanding conformity to the diversity agenda. And separatists of all sorts will claim a right to simply go their own way. Meanwhile, ordinary citizens are likely to rightly sense an ever-deepening cultural confusion.

The Curse of Policy Self-Consciousness

It was not too many years ago that the term "policy" was seldom heard in public discussions. If the immediately preceding centuries were a time when Western man began discovering himself as a spectator living in "history" and "society" (Manent 1998), the twentieth century is surely the era in which people discovered they were living surrounded by public policies. This dawning awareness no doubt had to do with the increased activism of national governments, not least of all in the realm of social welfare programs. In particular, "policy consciousness" seems to have crystallized in many

Western countries sometime around midcentury when the way of thinking about government activity changed from a program to a policy orientation. In other words, as national government spending, taxing, and regulation grew, attention shifted from public sector inputs to outputs—from distinct, statutorily authorized, program operations to interrelated, "system" results that were seen to be rich in unintended consequences.

In this sense, the world view promoted by the consolidated mixed-economy welfare state has more far-reaching implications than might first appear. As its subtext, modern social policy entails an increasingly self-aware society that perceives government in terms of policy, and policy manifested in terms of whatever conditions happen to prevail in society. In acts of commission or omission— whether government does something, or stops doing something, or refuses to begin doing something—policy is now seen to be everywhere. In this situation, almost anything that happens is charged with political potential and poised to break out as a policy dispute before the public, from the design of toilets to sexual innuendo in the workplace. Left behind is a time when Western societies governed themselves in small local ways with simple views of government action. For the foreseeable future—whether one is for or against Big Government—it is a time of governing ourselves in very large ways as policy-preoccupied national societies. But we must do so in the context of divisive inclusiveness where multiple personal visions and loyalties, because individually chosen, are all equally legitimate. The burden thus loaded onto already weakened common cultural understandings becomes immense.

Thus the curse is that nothing can be a matter of collective indifference because everything is policy. Nondecision is decision. If the state is not to pass judgment on who and what shall be genetically engineered, on euthanasia, on abortion, or on anything else, then this is to say as a matter of policy, with the full weight of state power, that such things should be legal. There is no place of neutrality. Everything is a choice, contestable as a cultural issue because the things people want government either to do or to stop doing are also projections of who we think we are as a people and what we think we owe to and are owed by others. And thus too, awareness of the cultural ramifications of social policy is likely to grow, if only because of the profundity of the issues at stake. More people are likely to realize that the real distinction is not between a secular public life and a religious private life—or even a religious public life. Rather, in an era of policy consciousness, the decisive distinction is between public policies shaped by a secular religiosity and public policies shaped by the traditional religiosity to which it is hostile. That is not a recipe for peaceful social policy making in the future.

The Angst of Self-Affirmation

As people in twenty-first century societies face proliferating choices, many do so with diminished conviction that there are firm moral foundations for guiding those choices. Choice-based social life is the widely held standard, but it risks becoming a self-contradiction for people awash in a sea of relativism.

While their evaluations and explanations differ, cultural and intellectual historians are generally agreed that, sometime over the course of the last one-hundred years, a fundamental change has occurred in how Western culture views and justifies its rules of conduct (Taylor 1989; Turner 1985; Delbanco 1995; Himmelfarb 1995; Bellah et al. 1985; Lears 1983).

At issue is the source of authority used for answering questions about how one should live. Almost universally upheld by "respectable opinion," the older world view was basically an expression of Judeo–Christian theism. Clearly not everyone in Western societies believed in, much less practiced, those religious virtues. But no less clearly, there actually was a dominant cultural perspective understood to sanction some choices and not others. Ultimately, that perspective framed human choices in terms of the superintending authority of the God of the Bible. Matters of heaven, evil, judgment, hell, and the like were conceived as something objectively real and not matters of opinion, social utility, or psychological wish fulfillment. The point was not simply that "values matter." It is that values (or, more precisely, in those days, virtue or righteousness) were seen as fixed by the authority of a timeless external reality, where the validity of standards was not contingent on what human beings feel, want, or choose to believe (Howe 1997; Abzug 1994; Eisenach 1994).

If the older view taught that lived answers to the big questions were a choice between good and evil, the modern view is what has been called "radical choice." Man has the prior choice whether to choose in terms of good and evil. In other words, a modern person is free to choose his first principles, just as different societies in history make different choices about what is right for them. Thus whether to treat any reason as having force (e.g., God commands thus; our tradition teaches this) is always the prior choice for which no reason exists. The criterion of legitimate authority is self-selected authority, which essentially means it is oneself. What the old culture would call arbitrary and licentious, the new would call "personal" and "liberated." Violations of right behavior had been called sins against God; in the new cultural perspective they are antisocial behavior. Essentially the same modernist mindset has been expressed by the twentieth century's growing insistence on an inherent split between faith (private, subjective, and unprovable) and knowledge (public, demonstrable, and objective reality of the natural world), between religion and science, supernaturalism and naturalism. As a number of historians have observed, the difficulty of conveying the older cultural world view to modern readers is itself a mark of how much has changed.

Overturning of the older cultural premises occurred in many ways on many fronts, and it covered large parts of the wider culture, including virtually all of the higher education system and popular culture, where more young citizens of Western democracies were spending more of their time (Marsden 1994; Sloan 1994). Writers about modernity's norms of social character have tried to describe the resulting change in various ways since the 1950s: as a growing commitment to "secularism" and "therapeutic self-realization," as a change from "inner-directed" to "other-directed" character formation, as a "domestication of the sacred" that replaces external divine authority with the personal spirituality of "God as our buddy" (Bellah et al. 1991; Susman 1984; Riesman 1961; Wuthnow 1994a). The general conclusion is that while belief in God and the importance of religiosity commands widespread verbal assent in opinion polls, deeper questioning shows this is not often the kind of cultural reality that would have been recognizable a hundred years ago. For example most Americans—by all accounts the one exceptionally "religious" people among Western nations—claim to believe in God. But most of even these "believers" also hold that standards of how to live are matters of individual judgment not to be governed by restrictive norms of external authority or absolute truth; these judgments of right and wrong are widely seen as a matter of personal opinion based on one's own experience in a search for self-fulfillment and authenticity (Yankelovich 1981; Patterson and Kim 1991; Leinberger and Tucker 1991). Nor is this theme a simple divide separating secular Americans from religious Americans. It infuses the culture's religious scene itself. As one careful opinion researcher has described the trend, the readily definable religious and theological landscape of the past has dissolved in an America "transitioning from a Christian nation to a syncretistic, spiritually diverse society" possessing "a new perception of religion: a personalized, customized form of faith-views which meet personal needs, minimize rules and absolutes, and which bear little resemblance to the 'pure' form of any of the world's major religions."[2]

Hence, insofar as people expect government policy to express "values," they expect it to do so in a cultural context where moral foundations are a kaleidoscope of self-legitimating personal views. Figuratively, Western societies are no longer places where there is one hometown movie house playing a single cultural story but a cineplex theater through whose showings people move freely to construct their own stories of authentic value. For example, a recent study of Americans suggests how people in their everyday work lives combine moral world views in complex ways, with theistic morality—trying to obey God—endorsed as the first priority by very few people (Wuthnow 1994b). The same researcher has shown that nowadays even those engaged in compassionate activities in civil society express uncertainty about their motives and hesitate to provide reasons why they have put themselves out to help other people.[3]

When ordinary citizens should look to intellectuals for orientation, the picture becomes more rather than less murky. One hundred years ago the Western intellectual elites were all but monolithically of the Christian theist school. By the mid-twentieth century, the so-called thinking class was no less overwhelmingly on the secularist, classic humanist side (i.e., man is the measure of all things but the standards of civilized life are not relativistic). By contrast, in today's intellectual circles the foundations of thought exhibit a thorough fragmentation. Humanists, modernists, postmodernists, traditional religionists, and neoevangelicals now counterattack each other with immense vigor but offer little coherent guidance to the general culture (Wuthnow 1991).

Since people tend to live the way they perceive themselves, it makes sense that a society convinced there really is no holy, supernatural power sitting in judgment over human beings will behave differently than one that does. Denying one's personal precariousness in the face of such a superintending power carries its own distinctive anxiety. If this world, not a transcendent reality, is the only place to look for satisfaction, then departures from total justice, self-affirmation, and well-being are not temporary setbacks and sufferings to be borne in a fallen world. They are a crisis of failed purpose. Hence not only is it difficult to get one's bearings in world of choice without foundations. The stakes in doing so are immense, the urgency for fulfillment intense. A world of choice-based living can become strangely frightening. When the only order is arrangements we make for ourselves individually and collectively, any and every lapse from personal well-being implies a threat to the cosmic order.

It is at least reasonable to wonder if something like this angst of self-fulfillment might not lie at the heart of a curious paradox that seems to have developed in recent years. By almost any outward measure of well-being—lifespan, income, consumption levels, years of schooling, and the like—Western societies at the end of the twentieth century have never had it so good. Virtually every available long-run measure of material human welfare shows remarkable improvement over the decades and centuries up to the present (Simon 1995). But at the same time, opinion research studies describe widespread feelings of unease and self-doubt, and that much of life seems to be spinning out of control—not only the momentum of technology and economic change but the childhood of our children, the meaning of education and working life, the rules of the game in family life, and even elementary moral discernments (Whitehead 1927, 88). With the ground seeming to move under them, people seek something to hold onto in a culture that indicates they have nothing to trust but themselves. Thus, regardless of trends in material well-being, cultural uncertainties constitute a powerful undercurrent of insecurity that often seems to be projected onto public policy for solutions. At some deep level, things just don't seem to add up. Self-protective nonjudgmentalism casts the shadow of a seemingly stable, peaceful society, behind which few people can really feel at peace.

CONCLUSION

What usable conclusions might be drawn from all this? If nothing else, it is worth recognizing that things are not going to somehow "settle down" or go back to "normal" anytime in the years ahead. On the contrary, things are going to become more unsettled for social policy in the long run. Our very idea of normal can be part of the problem. Views of current economic, social, and cultural developments are understandably conditioned by the hangover of expectations built up during the remarkable postwar period of affluence, the challenge from left and right, and the eventual consolidation of affluent welfare states. That is the natural reference point in the minds of the huge, loud, and demanding baby boom generation that is now shaping many nations' futures. But it is an unsustainable point of reference, and not because this age cohort will soon be old and dying.

Things are not going to settle down and normality be restored because the changing technological, demographic, and cultural conditions—the happenings that powerfully affect everyone's lives—are immense and irreversible phenomena. Processes on a scale beyond the scope of any government's ability to "cause or cure" are at work. It is simply unrealistic to think there are policies that will neatly solve the emerging cultural challenges and restore public peace of mind. The challenges are with us for the long haul. Battle lines may be drawn between different nations where priorities of secular versus traditional–religious grounds of morality are weighed differently. They will certainly be drawn within nations, where different groups reflect these same divergent weightings. And in many cases, no doubt the battle lines will also be drawn within hearts and consciences of individuals.

And yet the greatest danger may not be battles over the cultural uncertainties manifested in social policy making. The real danger may be that Western societies will turn out to be insufficiently bewildered. The easy and tempting route will be to conceal the reality of inner tensions and dilemmas of the coming times with wishful thinking and other deceits.

Insufficient bewilderment means first a tendency to overlook the truth of conflicting goods—the unfortunate fact that errors typically come as paired opposites. Fearing one thing, we are indirectly drawn to its opposite; or wanting one good thing, we inadvertently abandon another. Are we for freedom or equality? Security or entrepreneurship? Materialism or spirituality? Compassion or self-reliance? Overlooked in all this is the truth of genuine dilemmas. Hence following one good thing to the end may be disastrous, not because it is not good, but because there are other goods which are sacrificed in the process. Down this path a society is destined for the disorder of lurching from one extreme to the other.

But there is a much greater danger of insufficient bewilderment. It is danger of becoming so obtusely tolerant that we forget there is any necessity in having a serious debate about policy morality at all. It may be possible for a modern society to become so debauched by the norm of choice that it forgets how to even accept the invitation and pursue a public conversation of moral weightiness. That weighty invitation was well articulated in Alfred North Whitehead's observation that "the major advances in civilization are processes which all but wreck the society in which they occur. . . . The art of free society consists, first, in the maintenance of the symbolic code, and secondly, in fearlessness of revision. Those societies which cannot combine reverence for their symbols with freedom of revision must ultimately decay from anarchy or from slow atrophy" (Whitehead 1927, 88).

Well into the twentieth century the Judeo–Christian tradition saw the great source of evil to lie in absolutizing the relative, interpreted to mean substituting things of the world—religion, moral ritual, church, or anything else—for God. The line of least resistance in the future risks making the relative absolute in a different sense—in mindlessly assuming that choice itself is the ultimate value for legitimizing actions. In that case we will have absolutized a relativism such that no truth is the only truth. We will have returned to what Scripture teachers once taught to be the founding lie of God's image bearers: "Just trust yourself, then you'll know how to live."[4]

"The World was all before them, Where to choose their place of rest." So the poet of *Paradise Lost* observes as humanity's founding couple leave Eden behind. In the material sense—in the framework presumed and continuously reenforced by modern social policy and today's technologically-driven market cultures—the twenty-first century world does indeed seem all laid open to human choice. Broadly understood, social policy commitments will be the expression of whatever self-made places of rest societies might choose. But then again that future rest will prove a mirage, should the older religious teaching that lay at the heart of Western culture really be true, the belief that, in St. Augustine's words, "You have made us for Yourself and our hearts find no rest until we find our rest in Thee."[5]

NOTES

1. The phrase "inclusiveness that divides" is elaborated in a religious context by Peggy Shriver, "The Paradox of an Inclusiveness That Divides," *Christian Century*, 21 January 1984. This is different from the conventional us–them distinction created, because "attachment to the group is at once an act of solidarity and an act of exclusion" (from Tsvetan Todorov, *On Human Diversity* [Cambridge: Harvard University Press, 1993], 173).

2. George Barna, *The Index of Leading Spiritual Indicators* (Dallas: Word Publishing, 1996), 129–130. Almost a half century earlier the authors of the Princeton Studies of Religion in American Life perceived the same developing condition in which the intellectually sophisticated "seem to have given up on God altogether, while the naive masses simply 'infinitize' their personal and social values and call the nebulous aggregate 'God'" (from James Ward Smith and A. Leland Jamison, eds., *The Shaping of American Religion, Religion in American Life* [Princeton, N.J.: Princeton University Press, 1961], 1: 5).

3. This appears the common theme in reports from both leading Republican and Democractic opinion researchers to their clients. See for example the interchanges between Frank Luntz of Luntz Research Companies and Celinda Lake of Lake Research on "Values and Politics," *Diane Rehm Show*, National Public Radio, 22 July 1994.

4. Goethe, *Faust*. I. Mephistopheles speaking to Faust, line 2062.

5. The two quotations in the final paragraph of this chapter are from Milton, *Paradise Lost*, 12: 646; and St. Augustine, *The Confessions*, 1, ¶1.

REFERENCES

Abzug, R. H. 1994. *Cosmos Crumbling: American Reform and the Religious Imagination*. New York: Oxford University Press.

Alasdair, M. 1984. *After Virtue*. 2d ed. Notre Dame: University of Notre Dame Press.

Bellah, R. N., Madsen, R., Sullivan, W. M., Swidler, A., and Tipton, S. M. 1985. *Habits of the Heart*. Berkeley and Los Angeles: University of California Press.

————. 1991. *The Good Society*. New York: Knopf.

Delbanco, A. 1995. *The Death of Satan*. New York: Farrar Straus and Giroux.

Eisenach, E. J. 1994. *The Lost Promise of Progressivism*. Topeka: University of Kansas.

Gillis, J. R. 1997. "Creating Families—Then and Now." *Woodrow Wilson Center Report* (Spring): 11.

Gould, S. J., in Friend, D., and the editors of *Life*. 1991. *The Meaning of Life*. Boston: Little, Brown.

Gurstein, R. 1996. *The Repeal of Reticence: A History of America's Cultural and Legal Struggles over Free Speech, Obscenity, Sexual Liberation, and Modern Art*. New York: Hill and Wang.

Himmelfarb, G. 1995. *The De-Moralization of Society*. New York: Knopf.

Howe, D. W. 1997. *Making the American Self*. Cambridge: Harvard University Press.

Jeffrey, S. P., and Edmonston, B. 1992. *Immigration and Race in the United States: The 20th and 21st Centuries*. Washington, D.C.: Urban Institute, January, PRIP-UI-20, Figure 9.

Lears, J.T.J. 1983. *No Place of Grace: Antimodernism and the Transformation of American Culture, 1880–1920*. Chicago: University of Chicago Press.

Leinberger, P., and Tucker, B. 1991. *The New Individualists*. New York: HarperCollins.

McLeish, A. 1967. "When We Are Gods." *Saturday Review*, 14 October.

Manent, P. 1998. *The City of Man*. Princeton, N.J.: Princeton University Press.

Maranto, G. 1996. *Quest for Perfection: The Drive to Build Better Human Beings*. New York: Scribner.

Marsden, G. M. 1994. *The Soul of the American University: From Protestant Establishment to Established Nonbelief*. New York: Oxford University Press.

Passel, J. S., and Edmonston, B. 1992. *Future Immigrant Population of the United States*. Washington, D.C.: Program for Research on Immigration Policy, Urban Institute.

Patterson, J., and Kim, P. 1991. *The Day America Told the Truth*. New York: Prentice Hall.

Pernick, M. S. 1996. *The Black Stork: Eugenics and the Death of "Defective" Babies in American Medicine and Motion Picture since 1915*. New York: Oxford University Press.

Riesman, D. 1961. *The Lonely Crowd*. New Haven, Conn.: Yale University Press.

Simon, J. L., ed. 1995. *The State of Humanity*. Cambridge: Blackwell.

Sloan, D. 1994. *Faith and Knowledge: Mainline Protestantism and American Higher Education*. Louisville, Ky.: Westminster John Knox Press.

Smith, B. H. 1997. *Belief and Resistance: Dynamics of Contemporary Intellectual Controversy*. Cambridge: Harvard University Press.

Susman, W. I. 1984. *Culture as History: The Transformation of American Society in the 20th Century*. New York: Pantheon.

Taylor, C. 1989. *Sources of the Self*. Cambridge: Harvard University Press.

Turner, J. 1985. *Without God, Without Creed: The Origins of Unbelief in America*. Baltimore: Johns Hopkins University Press.

Whitehead, A. N. 1927. *Symbolism: Its Meaning and Effect*. New York: Macmillan.

Wiebe, R. H. 1995. *Self-Rule: A Cultural History of American Democracy*. Chicago: University of Chicago Press.

Wuthnow, R. 1991. *Acts of Compassion*. Princeton, N.J.: Princeton University Press.

————. 1994a. *God Mammon in America*. New York: The Free Press.

————. 1994b. *Sharing the Journey*. New York: The Free Press.

Yankelovich, D. 1981. *New Rules: Searching for Self-Fulfillment in a World Turned Upside Down*. New York: Random House.

FURTHER READING

Herrnstien, B. S. 1997. *Belief and Resistance: Dynamics of Contemporary Intellectural Controversy*. Cambridge: Harvard University Press.

Howe, I., ed. 1982. *Beyond the Welfare State*. New York: Schocken.

Marshall, T. H. 1965. *Class, Citizenship and Social Development*. New York: Doubleday.

McFate, K., Lawson, R., and Wilson, W. J., eds. 1995. *Poverty, Inequality and the Future of Social Policy*. New York: Russel Sage Foundation.

Myrdal, G. 1972. "The Place of Values in Social Policy." *Journal of Social Policy* 1 (1): 1–4.

Pierson, P. 1994. *Dismantling the Welfare State*. Cambridge: Cambridge University Press.

Selznick, P. 1992. *The Moral Commonwealth*. Berkeley and Los Angeles: University of California Press.

Index

About the Editors
and Contributors

Asher Ben-Arieh is the Associate Director for Research and Development at the National Council for the Child in Israel and heads its Center for Research and Public Education. He is a faculty member of the Paul Baerwald School of Social Work at the Hebrew University of Jerusalem. Since 1990 he has been the project director and the editor of the annual *State of the Child in Israel—A Statistical Abstract*. He spent the 1999–2000 academic year as an International Research Fellow at the Chapin Hall Center for Children at the University of Chicago. Dr. Ben-Arieh was a member of the Israel national committee for reducing poverty prevalence and was recently appointed as a member of the National Council for Reducing Economical Gaps in the Israeli Society and the National Council for Children's Health and Pediatrics. He was a faculty member at the Salzburg Seminar Session 320 "Beyond Child Survival—Promoting the Well-Being of Young Children." Dr. Ben-Arieh has published a number of articles on the politics of social policy in Israel, child poverty in Israel, deprived families, and reports on the state of new immigrants and Arab children in Israel (in English and Hebrew).

John Carrier is Senior Lecturer in Social Policy at the London School of Economics and Political Science. In addition to teaching Social Policy and Housing Law at London School of Economics, he teaches Health Care Law at the London School of Hygiene and Tropical Medicine. His most recent major publication was *Health and* *the National Health Service* (with Ian Kendall, 1998). Currently he is working on a book on law and social policy with Ian Kendall.

Francis G. Castles is Professor of Political Science in the Research School of Social Sciences at the Australian National University. He has been writing on issues of comparative public policy and the welfare state for more than twenty years.

Abraham Doron has been with the Paul Baerwald School of Social Work at the Hebrew University in Jerusalem since the 1960s. His main field of teaching and research interest is social welfare and social security policy in Israel and in a comparative cross-national perspective. He has published extensively in this field and his publications cover the most important issues concerned with the evolution of social policies in Israel and the functioning of its major social programs. His recent books include *The Welfare State in Israel: The Evolution of Social Security Policy and Practice* (with Ralph Kramer), and *In Defense of Universality*. He is the recipient of the Itzhak Kanev Prize for Studies in Social Security and the Paul Baerwald Award for distinguished service in the field.

John Gal is a lecturer at the Paul Baerwald School of Social Work at the Hebrew University in Jerusalem. His research focuses upon issues of social policy, social security, poverty and unemployment in Israel and in a comparative perspective. He has edited a book on child poverty in Israel and has published extensively on these issues in academic journals in English and in Hebrew.

Ian Gough is Professor of Social Policy at the University of Bath. Until 1995, he was Professor of Social Policy and Political Economy at the University of Manchester. He is author of *The Political Economy of the Welfare State* (1979) and coauthor of *A Theory of Human Need* (1991), winner of both the Deutscher and the Myrdal prizes. Other books include *Can the Welfare State Compete?* (1991), *Social Assistance in OECD Countries* (1996), and *Capitalism and Social Cohesion* (1999). He has lectured on all continents of the world except Africa.

Jack Habib is the Director of the JDC–Brookdale Institute of Gerontology and Human Development and Professor of Economics and Social Work at the Paul Baerwald School of Social Work at the Hebrew University of Jerusalem. He also serves as the Director of the Center for Children and Youth, which was established in 1995 at the JDC–Brookdale Institute. Habib has served on many national commissions, most recently on an interministerial commission on the measurement of poverty and income distribution and an interministerial committee examining the retirement age in Israel. He is the author of numerous books and articles in the field of social welfare, including the book *Children in Israel: Social Educational and Economic Perspectives*. His recent articles include "Resettling Elderly Soviet Immigrants in Israel: Family Ties and the Housing Dilemma" and "Strategies for Assisting Frail Elderly to Maintain Dignity and Independence."

Hugh Heclo is Robinson Professor of Public Affairs at George Mason University in Fairfax, Virginia, coming to his current position from a professorship at Harvard University. A former senior fellow at The Brookings Institution in Washington, D.C., and recipient of a Guggenheim Fellowship, he has received national awards for his books, *A Government Strangers, Modern Social Politics in Britain and Sweden*, and *Comparative Public Policy*. His most recent book is a coauthored volume, *The Government We Deserve: Responsive Democracy and Changing Expectations* (1998).

Ian Kendall is Professor of Social Policy at the University of Portsmouth. His academic interests include health policy, the changing role of the voluntary sector, and welfare theory. His most recent major publication was *Health and the National Health Service* (with John Carrier, 1998). Currently he is working on a book on law and social policy with John Carrier.

Ernie S. Lightman has, for many years, been Professor of Social Policy on the University of Toronto Faculty of Social Work. He has published widely in the field of social policy, focusing on the interrelationship between economic and social policy.

Julia S. O'Connor is Director of the National Economic and Social Council in Dublin, Ireland. She is on leave of absence from McMaster University in Canada. She is the author of *From Women in the Welfare State to Gendering Welfare State Regimes* (1996). She is coauthor of *States, Markets, Families Gender, Liberalism and Social Policy in Australia, Canada, Great Britain and the United States* (1999) and coeditor of *Power Resource Theory and the Welfare State* (1998). She has published several articles on comparative public policy.

Wim van Oorschot is Associate Professor of Sociology at Tilburg University, The Netherlands, and researcher at the Tilburg Institute of Social Security Research (TISSER). Besides take-up of benefits he has published on poverty, local social policy, welfare state legitimacy, issues of solidarity, and equity in social security administration, disability benefits and reintegration measures, activation of unemployed people and on occupational welfare arrangements. Most of his work is based on the use of national and international quantitative data sets, and an important part is funded through external contracts. He has carried out studies commissioned by the European Commission, the Dutch, British, and Danish government, pension funds, and various nongovernmental organizations in The Netherlands. He is Editor of the Dutch journal *Sociale Wetenschappen* (Social Sciences).

Martin Rein is Professor of Social Policy at MIT in the Department of Urban Studies and Planning. His research is on rethinking the welfare society which focuses on an examination of the different institutional spheres in which welfare is financed and administered, not only on the activities of the welfare state. A major aspect of this work is the study of the changing welfare mix in affluent countries. His most recent books include *Enterprise and the Welfare* (with Eskil Wadensjo), *Enterprise and Social Benefits After Communism* (with Barry Friedman), and *Frame Reflection* (with Don Schon).

Graham Room has been Professor of European Social Policy at the University of Bath since 1992. He has acted as consultant to the European Commission on the development of its programs in the field of poverty and social exclusion. He was Special Advisor to the U.K. House of Lords Select Committee on the European Communities in 1994. He is founding editor of *The Journal of European Social Policy*. Among his publications are *The Sociology of Welfare: Social Policy, Stratification and Political Order* (1979) and *Beyond the Threshold: The Measurement and Analysis of Social Exclusion* (1995).

Uri Yanay is Associate Professor at the Paul Baerwald School of Social Work at the Hebrew University of Jerusalem. Together with Abraham Doron, he studied major changes in the Israeli basic income maintenance programs and the provision of personal social services. His current research deals with support services and income maintenance programs designed for victims of crime and terrorism.

Yael Yishai is a Professor of Political Science at the University of Haifa. She has published extensively on interest groups, health policy making, and civil society in Israel.

Lightning Source UK Ltd.
Milton Keynes UK
UKHW040122191221
395907UK00002B/9